SELECTED WORKS OF PEARL JEPHCOTT: SOCIAL ISSUES AND SOCIAL RESEARCH

Volume 3

MARRIED WOMEN WORKING

MARRIED WOMEN WORKING

PEARL JEPHCOTT

with
NANCY SEEAR and JOHN H. SMITH

Foreword by
RICHARD TITMUSS

LONDON AND NEW YORK

First published in 1962 by George Allen and Unwin Ltd

This edition first published in 2023
by Routledge
4 Park Square, Milton Park, Abingdon, Oxon OX14 4RN

and by Routledge
605 Third Avenue, New York, NY 10158

Routledge is an imprint of the Taylor & Francis Group, an informa business

© 1962 George Allen and Unwin Ltd
© 2023 Josephine Koch

All rights reserved. No part of this book may be reprinted or reproduced or utilised in any form or by any electronic, mechanical, or other means, now known or hereafter invented, including photocopying and recording, or in any information storage or retrieval system, without permission in writing from the publishers.

Trademark notice: Product or corporate names may be trademarks or registered trademarks, and are used only for identification and explanation without intent to infringe.

British Library Cataloguing in Publication Data
A catalogue record for this book is available from the British Library

ISBN: 978-1-032-33020-4 (Set)
ISBN: 978-1-032-33014-3 (Volume 3) (hbk)
ISBN: 978-1-032-33019-8 (Volume 3) (pbk)
ISBN: 978-1-003-31777-7 (Volume 3) (ebk)

DOI: 10.4324/9781003317777

Publisher's Note
The publisher has gone to great lengths to ensure the quality of this reprint but points out that some imperfections in the original copies may be apparent.

Disclaimer
The publisher has made every effort to trace copyright holders and would welcome correspondence from those they have been unable to trace.

New Foreword to the Reissue of *Married Women Working*

The study of gender, family and work and how they intersect are now mainstream within sociological analysis. Following the ground-breaking works of writers such as Ann Oakley, Hannah Garavon, amongst others, the household allocation of domestic tasks, the dual shift of work and homework experienced by women and the problems of childcare feature heavily within sociological publications. Yet, this was not always the case with the private troubles of how women managed home and work life viewed by some as analytically unimportant and separate from the more worthy public issues of the day. It is hard to imagine now, through the prism of the present, that gender or how gender intersected with ethnicity or class were deemed less worthy topics of analysis. Moving gender from the periphery to the centre of sociology has largely been attributed to the successful feminist critique of malestream sociology and the questioning of positivism. However, as Oakley (1989) notes, there were pioneering women writing about gender and class well before this feminist critique of sociology and who often wrote without an overtly feminist orientation. One such writer was the sociologist Pearl Jephcott (1900–1980).

Jephcott's *Married Women Working* (1962) is a ground-breaking study of gender and work and positioned as an investigation in one firm and one locality of the implications of married women's employment. The research site was the Peek Frean & Co. Ltd biscuit factory in Bermondsey (so called 'biscuit town') in Southeast London and Metropolitan Borough of Bermondsey. With a workforce of over 5000 workers of whom 82% were women, supplemented by data from the Metropolitan Borough of Bermondsey, means that *Married Women Working* is supported by a rich, detailed, reliable and rigorous amount of data that really sets an early standard for studies of this type. Typically, the book also contains a very detailed methodological discussion in appendix one which, so characteristic of Jephcott's work, details the multifaceted approach to research as well as the fact that Pearl herself went to work in the biscuit factory. How better to understand the realities of work for this group of women than immersing oneself into the research site. The result is an incredibly detailed text that documents and explores the reality of working in the biscuit factory, how Bermondsey as a space has been shaped by the biscuit factory overtime, and the challenges that full or part-time working poses for homemaking and childcare. Moreover, Pearl details the work situations of many of the women, from their working hours and the positions they occupied on the conveyor belts right down to what happened to the broken biscuits. This is a book that deserves to be read by anyone with an interest in gender in work, social class, or every day working lives.

However, beyond the book is another story. It is a story of academic politics, of power, and one that would see Pearl ultimately leave the London School of Economics. First, the grant holder for the research was not Pearl Jephcott but instead Professor Richard Titmuss. In the book Titmuss is credited with directing the study and he also writes a foreword to the book. However, what remains uncertain is the extent to which Richard Titmuss made any intellectual contribution to the research, fieldwork, research design, or the wider writing of the text. As first author, and as revealed in the publishers' archives at the University of Reading, Pearl was more than an 'assistant' to the established Professor. Second, in relation to academic politics, a version of the study was offered to the University of Leicester by Richard Titmuss. Along with Ilya Neustadt, the variant looking at the employment of women in Leicester hosiery factory, was designed and data began to be collected in the early 1960s. Although ultimately this research never delivered on its promise, what is unclear is the extent to which Pearl was ever consulted or involved in the variant. As far as one can tell Pearl is not involved at all. Finally, as others have written (see Oakley 2014) the success of *Married Women Working* was to be Pearl's last contribution to the LSE. Despite senior colleagues wanting to retain this imaginative and creative researcher in London, Richard Titmuss thought differently and after a short meeting between the two Pearl left the LSE to a career of contract research.

Despite my not knowing about Jephcott's work before a random encounter with an oblique reference to one of her books, since rediscovering her work, Pearl Jephcott has changed my orientation towards sociology and sociological practice. What started as a side interest transformed, for me, into an academic obsession to uncover as much about Pearl's life and work and a desire to share my findings with others so that they may also benefit from her writings. By her death in 1980, Pearl Jephcott had spent considerable time immersed in the field, observing, recording, and reflecting upon what she saw in the social world around her. The result is a legacy of richly detailed, keenly observed social studies that give voice to her respondents, and which continue speaking to many contemporary debates.

John Goodwin
University of Leicester
October 2022

References

Oakley, A. (2014) *Father and Daughter: Patriarchy, Gender and Social Science*, Bristol: Policy Press.

Oakley, A. (1989) Women's studies in British sociology: To end at our beginning? *British Journal of Sociology* 40(3): 442–70.

Married Women Working

BY

PEARL JEPHCOTT

WITH

NANCY SEEAR AND JOHN H. SMITH

AND UNDER THE DIRECTION OF

PROFESSOR RICHARD TITMUSS

With a Foreword by
Richard Titmuss

London
GEORGE ALLEN AND UNWIN LTD
RUSKIN HOUSE MUSEUM STREET

FIRST PUBLISHED IN 1962

This book is copyright under the Berne Convention. Apart from any fair dealing for the purpose of private study, research, criticism or review, as permitted under the Copyright Act, 1956, no portion may be reproduced by any process without written permission. Enquiries should be addressed to the publisher.

© George Allen and Unwin Ltd, 1962

PRINTED IN GREAT BRITAIN
in 10pt Times Roman type
BY HAZELL WATSON AND VINEY LTD
AYLESBURY AND SLOUGH

FOREWORD

BY RICHARD M. TITMUSS

Head of the Department of Social Science and Administration,
London School of Economics and Political Science

IN 1961 more than one-half of all the women in paid employment in the United Kingdom were married. The proportion had been rising steadily for over a decade. It is now higher than the figure reached during the peak years of employment during the Second World War; the highest, indeed, in Britain's industrial history, and probably the highest in the Western world.

Changes in the age of marriage as well as the trend towards more marriage have both been contributory factors. The re-entry into paid employment of older married women represents another and perhaps the most important quantitative element. The married worker has, in consequence, replaced the unmarried worker as the typical employee. From the viewpoint of the employer, concerned to take account of family loyalties and obligations, this is an important change. Compared with the 1930's, for instance, a far higher proportion of all employees, both men and women, are now married with family responsibilities.

In round figures, we can say that in 1960 one in six of Britain's labour force was a married woman; over four million in total, of whom a substantial proportion were working part-time. During the preceding ten years of a rising demand for workers, married women made by far the largest contribution. Their numbers increased by 1¼ million while, according to official figures, the total working population of both men and women rose by under 1½ million.

These are the bare facts for the country as a whole. What do these remarkable changes portend for family life, for the woman herself, for employers and for society in general? They seem to have taken place without any obvious and immediate signs of social stress. Priorities in the educational field have not been markedly changed, for instance, by any greater emphasis on nursery school provision for the young children of mothers at work. Indeed, it is one of the puzzling features of this decade of change that such provision has declined in relative importance. Nor has policy in respect of national insurance been affected by the social as well as the economic need for more part-time work. If anything, the tax on part-time employment in the name of 'contributions' has become heavier.

But these are only two of a large number of searching questions

FOREWORD

that can be asked about the causes and consequences of these changes in the roles of women, wives and mothers. In this study, no attempt has been made to answer them on a national scale. When it began, over six years ago, the authors hardly knew the appropriate questions to ask. There was little information available, for instance, on the social and biological characteristics of the women who worked and their families to enable the authors to see behind the popular stereotype of the neglectful mother. Nor was anything known about the characteristics as workers of the increasing number of married women working part-time.

To make a beginning, therefore, it was decided to embark on an intensive local study, and to examine the problems more or less simultaneously from the angle of the home and the workplace. In this, the authors were greatly helped by financial assistance from the Department of Scientific and Industrial Research;[1] by the management and workers of Peek, Frean & Co. Ltd., and by the London County Council, the Bermondsey Borough Council and many other authorities. The organization of the research itself entailed some division of labour. Miss Jephcott has been responsible for those parts of the study concerned with the home and the community; while Miss Seear and Mr. Smith, as the members of the department concerned with teaching for its graduate course in personnel management, were more directly involved in examining the problems of employment in the industrial context.

The difficulties and time-consuming nature of social research of this kind are not always appreciated by a public which is often led to think that the world is an uncomplicated place. The findings of this study show—if they do nothing else—the great dangers of generalizing, even in a local context, about cause and effect. The problems here examined cannot be isolated from the broad stream of secular changes in the roles and functions of the family as a social unit in relation to other social units in society. We cannot understand the wife who goes to work nor, we should add, the husband who goes to work, unless we also understand at the same time the changing place of the family in modern industrial societies.

[1] A short interim report of this study was published as a booklet by the Department of Scientific and Industrial Research in October, 1960, under the title *Woman, Wife and Worker* (H.M.S.O., 2s.).

ACKNOWLEDGMENTS

THANKS are due to the many people who helped with this study, both in providing and in eliciting information. Particular thanks should be made to the Department of Scientific and Industrial Research who financed the study; to the Directors and staff of Peek, Frean and Co. Ltd.; and to the London County Council, Bermondsey Borough Council, and the Ministry of Labour.

The following have given particular help as members of the research team: Mrs James Meade, Mrs Phillip Sober, Miss Shirley Malin, John Rogers, Douglas Webster, Tony Lynes, and those responsible for the secretarial work. So many other people, in Bermondsey and elsewhere, have assisted the work that it would be invidious to mention names. Our gratitude is non the less real.

CONTENTS

TABLES IN TEXT		*page*	13
TABLES IN APPENDIX			15
I.	*Work and family*		19
II.	*Perspectives and methods*		30
III.	*Bermondsey's past*		38
IV.	*Bermondsey today*		54
V.	*The Peek Frean factory*		63
VI.	*Married women as employees at Peek Frean's*		71
VII.	*The Bermondsey wives who worked*		91
VIII.	*Home making*		115
IX.	*The children*		136
X.	*Conclusions*		164

APPENDICES

I.	*Method*	177
II.	*Tables*	194
	Index	205

ILLUSTRATIONS

1. *Peak Freen's*   *facing page*   **64**
2. *Women's beanos, c. 1925, 1954*   **65**
3. *A Bermondsey home*   **128**
4. *Five generations of Bermondsey women*   **129**

TABLES IN TEXT

Table No.   *Page*

1. Males aged eighteen and over by Social Class (Registrar General's Classification) in Bermondsey; County of London; and England and Wales — 54

2. Approximate numbers employed in selected principal industries in Bermondsey. 1958 — 55

3. Women employees at Peek Frean's by % in shift; and average age of shift. 1955 — 67

4. Women employees at Peek Frean's by shift; numbers leaving; turnover rate. 1955 — 72

5. Women employees leaving Peek Frean's in 1955 by shift; and main reason for leaving — 73

6. Views of women employees at Peek Frean's on quality of supervision — 82

7. Woman's marital status in relation to her work situation. 'Wives and widows' — 93

8. Woman's type of occupation—percentage distribution. 'Wives and widows' — 94

9. Woman's age in relation to her work situation. 'Wives and widows' — 95

10. Mothers (with a child in age groups 0–4 and 5–10) who worked, as a percentage of all mothers with a child in these age groups. 'Wives and widows' — 96

11. Number of children (all ages) living in household in relation to woman's work situation. 'Husbands and wives' — 97

12. Age of youngest child at home in relation to his mother's work situation. 'Wives and widows' — 98

13. Husband's occupation in relation to his wife's work situation. 'Husbands and wives' — 99

14. Husband's earnings in relation to his wife's work situation. 'Husbands and wives' — 103

TABLES IN TEXT

Table No.   *Page*

15. Husband's income (as percentage of N.A.B. figure) in relation to his wife's work situation. 'Husbands and wives'   104

16. Woman's earnings (in week previous to interview) in relation to her work situation. 'Wives and widows'   116

17. Amenities in household in relation to wife's work situation. 'Husbands and wives'   118

18. Children's age in relation to their mother's work situation   138

19. Children's age in relation to the times of day at which their mother worked   139

20. General health from birth of children under five in relation to their mother's work situation at date of interview   146

21. Immunization and vaccination of children under five in relation to their mother's work situation   146

22. Children aged 11 and over by type of school attended and mother's work situation   147

23. Children's attendance at school (children of all ages) in relation to their mother's work situation   148

24. Children of sample households involved with Probation Office in relation to their mother's work situation   150

25. Bermondsey children in general involved with Probation Office in relation to their mother's work situation at date of offence   151

TABLES IN APPENDIX

Table No.   *Page*

26. Estimated numbers of employees in England
    and Wales 1951–1959   194

27. Heads of household—Bermondsey households   194

28. Work situation of women heads of household
    who are, or have been, married. 'Wives and
    widows'   194

29. Woman's type of work in relation to time of
    day she worked. 'Wives and widows'   195

30. Woman's length of two-way journey to work
    in relation to her work situation. 'Wives and
    widows'   195

31. Woman's main pre-marriage job in relation
    to her present type of occupation. 'Wives and
    widows'   196–7

32. Woman's type of occupation in relation to her
    age. 'Wives and widows'   198

33. Wife's spendable income ((as percentage of
    N.A.B. figure) in relation to her work situa-
    tion. 'Husbands and wives'   198

34. Family holiday (1957) in relation to wife's
    earnings. Husbands and wives. Annual holi-
    day (1954) 'Factory Shifts Sample and New-
    comers'   199

35. Possession of car and washing machine in
    relation to wife's work situation. 'Husbands
    and wives'   200

36. Amenities in household in relation to wife's
    work situation. 'Husband and wives'   200

37. Frequency with which families were in contact
    with relatives. 'Wives and widows'   200

38. Child or no child in the home in relation to
    the woman's work situation. 'Wives and
    widows'   200

TABLES IN APPENDIX

Table No.   *Page*

39. Minding of worker's child (in week previous to interview) in relation to his mother's part- or full-time work situation   201

40. Minding of worker's child (in last long school holidays) in relation to his mother's part- or full-time work situation   201

41. Attendance at clinic of mothers of children aged under five, during child's first year of life, in relation to the mother's work situation   202

42. Illness during school days of school child in relation to his mother's work situation at date of interview   202

43. Analysis of 222 of the 231 refusals to interview in Bermondsey households sample   203

SUBJECT AND SETTING

Subject   An investigation in one firm and one locality of the implications of married women's employment.

Place

(i) Messrs. Peek Frean & Co. Ltd., Bermondsey, London, S.E.16
Firm employing 5,000 workers
Estimated % of married women among all women operatives, 82% (and of part-time workers 66%)

(ii) Metropolitan Borough of Bermondsey
Population: 54,000
Estimated % of married women at work, 52% (of whom 56% part-time workers)

Date

Peek Frean study. 1954–56
Bermondsey study 1956–59

M.W.W.—2

SAMPLES AND GROUPS

	First Reference Page
Peek Frean Study	
Peek Frean Shifts Sample	31
Newcomers Sample	32
N.B.1 Sample	32
Leavers' Group	33
Visiting Families	33
Borough of Bermondsey Study	
Bermondsey Households Sample	33
Wives and Widows Sample	34
Husbands and Wives Sample	34
Children (aged under 18) of Bermondsey Households Sample	34
Visiting Families	33

CHAPTER I

Work and Family

Trends in work and marriage–'A woman's place'?–Finding out the facts–The choice of Bermondsey for study–Some basic questions

THE married woman who leaves her home each day and goes off to work has become a familiar, if controversial, figure in western society. Some see her as a symbol of freedom, but to others she is the epitome of irresponsibility and neglect. The viewpoint varies, but the fact remains that as industrialization has spread, many women have added to their traditional role of wife and mother that of paid employee. In Britain today more than half the women in the labour force are married. Of these, a sizeable proportion have young children at home, as a recent study by Viola Klein showed: in a sample enquiry she found that 26 per cent of the mothers with children under fifteen were at work.[1] Concern over the social consequences of such a trend is not confined to this country: news that the problems were being studied by the London School of Economics brought enquiries from Canada, Germany, the United States, and Yugoslavia. The working wife is not, of course, a new phenomenon: poverty has always driven some wives out to work; and all social classes have bred a scatter of originals who have elected to work outside the home because they accepted the claims of some cause. What is different today is that the decision to work seems to be taken on an altogether different basis from that of dedication or simple necessity. Whatever the reasons for this decision many people see it as a challenge to society, because it breaks with long-established patterns of family life, and with the values and beliefs supporting them. That it has profound implications no one can deny. It involves two of the most intimate of personal relationships, that of husband to wife, and of parent to child; it affects economic life from the bread-and-butter choices of the household to the long-term decisions of the board room; and its relevance to social policy is subtle and far-reaching. Yet discussion of married women's employment is often conducted with little respect for even the most elementary facts. This study is mainly concerned with providing a factual basis for discussion, by reporting what this trend has meant for factory and family in a London community. But this local study must first be set against the

[1] Viola Klein, *Working Wives*, Institute of Personnel Management, 1960.

MARRIED WOMEN WORKING

background of national trends and the divergent views that married women's employment arouse.

Trends in work and marriage

In England and Wales in 1959 approximately one worker in six was a married woman, and Ministry of Labour figures give a total of 3,683,000 married women in employment, just over half of all female employees. Estimates of the position at the turn of the century suggest that only 20 per cent of women in employment were married, which is a measure of the considerable change that has taken place within living memory. Nor is there any sign that this increase is slackening: throughout the 1950's more and more married women went out to work. In 1951 the percentage of all women employees who were married was 44 per cent; in 1957 this figure had reached 50 per cent; and by 1959 it stood at 53 per cent.[2] These official figures underestimate the number of married women who are out at work.

At least half of today's female factory workers are married; so are more than a third of full-time women teachers, and perhaps a quarter of the nursing profession. Analysis of the traditional women's occupations and professions provides clear evidence of the necessity of the married woman to the labour force of an advanced industrial society. The demand for female labour has steadily increased since the beginning of the century. In industry itself, labour-saving machinery and the expansion of light engineering have greatly extended the range of industrial jobs a woman can tackle. Indeed, in much of factory employment, the woman has been the principal beneficiary of the machine. The demand for clerks and typists generated by the spread of the large-scale organization in industry, commerce, and public administration has been an important factor in increasing women's employment generally; while the growth of light servicing industries such as laundries and dry cleaning, of retail distribution, and of catering and entertainment, has helped to provide alternative jobs for many women who in former times would have had no option but to take up domestic service.

Economic expansion and full employment have increased the demand for women as members of the labour force. Assuming the supply of single women to be constant, this would imply the increased employment of married women as the last important reserve under conditions of labour shortage. But, in fact, the supply of single women is diminishing, owing to a complex of social forces among which changing patterns of marriage and of family size are the most

[2] Appendix II, Table 26.

WORK AND FAMILY

prominent. In the first place women are marrying earlier, thus reducing the numbers of single women available for work. An employer recruiting women aged 20–25, for example, will find that today twice as many are likely to be married as was the case thirty years ago.

Secondly, falling birth rates and shrinking families have revolutionized the life of today's mother, especially when she is in her thirties and forties. In a matter of only three or four generations, the outsize family has disappeared just as Septimus and Octavia have vanished as Christian names. The physical and social freedom which the smaller family have conferred on the mother can be demonstrated most effectively by comparing the life of today's mother in terms of pregnancy with that of the mother of sixty years or so ago—a past still within living memory. Professor Titmuss has estimated that in the 1890's the typical working-class mother spent about fifteen years in a state of pregnancy and in nursing a baby for the first year of its life, as compared with four years or so today.[3] Nowadays most families seem to be completed within ten years of marriage; and certainly many mothers have had their last child by the age of thirty—fifteen years earlier than at the beginning of the century.[4]

When to this is added the wife's greatly increased expectation of life after childbearing is over, the dramatic widening of life's perspectives beyond the immediate and traditional duties of family and home can be fully appreciated. A woman aged forty can now expect to live thirty-seven years; in other words, by the time most women have completed the cycle of motherhood nearly half their total life expectancy still lies ahead. In short, more married women are able to go out to work for three major reasons—because there are more jobs available, because there are fewer single women to fill them, and because reduced family responsibilities and a longer life allow the wife and mother to commit herself to work outside the home.

This, of course, only explains *how* the trend has been possible; it does not explain *why* married women should want to seize these new opportunities to work. That is a question to which any snap answer is almost certainly inadequate. One cannot escape the conclusion that, with all the advances in woman's physical and social freedom in the twentieth century—including the ending of so much routine drudgery in the home—it would be surprising if working-class wives were today prepared to confine themselves to a life that is solely domestic, or to a spending power solely dependent on their husbands.

[3] R. M. Titmuss, *Essays on 'The Welfare State'*, London, Allen & Unwin, 1958.

[4] A. M. Carr-Saunders, D. C. Jones, and C. A. Moser, *Social Conditions in England and Wales*, Oxford University Press, 1958.

MARRIED WOMEN WORKING

'A woman's place'?

Many people find this trend not only surprising, but wholly regrettable. Certainly few are willing to argue the question of married women's employment calmly, or to talk about it lightly. Before any facts have been introduced, altar and hearth have been invoked and moral judgments fill the air—a married woman ought, or ought not, to work; a doctor 'appeals' to husbands not to let their wives leave home; and so on. More specifically, public reference continually links working mothers with delinquent children. A woman barrister speaks of the direct relationship between the number of married women in industry today and the anti-social conduct of many children; a book on child welfare argues that the emancipation of women has in many ways led to the neglect of the child; and an educationist claims that the mother who works constitutes an insidious danger of greater destructive force than anything uncovered by the Wolfenden Report. In all this it is plain that many social analysts see the working wife only as a problem likely to cause serious harm to children. When the field studies on which this book is based were being made, the mere mention that they related to married women's employment frequently led to a raised eyebrow, if not to the positive charge that, had the research anything whatever to do with taking mothers out of their homes, then it must be suspect. Indeed one critic contended that part-time *marriage*, the result of wives being so much away from their homes, would prove more profitable to investigate. Where convictions are so deeply held there are clearly genuine problems, even if the arguments are confused.

The hostility to married women working is probably in part a legacy from its nineteenth-century associations with misery and exploitation—in particular with child mortality and the horrors of baby farming. But although anxiety still exists as to the physical risks, current fears centre on the possibility of ill effects if the finely balanced relationship between mother and child is disturbed. Society itself has created a dilemma by developing on the one hand a greatly increased concern for children's happiness and health generally, and by extending the provision for deprived children; and on the other, by emphasizing women's freedom as individuals and their right to compete for jobs and status with men. There are those who, in defending woman's new freedoms in the modern world, passionately assert her right to do as she pleases with her life; in particular they argue that her traditional responsibilities as wife and mother need be no restraint on her working outside her home if she chooses.

Hemmed between these contradictory forces, it would not be sur-

WORK AND FAMILY

prising if the wife who works showed some feeling of guilt. Yet little evidence exists which can be said to justify this particular anxiety; and none of these criticisms allow that wives might successfully divide their time between work and home. At least, none seem to grant the working-class wife this ability, for the stereotypes condemning the wife who works invariably concentrate on her. Perhaps these wives would be less often accused of forsaking their homes if they could represent themselves as a 'movement'; or if they could find an advocate for their 'rights' as forceful as Mrs Hubback in her plea for the employment of graduate wives.[5] Possibly the stereotypes derive in part from middle-class apprehensions about the increasing affluence of the working-class; or even from nostalgic memories of the army of resident domestics long since decimated by social and economic change.

These expressions of doubt and disapproval are not confined to the family life of the woman worker. She is also criticized adversely by employers. There are certain important exceptions, notably in the textile industry. Here the level of skill required of some women operatives has long made them an investment which the Lancashire cotton manufacturer has been reluctant to lose—even at the cost of turning a deaf ear to the stern warning of Samuel Smiles that 'wherever woman has been drawn from her home and family to enter upon other work, the result has been socially disastrous'.[6] Surveys at the turn of the century, in particular that made by Edward Cadbury in Birmingham,[7] show that the employment of married women in manufacturing industry was not confined to the north west. It was during the First World War, however, that women were employed on a large scale by manufacturing industry as a whole. The number so employed was reduced between the wars by a return to convention and to unemployment, so that many, though by no means all, industries excluded married women. In the Second World War the mobilization of the nation's human resources led to the greatest possible utilization of womanpower. Company rules and customs which had prevented the employment of married women were abandoned, and, as the war developed and the labour shortage became more acute, a variety of special part-time shifts and other concessions were introduced to facilitate the employment of women with domestic responsibilities. The exceptional nature of these war-time conditions, however, did not result in management revising its views on the

[5] Judith Hubback, *Wives who went to College*, London, Heinemann, 1957.
[6] S. Smiles, *Character*, London, John Murray, 1887.
[7] Edward Cadbury and others, *Women's Work and Wages*, London, T. Fisher Unwin, 1904.

undesirability of employing the married woman; indeed, in some cases, it served only to confirm the apprehensions. The influx of women into industry in the First World War had coincided with a marked increase in statutory regulations covering working conditions, which many employers found irksome and restrictive. But these regulations applied to all employees, and not just to married women. In the Second World War, the problems of employing married women with family responsibilities were exaggerated in the eyes of the employers by the selective operation of the Essential Work Orders. Employees of firms scheduled under these Orders could not leave or be dismissed without the permission of the Ministry of Labour: they could also be severely disciplined for absenteeism and bad time-keeping. The woman with dependent children, however, was exempt from the conditions of the Orders and was therefore free to behave in a way which inevitably led managements to compare her unfavourably with men and women workers forced to conform with far more stringent conditions. The persistence of unemployment until 1940 had made it unnecessary for management to develop a more tolerant attitude to married women workers, since they were enabled by economic conditions to enforce standards and regulations which paid little heed to the personal circumstances of employees who could not or would not accept the employers' requirements: for example, many firms applied rigid codes of time-keeping and would not tolerate occasional absence. As long as there was still a substantial surplus of women over men in the population, and while the school leaving age was still fourteen, there were sufficient single women who, since they had to earn to live, were prepared to comply with the employer's conditions.

The married woman was regarded as an exceptional type of employee. She was not normally dependent on what she earned, and had other and over-riding claims on her time and energy. After years of domesticity she did not fit easily into the accepted ways of factory behaviour; she had not the same pattern of home life as that of the single factory 'girl'; and her objectives and outlook were different. Fairly or unfairly, many managers believed her to be an unreliable worker, likely to be here today and gone tomorrow, a poor time-keeper with a high rate of absence and little interest in the job. Such views were not, of course, universal, but they were sufficiently widespread to make the alleged unreliability of the married woman tell against her as an employee.

Under these circumstances, many managers clearly preferred to believe that the employment of married women was a temporary measure to tide over unusually difficult periods in the labour market

WORK AND FAMILY

or in times of national emergency. The phase would pass and there would be a return to normal. The demographic and social changes already discussed were rarely perceived; in particular few people realized that the decline in the supply of single women was in truth the writing on the wall for those industries relying on unmarried women workers.

Finding out the facts

For the most part the legion of stereotypes about married women's employment represent an exaggerated response to changes in the economic situation and social structure. As a result, the essentials of these changes are often overlooked. Married women workers are roundly criticized for neglecting their children, yet it is well known that many mothers only go back to work when the last child is old enough to have left school. Again, the wife who works is assumed to be away from home all day, whereas Dr Klein found that about half of those at work did so part-time only.[8] As workers, married women are criticized for unreliability and lack of staying power, yet many firms which are heavily dependent on such labour manage to stay in business. Furthermore, despite the fact that the stereotypes stress the exceptional defects of the *part-timer*, more and more married women have been able to find part-time work.

These stereotypes and contradictions can only abound in the absence of well-established facts about married women's employment today, and its social and industrial consequences. Such facts are not easy to come by; in particular, official statistics have done little to illuminate the important trends in women's employment under consideration here. It is possible, of course, that to draw public attention to these developments might require an official attitude to be expressed; and that in view of the lack of public policy on such questions, even greater controversy might be aroused. Whatever the reasons, there is scant information to rely on in public discussion. As a result the more extreme views go uncorrected and a realistic appreciation of the economic and social significance of married women's employment cannot develop. That many more women are now working on a part-time basis than formerly is self-evident; but official information about part-time work and its distribution among different occupations is incomplete and certainly understates its true extent.[9]

The social and industrial implications of the steady increase in married women's employment are such that there is an obvious need for more factual information to be made available. When the case

[8] Klein, *op. cit.*   [9] Klein, *op. cit.*

25

for research is accepted, there is still the question of what should be studied, and in what setting. From the research worker's point of view, the central difficulty is just how his attention on married women's employment ought to be focused, since the wife who works plays so many roles in our social structure. She is a citizen, a consumer, an employee, a wage earner, a member of a working group, a wife, probably a mother—not to mention a person in her own right. The firm in which she works, too, can have varied functions. It may be a manufacturing unit, a workplace, a source of wages, a social organization, a supplier of goods, and an investment. Separate studies of different aspects of the problem would not add up to a total study of the whole situation. It must be examined from different angles with, so far as possible, all relevant considerations held simultaneously in focus. Within the limits of its resources the research team attempted an overall survey of a situation in which many married women were at work. This was found at Peek, Frean & Co. Ltd., a large biscuit factory which during the war had become dependent on the married woman as its principal source of labour; and in the borough of Bermondsey where married women's employment was believed to be extensive and traditional. In the field work no artificial barriers were established between domestic and industrial issues: and in the interviews with managerial staff, factory workers and Bermondsey households, the points touched on were often similar. What is reported here, therefore, is a case study of married women's employment. Since this study is not a national survey it is not possible to arrive at any firm conclusions for which general validity can be claimed. But it has at least isolated some of the factors which are believed to be relevant and of general importance.

The choice of Bermondsey for study

Bermondsey was an exceptionally suitable setting for the enquiry. A good deal was already known about its social and economic characteristics, as one would expect of an area studied by Charles Booth towards the end of the nineteenth century, and his successors of the *New Survey of London Life and Labour* forty years later. Traditionally a district of casual labour and widespread poverty, it had long attracted the attention of social workers and reformers—among them such illustrious names as Temple, Paterson, and Scott Lidgett. For many years, students of the Department of Social Science and Administration of the London School of Economics had found in Bermondsey plenty of opportunities for observation and practical work—in settlement, Social Service Departments and agencies, and in factories. The School's Anthropology Department

WORK AND FAMILY

had already made a study of kinship in Bermondsey.[1] In 1951, a group of students from the School's course in Personnel Management had investigated labour turnover at Peek, Frean & Co. Ltd., one of the largest firms in the area. This study revealed an unusually high proportion of married women working part-time at the factory—some 2,000 out of its 3,000 women operatives. Furthermore, this was a firm which, until the war, had set its face against the married woman employee, to the point of recruiting only single girls and of dismissing them on marriage. Labour shortage in the war years, continuing into the 1950's, had forced a drastic revision, not only of the firm's recruiting policy, but also of its overall organization of womanpower. In Bermondsey the post-war, nation-wide shortage of workers was aggravated by the wartime drop in the borough's population to about half of the pre-war figure. Even after the war, the dwindling number of Peek Frean's full-time women workers (now married as well as single) had to be supplemented by women prepared to work part-time only. Their insistence on part-time work was a signal that, in the wife's eyes, work took second place to home. As the number of part-timers increased, the system of production came to be governed by the needs of overlapping and interlocking 'shifts' lasting not more than four or five hours.

Peek Frean's, therefore, seemed to offer a dramatic illustration of the growing necessity, because of changing social and economic conditions, to employ married women; a study there would be likely to illuminate the industrial problems posed. After discussions with the directors, managers, and Works Council, permission was given for research to be undertaken. This, financed from the Department of Scientific and Industrial Research, began in September 1954.

Towards the end of this study, in 1956, the research team asked for further financial assistance, putting forward four main reasons why the research should be extended. First, the study's emphasis had so far been placed on married women as employees; but it was evident that this was a secondary role in the lives of the women and their families. Second, at the interviews, the women had been the sole assessors of the extent to which their domestic life was standing up to the strain; clearly they were unlikely to admit to failure. The unexpectedly rosy picture they reported contradicted so many of the stereotypes about the ill-effects of married women working, that closer investigation was obviously needed. Third, Peek Frean's provided exceptionally favourable conditions for its married employees, particularly for those who wanted a choice of part-time hours. Other

---

[1] Edited by Raymond Firth, *Two Studies of Kinship in London*, London, Athlone Press, 1956.

employers might be offering less favourable conditions. Fourth, it was evident that these wives who worked were very dependent on outside help and that in this they relied less on official agencies than on relations and friends. This applied not only to child-minding but to such matters as shopping, washing, and the provision of the midday meal. All these important aspects of married women's employment could only be adequately investigated by extending the study to the whole of the local community; a picture of family life in Bermondsey was needed, covering households of all types, including women who worked elsewhere than at Peek Frean's, and those who did not go out to work at all.

Bermondsey's population of 54,000—comparable to that of East-bourne or Wakefield—made it a manageable size for the kind of study envisaged. The Peek Frean phase had shown that a third of their women employees lived actually in Bermondsey; and a considerable store of background information had been gathered on the area, both from these women and from other local people. Part-time jobs suitable for the working-class woman were plentiful in the vicinity and there was a tradition of married women working. Finally the borough had clearly defined geographical boundaries, was solidly working-class in character, and possessed a strong sense of community. A setting of this type would possibly avoid some of the complexities that surround the causes and effects of married women's employment in less homogeneous areas.

Some basic questions

The scope of the enquiry is more fully described in the next chapter, together with an account of the methods used; but it should be noted that throughout the study's two phases—at the factory and in the borough—the team kept certain basic questions firmly in mind. At its simplest the guiding purpose was to provide a balanced picture of married women's employment in one area; and the consequences for family and factory. To realize this, essential questions had to be answered, and these were of more than local relevance. Any comparative studies (such as that now being undertaken by the Sociology Department at Leicester University) would need to concern themselves with these basic questions: and all are matters which would require exploration if a fully national survey was ever attempted.

In the factory phase of the work the questions asked concerned the main characteristics of the women employed, married and single. They included such points as the proportion of the labour force the married women accounted for; their ages; their type of work and earnings; the structure of their households in relation to the five shifts obtaining at the factory; their domestic commitments; and the time of day their work took them away from home. A question about which little information existed was the age at which the married woman returned to work. This was important from the family angle because it involved assumptions as to the age at which the youngest child could be safely left.

A second set of questions was concerned with the impact on the firm. Having been forced to embark on the large-scale employment of married women, what difficulties had Peek Frean's encountered, and how and to what extent had these been overcome? What differences were to be found between full- and part-time work in terms of absenteeism, turnover and output? In particular, were there new and intractable problems connected with this kind of labour force? What changes in the attitudes of managers and others might be called for?

A third set of questions related to the impact on the family. Did married women alter their daily lives to cope with the extra load? Did they re-plan their day and week on starting work? And from where did they get help, particularly in relation to the essential job of child-minding? What were the effects on housekeeping efficiency; did standards fall because of shortage of time, or rise because of improved finances? How did husbands react to their wives' financial independence? Above all there was the major question of the effects on the children. The cost of the dual role to the women themselves also had to be considered, the physical demands in terms of energy required, the length of their working day, and the personal inconvenience. What effect, if any, had work on the women's own leisure?

Finally, there was the question of why these wives chose to shoulder this extra burden, and how they viewed their job. Did they work primarily for economic 'need', or for pin money, or for such laudable ambitions as house purchase and education, or for less compelling reasons? What did they expect of their job, what kept them with a firm, and under what circumstances did they leave? These, the wife's motives for working, although more complex and less concrete than perhaps any other part of the study, occupied more and more of the team's attention as the research proceeded. Properly interpreted, the married woman's reasons for wanting paid employment can undoubtedly help to explain the significant changes now taking place in the life and outlook of women in modern society.

CHAPTER II

Perspectives and Methods[1]

Settling in—The factory study (1954–56)—The Bermondsey study (1956–59)

Settling in

BEFORE selecting samples and beginning systematic investigation, the research team established itself in Bermondsey in order to make formal and informal contacts and to get the feel of the neighbourhood. The senior research worker spent three months as a part-time domestic worker at St Olave's, Bermondsey's main hospital, and three women members of the team worked for a fortnight at Peek Frean's, on all five of the shifts. To elicit the local attitudes on the working wife, the effects work had on her domestic life and on the welfare of her children, some forty people holding responsible jobs in the borough were consulted. These included councillors, teachers, clergymen, doctors, health visitors, employment exchange staff, probation officers, and settlement workers. A dozen of Bermondsey's very old residents were also encouraged to tell what they remembered of women's life at the turn of the century, and what they thought about the wives of today who worked.

The senior research worker went to live in Bermondsey; this proved to be of the greatest value when the material from the interviews and other sources came to be interpreted. The fact that she was a Bermondsey householder was particularly useful in gaining confidence for the team among the women employees in the critical early days of the factory study.

Peek Frean's helped the team by placing at its disposal two small offices in a house just outside the main factory gate. These rooms were used for interviewing and their nearness to the factory facilitated daily contact with the firm's staff and employees. That these offices were physically outside the actual factory was another advantage, suggesting that the study was not too closely linked with management. The team was given regular access to the factory, which enabled them to appreciate the complexity of organization in a unit which has the population of a small town, and where the timetable of each department is governed by a carefully planned production programme for the whole factory. They also saw for themselves the contrast between the bustling environment where

[1] See Method, Appendix I.

30

PERSPECTIVES AND METHODS

action is closely controlled, and the self-organized, possibly leisurely, and possibly lonely life of the housewife. Brief talks with the women and their supervisors at their work benches suggested what topics needed to be explored more fully in the formal interviews. When these were under way, the team kept up its informal contact by holding two tea-and-talk parties after work at the senior research worker's home. Supervisors and members of the Works Committee were invited, people who knew the factory from a rather different angle from that of the ordinary employee. Daily visits to the workrooms meant that, throughout the Peek Frean study, the team had frequent, short, talks with the women while actually on their jobs; with the supervisors immediately responsible for them; and with management at various levels.

The factory study (1954–56)

The factory study had two principal objectives; first, to select a representative group of married women who worked, and to collect information from them about their home life and their attitudes to work; second, to analyse the managerial problems created by the employment of married women on a large scale. These objectives were pursued by any means that the team thought reasonable and useful: as has been said, a good deal of emphasis was placed in the early stages on frequent but informal contact with the women both inside and outside the factory. But the systematic collection of information was undertaken for the most part by interviewing randomly-selected samples of workers. The main sample of women chosen, referred to henceforth as the Peek Frean Shifts Sample, numbered 250: it was made up of a stratified sample of fifty persons from each of the five shifts as recorded on the firm's pay-roll in January 1955. Each employee was first sent a letter to her home address telling her that a university study, 'Home and Work', was about to be undertaken at Peek Frean's. Later on she was visited while at work by one of the team and asked if she would agree to be interviewed in connection with the study within a day or so. The firm allowed her the necessary time off with no loss of pay. Of the 250 women so approached, 202 were interviewed; and of these, 151 gave a second interview (on a different schedule) six months later. If the employee had left during the six months she was approached at her home for this second interview.

The basic points examined in the interviews with the Shifts Sample were the structure of the woman's household, the normal timetable of each of its members, details of the woman's own daily and weekly routine, and any provision she found necessary to make

MARRIED WOMEN WORKING

for the children at times when both parents were out. The interview also elicited the main facts about her personal and employment history since she had left school, and about her current job, including her attitude to positions of responsibility. As the pilot interviews had revealed considerable hostility among the women to any detailed questions on earning and spending, financial matters were excluded from all the interviews undertaken in the Peek Frean study. The final section of the interview tried to elicit the woman's views on the pros and cons of working, and the attitudes taken to this by the various members of her family. In the second interview, more attention was paid to the woman's leisure, to details of any child-minding that was taking place, and to the sources and extent of domestic help she received.

A second sample interviewed consisted of one in three of all the new employees engaged during a six-week period in the spring of 1955. This sample, referred to as the Newcomers, numbered 100 in all, ninety-six of whom were interviewed within a few days of their engagement. Fifty-seven of those who actually began work were re-interviewed either at the factory or their home after six months had elapsed. These interviews were focused on any changes that had taken place in the woman's domestic life since coming to Peek Frean's, on how her new job compared with any previous ones, and, in the case of those who had left before the second interview, on why she had done so.

The study of managerial problems included an analysis of factory records for the year ending December 31, 1955. Comparisons were made by department and shift of labour turnover and stability, absenteeism, and earnings. Managers of all levels were interviewed to discover whether they associated specific problems with the firm's high proportion of part-time workers. Their attitudes to the large-scale employment of married women were explored, and an attempt made to relate these opinions to data collected in the factory. In addition to these interviews, the team had frequent informal discussions with the Production Manager and with senior members of the Personnel Department.

An important source of information was a detailed study of one of the packing departments, known as N.B.1. This workroom was so dependent on part-time labour that of its 241 daily roll (from 7.30 a.m.–9.30 p.m.) only twenty-six were full-timers. A detailed diary of the activities of the department's two supervisors was kept, and a sample of fifty-three employees interviewed. These are referred to as the Peek Frean N.B.1 Sample. In the same department a record of all transfers was made in order to explore the complaint made by many

PERSPECTIVES AND METHODS

of the Peek Frean Shifts Sample about the frequency of movement from job to job, and its adverse consequences. A further group of women interviewed, not a sample, is referred to henceforth as the Leavers. It comprised twenty-eight employees who had left the firm after working there continuously for at least three years. Reasons for leaving were discussed with these women in detail.

A group selected from the 250 Peek Frean Shifts Sample proved of great assistance in supplementing data from the factory study. These were thirty-six employees (most of whom subsequently enlisted the interest of their households) who had been particularly helpful in the study, possibly from curiosity, possibly because it encouraged them to clarify some of the personal problems arising from their own dual role. All had a husband at home; most had one or more dependent children; and no one was included whose household structure was markedly different from that of the general run of employees in the Peek Frean Shifts Sample. This group is referred to as the Visiting Families. Certain of these families remained on visiting terms with the senior research worker throughout the five years of the study, being called on and called in to corroborate doubtful points or to talk over new ideas. Neighbourly, informal contacts of this kind threw light on a good many of the less obvious aspects of married women's employment as seen in Bermondsey.

The Bermondsey study (1956–59)

In 1956 the borough of Bermondsey contained 20,000 households. The Bermondsey study was based on interviews with households living at a random sample of Bermondsey addresses.[2] This sample—referred to as the Bermondsey Households—numbered 770; it was drawn from the total of addresses on the borough's Electoral Register of February 1957. Interviews were sought at each of the households living at these 770 addresses in Bermondsey's forty-eight miles of streets. A member of the team knocked at the door, and whatever adult answered the knock was told that a university study, 'Home and Work', was in progress in Bermondsey. Would the family co-operate by giving an interview then or by appointment? Normally the person who gave the bulk of the information was the wife, or the husband, or someone who held the head of the household position; but the interview, though starting with one individual, often served as a framework for general discussion in which anyone who happened to be in the room might take part.

Compared with schedules used in the Peek Frean Shifts and Newcomers Samples, the interviews with the Bermondsey households

[2] See Method, Appendix I.

MARRIED WOMEN WORKING

tried to elicit more facts and fewer opinions. The questions on family structure, the family's hours in and out of the house, daily routine, and the woman's work and personal history, were amplified versions of those used in the factory interviews. A cursory examination was also made of the family's main leisure-time pursuits. Compared with the factory study, the information asked regarding any minding of the children was more precise; moreover, the answers given were cross-checked by those to certain questions in other parts of the schedule. Income and expenditure, which it had been thought wise to exclude from the factory interviews, were included in the Bermondsey ones. In general the interview was designed to distinguish between those households where the wife was or was not at work, and those where she had or had not worked since she had her first child. As will be shown later, this second comparison proved impossible to establish on any but broad lines. The older women, those aged sixty and over, were asked what they recalled of their mother's going out to work, and how much they themselves had worked when their children were young. Certain other opinion questions, such as the husband's attitude to married women working, and the parents' ambitions for the children, were relegated to the end of the interview on the principle that if anything got crowded out, it should be views rather than facts. A full interview, taking up to an hour and a half, was given by 517 households. Of those classed as refusals, 114 were chosen for a very short second interview on basic questions; in ninety-three cases this briefer interview was obtained. For purposes of comparison, the Bermondsey households sample was broken down in various ways; for example, Wives and Widows households were analysed separately from those of Husbands and Wives. These separate groupings are explained in Chapter VII.

As far as the dependent children were concerned, the Peek Frean study had dealt mainly with the mechanics of minding, and with the mother's own views on how going out to work affected them. Interviews with the Bermondsey households not only explored this key question of minding in more detail, but tried to assess the progress of each of the household's children aged under eighteen (435 in number) as seen through the eyes both of the home and, if the parents agreed to the matter being pursued, of certain outside agencies. These agencies were later asked to 'assess' the child's progress in relation to that of his peers; the team then set the total assessment against what was known of the mother's current work situation. The point examined was whether the worker's child appeared to have 'fared worse' than the housewife's. The agencies which it was thought were most likely to be able to provide relevant

PERSPECTIVES AND METHODS

information were the London County Council, the Children's Department, and the Health, Youth Employment, and Probation Services. Senior officers of these agencies gave considerable time to discussions with the team as to how the required material could best be obtained, and on the safeguards to be observed. The information they provided was treated as strictly confidential and neither their reports on the individual child nor any of the information given at the factory or household interviews was seen by any persons other than those directly responsible for the research.

As is explained in Appendix I, the team failed to get satisfactory information on those children living at home who had left school. On the other hand, the material provided by the outside agencies on the pre-school and school children was extensive, even if it was less often available than had been expected in a form that permitted the desired comparisons. At the period of the study, the junior school children were those of the post-war bulge in the birth rate. This age group was therefore much in evidence both at the interviews and in Bermondsey generally. This was valuable to the study since, in this area where few mothers go out to work till the child is old enough for school, the chief practical problems centre on the younger school children.

Two additional studies of children were made. These had no connection with the children of the sample households but related to Bermondsey children in general. The first analysed the mother's work situation in connection with every child with a Bermondsey address for whom a probation order was made because he had been brought before the local Juvenile Court in the last twelve months (April 1957–58). A similar analysis of the mother's work or non-work situation was made of every Bermondsey child who had been in any way connected with the Children's Department.

The Peek Frean study examined the relation between factory employment and family life: the Bermondsey study widened the focus, by looking at the connection between married women's work generally, and its place in community life. Neither phase of the study attempted to probe deeply into the psychological factors involved in married women's employment. Even within a limited sociological field it was hard to sort out the crucial variables, or to establish norms for such things as 'child neglect', 'economic need', or 'personal strain'. As the study proceeded the team became increasingly aware that there were special features about Bermondsey which made it even less desirable than is usual in surveys of this kind to claim any general validity for its conclusions. Both in terms of the present and of the recent past, Bermondsey appears somewhat out of the

35

ordinary. It has an unusually plentiful supply of part-time work at a wide scatter of hours. This makes it easier for the wife to relate her working hours to any variations that take place in the domestic calls made on her as her family's age structure changes. Then, too, life is lived within a solidly working-class framework; as many as 30 per cent of Bermondsey's men are in the Registrar-General's lowest social class, V—well over double the proportion for the population as a whole. The findings of the study relate, therefore, to a population with an exceptionally high proportion, not merely of manual workers, but of those in the less skilled jobs within this field. One must also bear in mind the powerful impact of prosperity on this area where, until just before the war, not some but nearly all the homes were poor and where families were still large. George Barker's phrase, 'I am the wife of the workman world with an apron full of children', would be a fair description even today of the mothers of many of those interviewed in connection with the study. Another of Bermondsey's special features is its homogeneous character, deriving from a closely-knit social life and extensive kin relationships. In such an area, should the mother work, the physical risks to the child and the practical problems and anxieties of the parents may well be lessened.

Some may conclude that these special features of the study's setting leave the argument about the harmful consequences of married women's employment exactly where it was. It is possible that the satisfactory nature of the team's findings are accounted for in this way. The only real answer to this argument is, of course, comparative study, such as the one now being undertaken at Leicester. On the other hand these limitations provided some advantages. The very homogeneity of Bermondsey meant that certain lines of enquiry— for example, into the local norms of child-care—could be pursued with greater confidence than usual. Further, in the factory study, the extreme nature of the situation—particularly the dramatic reversal of management's traditional rejection of married women—seemed likely to present the essential issues more sharply. To the criticism that the study thus dealt only in extremes, one can reply that it is difficult to say what the 'extremes' are in married women's employment.

All these considerations will crop up again whenever expeditions into this controversial territory are undertaken: the justification for adopting the approaches described rests on the extraordinarily limited knowledge of the specific consequences for factory and family of married women's employment. Bermondsey proved to be an exceptionally favourable setting for a specific study of this kind, not-

PERSPECTIVES AND METHODS

withstanding that, as an area, it had certain special features which might act as limitations on the general application of its findings. Of these limitations and difficulties, the team remained fully aware. But the data collected are of considerable interest in themselves. They also raise issues of far more than local interest; issues on which society urgently needs comprehensive and objectively-gathered information.

CHAPTER III

Bermondsey's Past

*Special features of Bermondsey–Geographical location–
Isolation–Nineteenth-century expansions–Housing (pre-
1914)–Health (pre-1914)–Employment (pre-1914)–Married
women's employment (pre-1914)–Poverty (pre-1914)–The
fight for improvement (1900–39)–Late persistence of
poverty–The war (1939–45)*

Special features of Bermondsey

WHEN this study was extended from Peek Frean's factory to a sample of Bermondsey addresses, the research team found that there was a higher proportion of married women in employment in the borough than that indicated by the national figures. Roughly 50 per cent of the women responsible for households worked, while the 1951 national average for women under fifty, although not exactly comparable, was 25 per cent.[1] Although no attempt has been made to generalize from this report, it must be emphasized that the choice of Peak Freans and Bermondsey was not made because they were 'typical' sites (as far as any place can be so called), but because of the large numbers of working wives known to be employed at the factory, and of the numbers believed to be living in the borough. To recount something of the history of Bermondsey may clarify the reasons why it is a somewhat unusual locality, and so add to an understanding of the various problems that were examined.

The Bermondsey population is, and has long been, homogeneous. Most families have shared, and to much the same extent, the rise to comparative prosperity from the extreme poverty of Victorian and even Edwardian days. The experience of the grandparents in the inter-related households of Bermondsey, where oral tradition is still strong, has an important bearing on today's attitudes. Not all the memories are painful, of course, and distance has sometimes lent a measure of enchantment; but no such distortion applies to the memories of the generation which, growing up between the wars, is still under fifty. For this particular study, this nearness of the bad old days, and the reversal from the then perennial insecurity, loaded with spells of deep poverty, to the relative ease of today, is probably the most relevant of the many radical changes which have taken place locally. It is this living background which, as was continually

[1] Census 1951.

BERMONDSEY'S PAST

illustrated during the study, has made today's parents determined that their children shall not undergo the privations and humiliations they themselves experienced.

There is another feature of Bermondsey life which bears closely on the subject of the research, viz. that the borough is generally agreed to be a decent sort of place, inhabited by self-respecting, inter-related families who feel rather more than the usual sense of local loyalty. 'One of ours' is a phrase used to describe not necessarily another of the household, but anyone who lives hereabouts. Few want to move away and many are proud to claim 'we are old Bermondsey people'.

These characteristics suggest that the place is somewhat different from many London working-class areas, and in ways which might distort both the good and ill effects of married women's employment. The incentive to work, for example, may be greater in this area where nearly every family holds its past poverty so vividly in mind; while the possibility of subtle, long-distance damage to the child may be masked in a locality whose stability minimizes the immediate physical risks.

Geographical location

Bermondsey lies on the south bank of the river, within sight of St Paul's and the Tower, and about two miles as the crow flies from Piccadilly Circus. It fans out east and south from London Bridge with two ancient highways, the Thames and the Old Kent Road, as its northern and southern boundaries. One of the smallest of the London boroughs, its size (1,700 acres) is approximately that of Marylebone or Wembley, but a fifth of this area is occupied by the Surrey Docks. The original name (Beamond's'ea' or island), denotes its ancient links with the river. Much of it is built on reclaimed marsh, nearly all lies below high-water mark, and building height has to be restricted because of the spongy foundations. Flooding, when the tides are high, has been a menace since the earliest records; the succession of 'Bermondsey walls' which bank the river date back to Roman times.

The oldest part of the borough is situated at a strategic point— the first place upstream at which the river could be bridged. From there down to Limehouse Reach, Bermondsey has three and a half miles of water frontage with the Pool, 'the most valuable sheet of water in the world', as the borough's front door. Twice in the twenty-four hours the tide makes a high-road of the river, but whether on the ebb or flow these reaches of the Thames bear the craft which have provided Bermondsey's livelihood since recorded history. The district known as Rotherhithe ('the sailor's haven') has been a port with a fringe of houses from very early times. Boat building and re-

39

MARRIED WOMEN WORKING

pairing, as well as the discharging and loading of cargoes, was the traditional work until the 1860's when steel ships replaced those of wood. The Surrey Docks are the centre of the Thames' softwood trade, and it is estimated that 85 per cent of the whole country's eggs, bacon, butter, etc., passes through Tooley (St Olave's) Street alone. In 1958 over 800,000 tons of food was landed in Bermondsey. The local industries have long included those connected with food processing. Characteristic kitcheny smells include hot jam, chocolate, chutney, roasting coffee, and newly baked biscuits, while hops, wine in the ancient cellars under London Bridge, and tobacco in the bonded warehouses of Cathay Street, are other indications of the goods handled.

Isolation

Bermondsey's relative isolation has helped to give it a well-defined character. Until Brunel's tunnel was built in the 1840's (and that was originally for pedestrians) London Bridge was the only roadway into Bermondsey from north of the river. Moreover, the great southward bend which the Thames takes by Waterloo Bridge, means that the main Kentish traffic bound for the south coast just by-passes the borough. As soon, therefore, as the day's work at the docks is over, Bermondsey's main roads are, for London, unexpectedly quiet. The fact that neither people nor land-borne trade moves in or out as readily as in other parts of the South Bank is reflected in local attitudes. Anyone whose home is north of the river is said to 'live up in London'; and anything which takes place across the water tends to be relegated to another world as 'no concern of ours'. The narrow strip of land in Rotherhithe between the river and the Surrey Docks is still a curiously self-contained and inter-related community. As late as 1935 it had no bus service, and traffic still has to cross one or other of its swing bridges. One small pointer to the borough's isolation is that old games like the July 'grotto' have hardly died out. All know the details of the local ghost stories—that 'Madam Merachiall' in St Mary's Churchyard puts pigs ears on to anyone she spots on Christmas Eve so that you'd best lock your doors that night if you live around there.

Nineteenth-century expansions

The urbanization and growth of this part of London was unusually spectacular because it involved on an enormous scale not only railways and docks but also the bridging and tunnelling of the Thames. There was a vast undertaking in Rotherhithe when, in 1864, the old docks were expanded into the twelve inter-connected basins of the

BERMONDSEY'S PAST

new Surrey Commercial Dock Company. Within a matter of nine years, three railway stations (London Bridge among them) and miles of line were built within what is now the borough of Bermondsey. As many as four of London's new north to south lines of communication across the river involved Bermondsey: they were Rennie's new London Bridge (1831), Brunel's Thames Tunnel (1843), Tower Bridge (1894), and Rotherhithe Tunnel (1908). Undertakings of such magnitude continuing for so many years meant that heavy manual work became even more characteristic of the area than in its shipbuilding days. New labour had to be brought in; and so many Irish day workers settled in Bermondsey that in the 1840's it was estimated that a third of the area's inhabitants were Irish. It was, however, particularly between 1850-70, and therefore only just out of living memory, that this part of London experienced the spectacular growth in population (from 65,000 to 107,000 for Bermondsey's two parishes) which characterized the nineteenth century.[2]

Housing (pre-1914)

As the population grew, the old Bermondsey which had clustered round the main focal points at London Bridge, at the crossroads at the Bricklayer's Arms, and at the shipyards of Rotherhithe, stretched south and east. The ten miles of Bermondsey streets which existed in 1830 eventually lengthened into the forty-eight miles of today. The great building period was the 1860's; and much of today's housing dates from then. Streets are wide and straight; and the two-storey, dun-coloured brick houses, with their plain parapets and flat fronts, give a genuinely urban, though naturally small-scale, character to this artisan housing. Like so much else about Bermondsey, the typical 'old' housing, though unpretentious, is not commonplace. This only applies to the New Bermondsey of the 1860's. In the more ancient streets, what contemporary reports described as the 'tyrannical side' of railway expansion, had a very different effect. Those families who could not afford to move out doubled up alongside the thousands of immigrants into 'the streets, lanes, yards, courts, alleys and passages' of earlier days. It was part of the expansion plan to use the arches of the new railway bridges as dwelling houses, an optimistic economy which was defeated even in those days by their dirt, damp, and din.

The dilapidated nature of the ancient housing, the lack of drains and drinking water and the constant and consequent outbreaks of cholera, were some of Bermondsey's disabilities. The congestion in the middle of the century is suggested by the fact that Bermondsey

[2] *Victoria History of the County of Surrey*, Vol. IV, 1912.

MARRIED WOMEN WORKING

was chosen for one of the first blocks of dwellings provided by the Metropolitan Association for the Improvement of the Industrious Poor, buildings still occupied and still so inscribed. By the late 1880's conditions were still so bad that the riverside alleys of Rotherhithe formed the subject of one of the early housing enquiries.

Health (pre-1914)

The changeover from a rural area to a densely populated urban one was made particularly disastrous in Bermondsey because of its marshy terrain. At the mid-century, Rotherhithe, in spite of its rapidly increasing population, was still criss-crossed by tidal ditches. These, into which the contents of the privies were thrown, were its sole water supply. Even when such an amenity as a stand pipe did exist, it was permitted for the water to be turned on for only half an hour in the day. The vital statistics tell their own story, and are peculiarly revealing in the case of the children. In 1865, when Bermondsey is believed to have reached its social nadir, 45 per cent of all deaths in Rotherhithe were those of children under five.[3] The children's general condition is illustrated by the following extracts from a report book written up each week by the Head Teacher of an Infants School still in use:

1877. Jan. 13. Thames has several times overflowed. Flooded numbers of the homes . . . so that many children were very ill and are so still.

Feb. 3. Much sickness.

Feb. 10. Several sent home in consequence of smallpox being in their homes.

May 12. Eleanor F. (teacher) away through ringworms supposed to have been caught at school.

1879. Nov. 20. The sickness in the neighbourhood very great, together with the distress and poverty causes many to be away from school.

1883. Jan. 20. Numbers of them have no garments to come in. Some of them are nearly naked.

1890. Mar. 3. Weather severe in consequence many have stayed away . . . the children are so poorly clad, have begged boots for five this week.

Sept. 27. Scarlet fever is very prevalent in the neighbourhood.

The sheer amount of child death appals one. The anxieties and grief occasioned by the constant death of children must have added greatly to the mother's personal load. Paterson, writing of Edwardian

[3] Connan. *A History of the Public Health Department*, 1935.

BERMONDSEY'S PAST

Bermondsey, noted that there was 'a memory of each one's face, remembered usually as it was in sleep, clear and distinct, which never leaves a mother'.[4]

Employment (pre-1914)

Bermondsey's long river frontage has helped to make it an area where unskilled manual work has predominated. Moreover, unemployment, the casual job, the sweated job, and the insanitary one, seem to have affected a larger proportion of the population than in the average nineteenth-century working-class urban area. Though there are few figures to support this contention, the nature of the dock and tanning work in which so many people were employed, presupposes it. The men who work actually on the water are by tradition an independent and unruly race. They have survived much; from the press-gang, and those hazards from fire and water which work on the river entails, down to the insecurity of employment which persisted until only a dozen years ago.

The labour unrest which characterizes dock work has been chiefly directed against the insecurity of employment. The 'Docker's Tanner' strike of 1889 when the men, championed by such leaders as Ben Tillett, Tom Mann, and John Burns, were out for nineteen weeks, is still held vividly in mind by the old people. Improvement in conditions was slow, and until the establishment of the Dock Labour Board in 1947, the dock worker's job continued to be below the level of that for industry in general. The memories of those who have lived all their life in Bermondsey linger less on the wretched wages which used to obtain, than on the casual nature of the work. 'You ran from here to there to get the day's job *and* had to fight for it' was one man's comment to the team; another said that 'once out you never got back'; a third that if you were put off at fifty 'that was the end'. Another man remembered his father being up at three o'clock in the morning and off round the barges to look for a day's work, 'and if he got it it was from six to six for 5s 10d with three halfpence for two and a half pints of black beer'. Well within memory, too, are the indignities of the docker's call stand with its physical fights; the filthy state 'black as Newgate's knocker' the men got into when unloading certain types of cargo; and the fact that the bargee and 'dock rat' were held to be at the bottom of the social, as well as economic, scale.

The old people's accounts of leaving school when they were nine, doing a part-time job at the age of eleven, and, at ten, of being sent out

[4] Paterson, *Across the Bridges*, Arnold, 1911.

43

MARRIED WOMEN WORKING

to clean steps (the twopence being handed over to the home) show how vital it was for even the young children to earn. The girls mostly went into the local factories. Here they washed bottles, labelled jars, and packed custard powders and biscuits. 'Factory girls exist in their thousands in Bermondsey' commented an appeal from the parish church,[5] listing such jobs as rag sorting, wood chopping, and tin soldering. A club helper, writing in 1908,[6] gives a pen picture of some of these girls who, numerically, formed so important a part of the local labour force. One girl, a bean sorter, said hers was an anaemic job 'owing to the foreign dust we breathe.' Another, a 15-year-old box maker, had just cut off her right thumb in a machine used for chopping up tin. She had previously lost two finger ends off her left hand and felt 'I'm no good for nothin' now, without my thumb! I don't know what we should do, but my muvver 'as two or three babies to mind at sixpence a week each!' These were the roughs, contemporaries of Somerset Maugham's *Liza of Lambeth* in the neighbouring borough. The 'better sort of working girls' were put to a trade like dressmaking, or exported to the suburbs and West End as domestic servants. One Bermondsey agency, St Olave's Branch of the Metropolitan Association for Young Servants, found situations for 103 local girls in 1899, and for 130 even as late as 1910.

Married women's employment (pre-1914)

Another source of earning power for the Bermondsey home was the mother herself. At the turn of the century Charles Booth was noting the increase in Bermondsey of cheap labour firms employing women on such jobs as jam making which he described as 'low-class work at low pay . . . and largely seasonal'.[7] Mission reports, too, show that the use of sweated labour abounded. Rag and bottle sorting suggests the level of work the unskilled, and probably married, woman was doing. When the borough installed a refuse destructor in 1902, this replaced the women who had 'wallowed like so many hens . . . each sat or stood behind a mountain of ashes sifting away for dear life. . . . The women worked for a few shillings a week amid the nauseating odours that arose from the semi-decaying vegetable and animal refuse'.[8]

Other part-time work undertaken by the married woman was office cleaning in the City, kitchen work in local pubs, and the scrubbing

---

[5] *A Dispatch from the Church Militant in Bermondsey*, 1896.
[6] *Church Army Review*, 1908. Article on Princess Club.
[7] Booth, *Life and Labour of the People in London*, 3rd series, Vol. IV.
[8] *Southwark and Bermondsey Annual*, 1902.

which the resident maids of the upper-class families across the water could not be expected to undertake. Then there was out-work proper. In this area, sack and bag making is a traditional job; so, formerly, was the hand stitching of leather; and dyeing and curling of hat feathers; fur pulling (a job associated with tuberculosis); and work like squib making at 2½d per five gross. Finally there was the job that the least skilled and most tied of mothers could undertake, the taking in of washing, mangling, and ironing for better-off homes. Of all the types of women's work then undertaken, this is the one that people today hold most bitterly in mind in connection with their own mothers and grandmothers.

Much of the work was seasonal and short-term, 'You'd get called off at the factory gate for one day's work'. It was also very local, 'You'd come home to dinner to feed the baby'. On the other hand, when the job was supposedly regular, the hours, both in industry and shop work, were much longer than today's, and of course included Saturday morning. In general, paid employment for the wife who also had a home to run must have been much harder than it is today.

There are no official figures to show the extent of work among the Bermondsey married women, but everything points to its having been common, persistent, and dictated by need. The occupation of the female patients of the local Nursing Association, as listed in their annual reports for 1891–1911, by no means suggest that those in employment were all girls or spinsters.[9] That wives continued to try to work even when conditions were slowly improving, is illustrated by the job history of today's older women. The employment record of a consecutive series of 100 women patients at the Bermondsey Medical Mission, all aged over sixty-five when they were asked about it, showed that fifty had been out at work in the inter-war years, and that in twenty-four cases this had been full-time factory work. Of those who did work, thirty-one were mothers of three or more children; whereas only ten of those who had not worked had had a family of this size. The economic implications are obvious.

All told, the information assembled, impressionistic as it must be in the absence of statistics, presents an astonishing record of the extent of married women's employment. The Bermondsey Settlement Annual Report for 1900 confirms this impression. 'These mothers', it said, 'lead hard self-sacrificing lives, their amazing powers of endurance are only equalled by the skill with which they contrive to keep their families on about half the weekly sum found necessary in the Poor Law Schools for each child's food and clothing.'

[9] St Olave's District Nursing Association, *Annual Reports* 1891-1911.

MARRIED WOMEN WORKING

Poverty (pre-1914)

Towards the end of the century, when Booth made his great enquiry and when a measure of reform had been effected by such legislation as the Artisans Dwellings Act, his analysis ran as follows. 'I know', he said, 'no set of people in London who look quite so poor as those who do their marketing in Bermondsey New Road on Sunday morning.'[1] Or again, 'I have written of this portion of London at considerable length because in it certain evils rise to their greatest height. It has not the Whitechapel Jew, the Hoxton burglar, or the Notting Dale tramp, nor is it, like parts of Fulham, a receptacle and dumping ground for the rejected from other quarters. . . . It is neither vicious nor criminal in any marked degree: it is simply low; but for debased poverty aggravated by drink this portion of Southwark and Bermondsey fall below any other part of London.'[2] This comment from a professional worker was echoed by that of a casual visitor of 1896 who wrote to the *Lincolnshire Echo* that he had found Bermondsey 'terribly poor, hideous to look at, hideous to listen to, and particularly hideous to smell'.[3] His observations were probably partly inspired by the number of offensive trades, glue boiling, skin dressing, manure making from dog dirt, which were a feature of local industry. As late as 1916 there were comments on Bermondsey's 'smell of dirt and congestion, the odours of fish and beer and the stink of decaying human life'.

The extent of the poverty was continually confirmed by what the older people in Bermondsey told the research team of their own childhood. Very many had poignant memories of inadequate food and shoes, of the humiliations of the Poor Law, of the cold charity of the 'Insistence Board', and of the 'sell that, and that, and that' of the Means Testman. One old lady of eighty-four recalled, 'I've seen my mother cry because there was nothing for us—you pawned the clock, chair, bedding,' and she remembered waiting in all day for something to eat until her father could get a can of soup at the Relieving Office. Another, speaking of the early 1900's, said that, as children, they just had one meal a day (and hers was a small and comparatively well-off home with only five children). Some of these old people still metaphorically lick their lips at the breakfasts which, if the child could get hold of a ticket, were obtainable at one of the missions. Another woman, comparing today's spending with her own ('A Saturday halfpenny and we thought we were rich! ') recalled

[1] Booth, *op. cit.* [2] Booth, *op. cit.*
[3] *Lincolnshire Echo*, May 1896. Quoted in *A Despatch from the Church Militant in Bermondsey*, 1896.

46

BERMONDSEY'S PAST

how she and her brother would walk the two and a half miles to Greenwich to blue their joint wealth, and on windfallen apples at that! Others vividly remembered the details of fetching back the clothes from the Monday morning line-up at the in-and-out shop, or being sent out with a cup for a halfpenny worth of jam. Illness was dreaded, 'We never had no insurance nor nothing'. Or again, 'When my mother had the smallpox no one ever came near us except the Vicar'. The continual borrowing was also mentioned, and the fact that credit, hard to get, was used only for essentials, not as is the case today, for extras. Paterson noted how often the woman eventually became content if she could just 'turn the corner of each week with the friendly aid of the pawnbroker'.[4]

Charity and relief, from the lying-in bundle to the black treacle of the Relieving Officer, was, at its best, distasteful. One woman could still see her father coming in with his hands all torn from the stone breaking he had had to do to get the pittance of the unemployed. Another, an elderly man, told a racy tale of how his father had outwitted a detested Relieving Officer by pinching the latter's coat and pawning it. The family considered that their Dad's odd days in jail were well worth the satisfaction of paying off old scores.

The Mission's reports are full of references to drunkenness, including its prevalence among women and the factory girls. 'Drink is the Citadel' as the missions so tirelessly proclaimed. Way back in the late 1890's, a little social survey which a Wesleyan mission carried out on a Sunday during 1–3 p.m. and 6–11 p.m. at certain pubs near one of the chapels showed 1,777 people entering one pub: and going into another, 826 men, 418 women (56 carrying babies) and 277 boys and girls (209 carrying jugs). That was seventy years ago, but the team noticed how often Bermondsey people still used phrases like 'He (or she) drank', or, 'My Dad was a good husband when sober', to indicate the character of their own childhood. The very old people, remembering the brawls that used to occur so regularly inside and outside pub doors, made the point that nowadays people keep their quarrels at home. They also recall the contrast between the pub and the wretched housing with a rabblement of children. Though most Bermondsey people never seem to have attached much social stigma to pub going, and do not do so today, nevertheless they still associate the heavy drinking of the past with low material standards for the family. If a gay-looking, comfortable home helps to discourage too much pub going, then, as will be stressed later, people feel this is one more justification for lavish spending on the home, the wife making her contribution by going out to work.

[4] Paterson, *Across the Bridges*, 1911.

47

The fight for improvement (1900–39)

The old people in Bermondsey often associate the marked betterment in their own lives with the disappearance of the 'halfpenny bumpers', the horse-drawn trams which stopped running in 1911. The general rise in wages and improved employment conditions of this period was particularly significant in a highly industrialized and impoverished area like Bermondsey. So was the social legislation which marked the decade before the First World War. The demographic changes, too, were of vital importance, and especially so to the women. Writing in 1935 Bermondsey's Medical Officer of Health[5] considered that the decline in population was the most pronounced of all changes he himself had seen locally since the turn of the century. It had fallen by 10,000 between 1901–17 and there had been a very steep drop in the child population between 1911–35.

Bermondsey's Council played an unusually active part in the general fight to improve health. In 1901 it took the advanced step of appointing a full-time Medical Officer of Health. By 1908 it had set up a school for mothers. This, one of the earliest Infant Welfare Centres in England, gave its first health visitor the nominal responsibility for a matter of 4,000 new babies a year. The Council's activity in the field of health developed still more after the 1914 war. It provided a convalescent home for mothers and children; and in the thirties was helping voluntary agencies with two day nurseries.[6] In 1926 it set up a sanatorium, and ten years later built a Public Health Centre. The Council laid emphasis on street preaching and other educational measures of preventive medicine, especially in connection with venereal disease and dental care.

Housing was another field in which the Bermondsey Council was ahead of the times. As early as 1914 it took over 227 dwellings, and between 1922–30, when the Homes for Heroes campaign was being fought, it launched various clearance schemes. Steady progress was made throughout the thirties, the Council pioneering to improve on the standards of housing thought suitable for the working class. It also set up a 'Beautification Committee'. This Committee is still in existence, but was at that date a surprisingly advanced step for an artisan area. In the late 1920's it began the extensive tree planting, the limes, planes, and poplars which add so enormously to the pleasantness of Bermondsey's streets today.

Hand in hand with the statutory provision, and often undertaken by the same people,[7] was a flood of voluntary effort. Such work had

[5] Connan, *op. cit.*   [6] Connan, *op. cit.*
[7] Fenner Brockway, *The Bermondsey Story*, London, Allen & Unwin, 1949.

BERMONDSEY'S PAST

a long history in this part of London. Kingsley, in *Alton Locke*, wrote of plunging into the wilderness of Bermondsey, and of the foul ditches in the district east of London Bridge known as 'Jacob's Island'. You emptied the slops into these 'with one hand, and filled your kettle with the other'.[*] Dickens, too, made repeated efforts to draw attention to the same area; he used it as the setting for Bill Sykes' last leap.[*] In Bermondsey, 'the poor' who so fascinated the Victorians, were both plentiful and conveniently get-at-able, and a surprising number of people did more than send their subscriptions and cast-off clothes or set up their anonymous ('The Gift of a Lady') granite drinking troughs. They came in person—doctors, business men, royalty, missioners, undergraduates, and above all 'ladies'—and some stayed for life. Once there, they founded settlements, medical missions, temperance lodges, cripples' parlours, children's holiday funds, and educational classes for all, from working men to factory girls. Most of this effort stemmed from religious conviction; direct action, directed by prayer, was the keynote of a Christianity which was muscular, efficient, and tireless. For the workers at St James' Mission, for example, 'time was always allotted each morning for Bible study and each afternoon for united prayer'. But 'no time was apportioned for recreation'.[1] Bermondsey has thus been worked on and lived in by a band of devoted men and women for the last eighty years. They included such distinguished names as Dr Scott Lidgett, Princess Christian, William Temple, Alfred and Ada Salter, Cecil Wilson, Dr Alex Paterson, Dr Selina Fox, Eveline Lowe, and Joe Blake. They, and the less eminent of Bermondsey's officials, clergy, teachers, club leaders, and nurses must have had peculiar insight into the area's needs since so many of their names are still evergreen. Nor should one omit to mention a point which came out in the research, that not all the effort came from outside. God-fearing, artisan families living in Bermondsey played their part in the social and evangelistic work among the poorer homes. A reminder of this is a drinking fountain to one 'Jabez West, Temperance Advocate'. Erected in 1884, it is London's first public memorial to a working man. The reports of these social workers suggest an extraordinarily remote world, especially in its minutiae. Writing of his boyhood one former boys' club member recalled how, at his first camp, their tent officer had put on a funny striped suit to go to bed in, and how it had made the boys laugh! Odd as some of these workers seemed to Bermondsey, and odd though some of them undoubtedly were, they established, in most difficult circumstances, that wealth of voluntary

[*] Kingsley, *Alton Locke*, 1876 ed.   [*] Dickens, *Oliver Twist*.
[1] *Faithful unto Death*, Memorial of Rose Colby, St James' Mission, 1909.

agencies which have so often sparked off, and later supported, the official measures for social betterment.

The late persistence of poverty

The most significant feature of this past as it affects the research is the relatively recent date to which minimum economic and social standards persisted. A local doctor giving evidence at a 1914 enquiry on the National Insurance Act[2] could still draw the following picture of the area:

'*Question*: What are these people for the most part?
Answer: I suppose the bulk of them are waterside labourers . . .

Q.: What are the women?
A.: They are chiefly in the jam factories, the tin factories, and the biscuit factories. Some of them who are a rather lower grade still are rag sorters and wood choppers.

Q.: What do they make in a week, do you think?
A.: Their wages vary. The rag sorters, I suppose, would only get from 5s to 7s 6d per week. The women at the biscuit works vary, but I think the average rate is about 10s or 12s.

Q.: Are they married or single, or mixed up together?
A.: They are mixed up together. The married women, I think, almost entirely work in the jam and pickle factories, and the single women are girls who work in the biscuit works and the tin factories . . . (It is a kind of reserve market for those people when the husband comes on bad time.)

Q.: What about the women?
A.: . . . The women who get employment in these factories are very steady, and not given to drink to the same extent as the men. The woman who drinks is the waster who will not work. She is the married woman at home who is not looking after her home.

Q.: You give eight cases of women in jam and tin-box factories working from 7 a.m. to 7 p.m., each having five children to care for after factory hours. You say none of these women were really fit for work for months before confinement or for months afterwards. Does that mean you would give them a certificate before confinement and afterwards?

[2] Appendix to the *Report of the Dept. Cttee. on Sickness Benefit Claims under the National Insurance Act 1914*, Vol. III. Giving evidence—Dr B. A. Richmond (of Bermondsey).

BERMONDSEY'S PAST

A.: I think that one could honestly say that they were incapable
of work. Because, as I have pointed out, these women have
already done heavy work at home, they are badly nourished,
and their health has suffered from the hard nature of their
lives.'

When the older people speak of the 1914 war as the watershed
between the consistently bad old days and the rather less severe
ones, and when they recall the depression years, they talk primarily
in terms of employment. In this dock area with so many homes
dependent on casual work, the national scramble for jobs in the
1930's was doubly urgent. In Bermondsey itself, in 1932, the percentage of unemployed among the insured population reached the
figure of 17·8, representing some 7,500 persons, compared with
London's average rate of unemployment which was 13·5. By 1950
Bermondsey's unemployment rate had dropped to under 1 per cent.
The war brought work and raised wages but it did not remove the
area's basic disability, the casual nature of the docker's job.

In health, too, the improvement was slow. Despite a decline in
population, deaths from diphtheria and scarlet fever remained at
roughly the same figure in 1931 as twenty years previously: so did the
tuberculosis rate for children and young adults. The extent of malnu-
trition is suggested by the fact that, in one of the mission reports for
1922 (that for the South London Mission working chiefly in Bermondsey and its immediate fringes), reference is made to over 50,000
free breakfasts provided for children under fourteen during the winter
months. For many of these children 'the large cup of cocoa, several
slices of bread and butter and jam' was believed to serve as their
'only good meal of the day'.[3] Dirt was another of the troubles which
persisted late. Even in 1935, the Medical Officer of Health was making provision for cleaning 4,000 verminous children per annum,
devoting a page of his memoirs (published that year) to the latest
methods of bug destruction.[4] He saw his last case of a child being
sewn into its clothes for the winter in about 1927.

Bad housing also persisted late. Any clearance schemes were
necessarily extensive in a locality which, as late as 1916, could still
contain such plague-spots as 'a street of 400 yards, with three-storied
houses on either side' in which lived 2,500 souls.[5] The mission which
referred to this particular street doubtless quoted the worst it knew;
but nearly eighteen years later, the Medical Officer of Health him-

[3] *City of Laughter—City of Tears*, South London Mission Report, 1922.
[4] Connan, *op. cit.*
[5] *South London and Deptford Mission Report*, 1916-17.

51

MARRIED WOMEN WORKING

self, making a careful comparison of various aspects of local housing in 1934 as compared with 1927, found that 'the figures do not indicate any material improvement'.[6] And this was a period when there was less overcrowding in the administrative County of London.

Education was another matter in which advance was late. Bermondsey had only one fee-paying school; and in 1923 the borough had a lower figure (1·1 per 1,000 elementary school children) of scholarship winners than that for any other of the London boroughs except Shoreditch and Finsbury. Between 1909 and 1926, the proportion of Bermondsey children in secondary schools actually declined, from 3·7 to 3·5 per 1,000 population; whereas in the neighbouring borough of Lewisham it rose from 11·9 to 19·9.[7]

The war (1939–45)

Bermondsey's location and the concentration of docks, bridges, factories, and railways made it an obvious wartime target. From the early blitz of May 1940, to the V2s of 1945, the area suffered intensely. It was the second most heavily bombed of all the metropolitan boroughs and 796 people were known to have been killed. Among many terrible incidents was one at London Bridge where at least sixty-three people died.[8] The bombing also destroyed many of the amenities which this poverty-stricken borough had built up with so much imagination and effort. Of Bermondsey's 19,000 separate dwellings, 3,200 were totally lost, and only a few hundred suffered no recorded damage.[9] Hundreds of acres of the docks, and many industrial premises were burnt out. At Peek Frean's 40,000 square feet were destroyed. By June 1947, and before any major rebuilding had begun, extensive repairs had to be undertaken in every street. Bermondsey's vulnerable position also meant that evacuation began early and continued late. This, and the wholesale physical destruction, had by 1944 reduced the population to a third of its pre-war figure of 120,000. In 1946 it had risen to 54,000, the size at which planning policy decided it should remain. Present-day Bermondsey, therefore, is one of the few central urban areas which although it has very many new buildings, nevertheless enjoys more elbow-room than formerly.

Two years after the end of the war, but closely connected with wartime experiences, the National Dock Labour Board was set up, revolutionizing the character of the docker's job. He was guaranteed

[6] Connan, *op. cit.*
[7] Flann Campbell, *Eleven-Plus and All That*, Watts, 1956.
[8] *A.R.P. Incident Book* (Stainer Street, 17.2.41).
[9] *Bermondsey Official Guide*, eighth edition.

BERMONDSEY'S PAST

a minimum weekly wage, though not a full week's wages. The change has, however, provided a minimum of security. One of Bermondsey's few public memorials, a statue to Ernest Bevin, typifies the significance that this riverside borough attached to the ending of casual work, in which Bevin himself played so important a part.

Though the war lengthened hours of work, it enlarged the range of jobs open to women, and removed many of the old prejudices and bans on work for the married woman. In particular it extended the opportunities for part-time work, and for work outside the normal hours. It also led to the setting up of certain provisions like day nurseries which enabled the mother of young children to be away from home. The effect of the war on the labour force at Peek Frean's has already been discussed; similar changes, if on a smaller scale, doubtless took place at many other local firms, and in a variety of types of employment.

The only justification for quoting the short and simple annals of these particular poor is that so many Bermondsey homes hold their past most vividly in mind. 'We don't want *them* days again' expresses their determination to keep on raising standards, and helps explain the wife's readiness to go out to work. While the younger couples feel that they are now secure enough not to bend to circumstances, people of all ages declare roundly 'We're not going down no more'. Nevertheless, someone or other in the room is always likely to add an uneasy 'Who knows?'. On the whole, however, the mood is confident. An inscription on one of the local war memorials, 'For his very ashes do cry out in triumph', might be held to apply not only to the men of the Queen's Regiment whom it commemorates, but to Bermondsey's own resurgence from the blitz, and her final emergence from want.

CHAPTER IV

Bermondsey Today

Structure of population–Housing–Employment–Women's employment–Services for children–A stable community

Structure of population

THE vital statistics of Bermondsey's population (54,000 in 1958) show that the 1951 birth rate was 17·6 per 1,000 as compared with the national average of 15·5; the marriage rate 19·3 as compared with 16·5; and the death rate 12·3 compared with the national figure of 12·0.

The following table gives Bermondsey's social structure. Even by East London standards its solidly working-class character is striking. It contains double the London average for Social Class V; and only five of London's twenty-eight boroughs have a lower proportion of Classes I and II.

TABLE 1

Males aged eighteen and over by Social Class (Registrar General's Classification) in Bermondsey; County of London; and England and Wales, 1951

Social Class of males aged 18 and over	Bermondsey per 1,000	London A.C. per 1,000	England and Wales per 1,000
I	8	40	33
II	80	130	145
III	461	542	530
IV	132	119	161
V	319	169	131

Housing

The most noticeable feature of Bermondsey's housing is the small number of families who are overcrowded or who share a home; the uniformity of the housing; and, for an old urban area, the high proportion of the population occupying a newly-built home. At the end of 1957, the Borough Council's waiting list (excluding transfer cases) was 657. The 1958 figures for overcrowding give only 105 families so affected, and the slums that do still exist are not overcrowded. The figures also show that about half of Bermondsey's 15,000 houses and flats are Council owned (5,385 Bermondsey Borough Council, 1,939 London County Council); and that over 3,000 have been built since the war. A combination of circumstances has produced these favourable characteristics. As late as the 1930's the state of Bermond-

BERMONDSEY TODAY

sey's housing was still grossly inadequate; the war damage was most extensive; the population has halved; and the local council has had an outstandingly vigorous pre- and post-war housing policy. All this means that by national standards there is an unusually large proportion of Bermondsey families living in fairly uniform housing of the high standard which Council ownership implies. As many as one in seven families live in a newly-built, and in most cases self-contained, flat or house. Chapter III has emphasized that today's housing is in striking contrast with that of former days, which is of course common enough in post-war England. The point here is that in Bermondsey not some, but nearly every family, has experienced very considerable improvement in the comfort and appearance of its home. And it has to be remembered that large re-housing undertakings are still going forward.

Employment

Bermondsey is one of the areas of high industrial concentration served by the Port of London. The employment of 20 per cent of its male workers is connected with the river, while a high proportion of its other workers are engaged in work that is immediately dependent on the port, in particular food processing and distribution. The borough's acute labour shortage, due to wartime reduction in population and the expansion of local industry, is reflected in the fact that about 26,000 people come into Bermondsey to work, which is double the number of those residents who are employed outside the borough. That this figure is not unlike that for the neighbouring boroughs of Southwark and Deptford emphasizes the shortage of labour in this part of London.

A rough guide to the character of employment in Bermondsey is given below, though the figures (kindly supplied by the local office of the Ministry of Labour) can only give a general indication, since Bermondsey is not a separate unit for purposes of National Insurance, and the area covered by these statistics does not coincide with that of the borough.

TABLE 2

Approximate numbers employed in selected principal industries in Bermondsey. 1958

Type of industry	Males (15 & over)	Females (15 & over)	Total
Wharf and dock work (approx.)	6,000	—	6,000
Biscuit manufacturing	1,719	3,172	4,891
Food processing	1,757	2,161	3,918
Road haulage	1,329	98	1,427
Railways	1,052	42	1,094
Food distribution	600	444	1,044

MARRIED WOMEN WORKING

Figures from the same source show that both the building and clothing trade are important, each employing about 1,700 persons. The National and Local Government services and Distributive Trades, excluded from the above table, employ about 5,000. The latter engage about 3,000 people, almost half of them females. Three smaller, but traditionally important industries, are the leather trade and the manufacturing of cardboard and of tin boxes; in these the chief firms employ some 3,000 people, half of them female.

Though unemployment in the accepted sense has been banished from dock work since the setting up of the Dock Labour Board, the periods of time when there is no work available and when the docker qualifies for attendance money only (£6 1s 0d for a full week in 1958) are still relatively high. In January, 1957, about 10 per cent of the men were so placed.

Dock work still has certain features which distinguish it sharply from that of the ordinary industrial worker. Of the 28,000 men working in any capacity in the Port of London, 18,000 are employed by the day and therefore have more uncertainty about getting work than the ordinary weekly wage earner. Quite apart from the fall in pay for a workless week (as compared with a full week's wage) there are also sharp variations in the earnings for a full week.

Of Bermondsey's own 6,000 or so dockers (as distinct from those employed in ancillary work) about 2,000 are employed on a regular basis. In 1958 the total average weekly earnings of these 2,000 regulars was probably £16 10s 0d. The other 4,000 odd men are employed in the Surrey Docks and are engaged week by week, or at least by short periods. Work in these particular docks is more seasonal than elsewhere since the cargoes, largely timber, are affected by the freezing of the Baltic ports. Most of these men spend as much as three months in the year on the pay which the Dock Labour Board makes to the man for whom there is no work in that week. A basic 44-hour, 5½-day week is worked, but there is a great deal of overtime when a ship has to catch a tide or to make a quick turn round. Minimum rates for an 8-hour day at the time of the study were £1 10s 0d, varying with the type of cargo. Ninety per cent of these men were on piecework. Though the weekly average earned throughout the year was about £12–£13, when the docks were busy a top figure of £30 might be made.

About another 1,000 workers do ancillary jobs. They include dock police, clerks, maintenance men, lock gate operators, and 'shore-riggers', the men who clean out the hold after a cargo has been discharged. Some of these latter men may be on a 48-hour shift which involves only five hours' actual work. Their minimum day's

BERMONDSEY TODAY

wage was £2 8s 0d, a night's wage £2 10s 0d. It is difficult to give any realistic figure for the earnings of these ancillary workers; the weekly average of a maintenance worker, such as an engineering craftsman, may be as much as £20; while £15 is common for four days of work by a 'shore-rigger'.

Work on the river has its own hierarchy, from the Trinity House job of the pilot down to that of the most unskilled labourer. A dock worker's life is no sinecure. The thick neck muscles of the typical docker are proof that even today the job still involves the pushing, humping, and lifting of heavy weights. In addition much of the work is undertaken in the open, and those actually on the barges have no protection whatever from the squalls and fierce east winds that blow up river.

Women's employment

Over half of Bermondsey's female population of working age, 11,000 girls and women, are in employment. Compared with work-ing-class boroughs north of the river, the needle trade is negligible, the food trades important. About half of those employed work in the food, drink, and tobacco industries, their firms including such well-known names as Hartley's, Crosse and Blackwell's, Pearce Duff's and, of course, Peek Frean's. Rather more than half work actually in the borough. In general the opportunities for part-time work are exceptionally good, and throughout this study the figures from the local Labour Exchange showed a market for both full- and part-time work in local industry and in cleaning and café work in the City and West End. To these must be added the small, part-time jobs for which no insurance card is issued. There is also a certain amount of part-time work in Bermondsey's own shops, and in those of the surrounding boroughs. Much of the domestic type of work can be undertaken by women of all ages and with little training or ex-perience. Any job which can be done at one's own pace and with a minimum of supervision is especially valued, not only by the older women but by those younger wives who are nervous about re-starting work after a considerable spell of domesticity. Much of this part-time domestic work is available from very early morning to late evening, and much of it is within, at most, a twenty minutes' journey. The following advertisements from the South London press in May 1960 indicate the type of job that encourages even the wife who has not worked for years to consider trying her hand:

CLEANERS (women) reqd. for mornings only.—Apply Trocadero, Elephant & Castle.

57

MARRIED WOMEN WORKING

CLEANER wtd for large hairdressing salon, mornings only; pleasant conds.; 6.15 a.m. to 9 a.m.; wages £3.—Apply Phyllis Earl, Ltd., 32 Dover-st., W.1. HYDe Park 7541.

CLEANER/Washer-up, 10 a.m.-4 p.m., Mon.-Fri.; £4 and meals.— Wee Astor Cafe, Quadrant Arcade, Regent-st.

CLEANER (female) reqd. by Lillywhites Ltd., of Piccadilly Circus; mornings, 6.30-10, Mon. to Sat. inclusive.—Apply Staff Manager, WHI 3181, for interview.

CLEANER reqd., early mornings, 5-day wk., 6.30 a.m. to 9.30 a.m.— Apply Hobson & Sons, 1/5 Lexington-st., London, W.1.

EARLY morning part-time male cleaners reqd.—Apply Mr. Cooley, 14 Sun-st., E.C.2. BIS 7281.

EARLY morning cleaners reqd. Regent St., 6-8.30 a.m., wages £2 10s.—Ring Mr. Wood, TRA 7175.

FOR THOSE WOMEN who seek early morning office cleaning situations, Office Cleaning Services Limited have a Staff Department at 80/84 Bondway, S.W.8, where further details will be given and women interviewed daily (Monday-Friday) between 10 a.m. and 4 p.m. (Tel.: RELiance 7151/2.)

EARN YOURSELF some extra money in the early morning; some women wanted for office cleaning.—Write or call (Monday-Friday) 3-6 p.m., Mrs. Sloane, 56a De Laune-st., S.E.17. (Tel. CENtral 1457.)

FULL or part-time waitresses, 3/1 per hr. and free meals on duty; uniform allowance.—Guy's Hospital College Catering Co., Great Maze Pond, S.E.1. HOP 2288.

KITCHEN asst. (female) wtd. for City canteen; hrs. Mon. to Fri. 8.30 a.m. to 4.30 p.m., and every fifth Sat. 8.30 a.m. to 11.30 a.m.; overalls free.—Apply Canteen Manageress, 119 Cannon-st., London, E.C.4.

KITCHEN hand (female) reqd.; Mon. to Fri. 8.30 a.m. to 3.45 p.m.— Mr. Redpath, London Stone, 109 Cannon-st., E.C.4.

KITCHEN hand, 8-4.30, no Sats.—Apply Mrs. Howling, Adelaide House, London Bridge.

Services for children

Bermondsey has an unusually good supply of amenities, statutory and voluntary, which provide for the formal and informal education, the leisure and the general well-being of its 12,000 children aged under fifteen. The school meals service of the London County Council is specially relevant to married women's employment. At the time of the survey there were four day nurseries provided by the Ministry of Health and one nursery school and six play centres provided by the London County Council. Bermondsey also has an uncommonly large and efficient supply of youth organizations, in

BERMONDSEY TODAY

1956–57 their junior (5–11) membership alone being about 2,000.[1] There are indoor and open-air swimming baths, and playgrounds with attendant staff and good equipment are sited in most parts of the borough. Both the London County Council and the Bermondsey Council organize open-air shows in the parks, at peak traffic hours, and group games sessions during the school holidays. The Bermondsey mother who wants to work can turn to many such services, and the mothers interviewed frequently referred to the incidental help with minding that they derived from such sources.

A stable community

Two aspects of Bermondsey life hard to substantiate but undoubtedly relevant to married women's employment are its respectability and its homogeneity. Despite past poverty and notorious slums Bermondsey has somehow long enjoyed the reputation of being a decent, social kind of neighbourhood. Even at the turn of the century, when its distress was extreme, Booth found it 'Neither vicious nor criminal . . . it is simply low . . . debased poverty aggravated by drink'.[2] When the Bermondsey figures for certain social characteristics are compared with those for other London boroughs, they appear to support this general claim to stability. In 1951 in Bermondsey divorced men and women accounted for 0·8 per cent of those who were or had been married compared with a figure of 1·1 per cent for the Administrative County of London. The suicide rate in 1958 was 0·148 per 1,000 compared with 0·17 for London; and the illegitimacy rate 4·1 per cent of live births compared with London's 9·9 per cent. Way back in the 1930's the Medical Officer of Health could comment that Bermondsey's 2·05 per cent illegitimacy rate for the last five years had been the lowest for the London boroughs. When the team came to study the number of all Bermondsey children involved in a year's Juvenile Court cases, the figure suggested that the incidence of trouble was relatively low, the offences light. Surface impressions too support this claim to 'decentness'. Bermondsey has not that aura of staleness with which centuries of overcrowding have impregnated so much of the East End. The city slicker and flashy-looking woman are seldom seen, nor are there hopeless-looking men lying about on park benches. It is rare to hear adults rowing with one another, or berating a child harshly, the groups of teenagers don't cause disturbances, and the smaller children don't seem unduly destructive, cadging, quarrelsome, unkind to animals, or prone to write rude words on the wall. The fact that disturbed marital rela-

[1] *Bermondsey Youth Committee Review*, 1956–57.
[2] Booth, *op cit.*, Vol. IV.

MARRIED WOMEN WORKING

tionships and anti-social conduct appear to be less common topics of conversation than in certain other working-class districts of London, also suggests that Bermondsey's claim to be a self-respecting place is well founded. None of this alters the fact that it is in most ways a quite ordinary working-class area. The cultural paucity of many homes is commented on by the teachers, it has a minimum of cultural organizations, and few public events of interest take place.

The 'very peculiar and exceptional characteristics' and the marked sense of unity of this part of London have long been recognized. A recent illustration is that the railway viaducts which slashed through the district so brutally a hundred years ago are still not accepted as the logical boundaries. As late as 1954 there was strong and successful opposition to revising the polling wards so as to align them with the new boundaries which the railway lines imposed a century ago. A strong Irish and Catholic element, the descendants of the men who navvied Bermondsey's docks, tunnels, railways, and bridges, is now an integral part of local life. One of this group, respected and popular throughout the borough, is the Parliamentary Member since 1940, Mr Bob Mellish. Despite the vaguely foreign air cast by the river, Bermondsey's shops and surnames are rarely foreign. There has been no settlement of West Indians to cause a colour problem, and the Jewish population is too small to maintain a synagogue. Though Bermondsey lies no further from Piccadilly Circus than Paddington, it has not experienced the corrupting influence of that rootless population which, irrespective of nationality, gravitates to any central area of cheap housing. Inter- and post-war housing policy has not given it any marked influx of families from other parts of London, nor has industry moved in to any large extent. At the 1951 census, Bermondsey's hotel and boarding house population numbered twenty, the lowest for any of the London boroughs. Since the district possesses little of historical interest and few places of entertainment like greyhound tracks and dance halls, it does not attract the casual visitor. Compared with other London boroughs therefore the disruptive forces have been inconsiderable.

The population is not only London bred, sharing with Bethnal Green the distinction of having a larger proportion (82 per cent) born in London than any other borough, but the team's own sample of addresses throughout Bermondsey showed that, in half those households which contained a husband and wife, both partners had been born in Bermondsey. This, together with the fact that the large family persisted late, and that rehousing has tended to shuffle households *within* the borough, means that the number of related households is high. The family living next door to the senior research worker was a case in point. The parents, in their forties, had twelve closely related households living locally, most of them within about fifteen minutes' walk. At another older household (taken at random from the interviews) this was the pattern. The husband and wife were both Bermondsey born, the man in his present house. One brother lived with the couple in question, another from Sidcup visited every Sunday, the wife's mother lived within five minutes' walk, a daughter lived in the next street, and they had seven other near relations living in the borough.

Another indication of unity is the extent to which Bermondsey shares a common pride in those of its citizens, past and present, who have fought to improve social conditions. Today's leading councillors, officials, doctors, clergy, and heads of schools are known by name to nearly everyone, and anyone in trouble reckons to consult them. To go round to 'Mellish's place' is a recognized way of tackling a problem. Every household is familiar with certain annual events, the Catholic processions, the Labour Children's Christmas Party, the Aylwin and the Bacon School Fairs, and the Parish Church Service when the Queens (T.A.) march alongside other local organizations. An admirable monthly news sheet issued by the Council presupposes an acquaintance with persons and places, again past as well as present, that is less reminiscent of the metropolis than of a small country town. Bermondsey is also proud of its local amenities, especially the Health Centre. Among other local facilities is a library service to whose efficiency and helpfulness the team can testify; well-kept public gardens and well-pruned trees; free toilet facilities that include water-soap-and-towel; and 300 entertainments a year, from quizzes and cinema shows to five-a-side football, some free and few costing more than a shilling or so.

As in a small town, certain spots act as informal meeting places to which people seem to flow naturally. The Park is one, visiting hours at St Olave's Hospital another and, of course, any doctor's surgery. But the chief centres for the collection and dissemination of information are the pubs and the shops. Apart from the Co-op there are no big stores, and even the branches of multiple firms are not large. Bermondsey's typical shop is still the small family concern where grandad and the children help out and where people are on Christian name terms, 'That'll be tenpence to you, Grace', or, 'Seen our Lil, Dick?' Even the little sixpenny advertisement boards have an intimate flavour, 'We have to nice kittens to give away', or 'Would anyone like to exchange there caravan for my nice . . .' The florist, writing the black-edged card for a wreath, knows all con-

MARRIED WOMEN WORKING

cerned and can confidently advise whether it is a case for 'deepest sympathy' or 'loving memories'. The carefully written letters so often to be seen pinned in house windows, and which begin 'Dear Neighbours' before going on to thank for floral tributes, also suggest how well people know each other. So does the frequent exchange of greetings in the street. This neighbourly attitude is not confined to natives. Visitors often remark how helpful the local people in the buses have been, and what trouble has been taken to identify an address for the stranger. The strongest evidence as well as reflection of Bermondsey's unity is, however, the tightly knit family unit which forms the core of local life.

For a population of 54,000, Bermondsey is thus very alike as regards ancestry, social class, education, and employment, nor, by national standards, are there wide differences in income. It still has as solidly a Labour vote as any of the London boroughs, and there is relatively little appearance of straining to climb socially. People are not particularly anxious to move to a better-class locality, they are not unduly worried about the 11 + exam, no one is ashamed of manual work, and a job such as office cleaning carries no social stigma. During the course of this study, Bermondsey happened to have two rather untypical connections, Mr T. Steele and Mr A. Armstrong-Jones. It was characteristic of Bermondsey that neither appeared to excite excessive interest locally, nor were they cashed in on. If undue stress seems to have been laid on the stable, near-villagey character of this part of London, it is because the sense of security it engenders is undoubtedly among the half-conscious factors which permit the mother who works to leave her home each day without too many qualms and anxieties.

CHAPTER V

The Peek Frean Factory

*The firm–The development of personnel policy–Changes
in the labour force–The reactions of management*

The Firm

PEEK FREAN'S, the firm which employed the women studied in
the first part of the investigation, was founded in 1857 on a site in
dockland. The present works, of which the oldest parts date from
1866, consists of a jumble of buildings of varying dates and heights,
hemmed into a triangular twelve-acre site adjoining the Southern
Region Railway and within earshot of the ships' sirens in the Pool of
London. Peek Frean's clock tower, topping one of the older blocks,
has long been a landmark in Bermondsey and to commuters on the
Southern Region Railway.

The firm has been a family business for most of its existence, and
control is still a family affair. Biscuits, the original product, are the
most important part of the factory output, and many varieties like
Pat-a-cake are household names. Peek Frean's Christmas puddings
have been on the market for over thirty years and an expanding
export trade sends the firm's products round the globe.

Peek Frean's has the reputation of being progressive, and has
certainly tended to be experimental in both its technical and its
personnel policy. A sharp contrast between ancient and modern is
evident throughout the factory. Adaptation and improvisation has
been called for in converting a production system once centred on
Victorian bakehouses and master bakers to one dependent on automatic ovens and 'bakehouse ladies'. Physical limitations are a per-
petual problem for management, and there is very little of the 'model
factory' in the appearance of Peek Frean's.

The development of personnel policy [1]

The personnel policy of the firm represents a modification of the
old by the new. Within a few years of its foundation a member of
the present controlling family became a partner, and later chairman
of the company. His benevolent and paternalistic attitude towards
the employees resulted in many practical welfare schemes, including

---

[1] This section incorporates information collected by a group of students
from the Personnel Management Course of the London School of Economics,
1955–56.

63

medical and dental services and sick clubs, all introduced before the end of the nineteenth century.

It seems that these schemes did not express that type of paternalism which maintains that the employer knows best, and that the representation of workers' views is unnecessary. Recognition was accorded to the trade unions before the First World War: and the firm responded immediately to the Whitley Committee's recommendation that works committees should be set up throughout industry to foster co-operation between management and labour. The establishment of a Works Committee in 1918 was seen as an important development in the firm's labour relations, as well as a means of dealing with the immediate issues of the transition from war to peace. Though there were many cases of short-lived and opportunist enthusiasm for Whitleyism, at Peek Frean's the Works Committee was no nine-days wonder; it has flourished ever since. Nor, as happened at some firms, did management attempt to use it as a substitute for vigorous trade unionism, though an early demand that only unionists should sit on the Works Committee was rejected by the directors. The strength of Trade Union activity was demonstrated by the many active unionists elected to the committee. The first proposal put forward by a woman representative on this committee was for 'a lecture on Trade Unionism to be given in the Works'.

The earliest Works Committee consisted of 14 men and 14 women, though the proportion of women later fell. At no time was the committee concerned only with minor items of welfare. From an early stage its recommendations on employment questions, on pensions, and on dismissals, were a prelude to action by the directors. The records of the committee make it clear that its women representatives have been among the most conscientious and useful members; they appear to have done a particularly valuable job in dealing with day-to-day problems in the departments. Married women workers have not yet taken an active part in the committee, though some older married women have lately been elected to it.

In 1919 a Joint Council was set up. This, a smaller body, did not supersede the Works Committee, but took over certain of its functions. Members of the junior management and of supervision sat on the council, together with senior management and workers' representatives. Sub-committees of both the Works Committee and the Joint Council were formed to deal with a variety of problems including accident prevention, works rules, works catering, and fuel watching. The range of activities was considerable, and though the minutes of meetings suggest fluctuation in the vitality of the various com-

1
PEEK FREAN'S

2. WOMEN'S BEANOS. Pub outing, c. 1925

Pub outing, 1954

THE PEEK FREAN FACTORY

mittees, there can be no doubt that the system of consultation has played an effective part in the life of the factory for the last forty years.

Parallel with the growth of the Works Committee and the Joint Council, the trade unions' relations with the firm developed and their role was clarified. The unions with which the firm negotiated included the Amalgamated Union of Operative Bakers, Confectioners and Allied Workers; the Union of Shop, Distributive and Allied Workers; the National Union of General and Municipal Workers; and the Transport and General Workers' Union. Wages and conditions of work at the factory are now governed by the National Joint Wages Council for the biscuit industry, on which Peek Frean's is represented through its membership of the Cake and Biscuit Alliance Limited. At factory level, the trade unions negotiate rates above the minimum. Furthermore, since 20 per cent of the men and 80 per cent of the women at Peek Frean's at the time of the study were working on some form of payment by results— under both individual and group incentive schemes—the unions play an active part in dealing with wage questions in the factory.

When the study began, in 1954, the system of control in the factory followed the pattern of many family businesses. Three members of the family sat on the Board—the Chairman and two of his sons, one as Managing Director and the other as Works Director. Executive control over the factory was exercised by the Works Director, and by senior management, consisting of the Production Manager, the Technical Manager, the Labour Manager, and the Chief Engineer, who reported to him. Under the Production Manager were five departmental managers, each responsible for one of the production departments. Reporting to the departmental managers were supervisors; in the departments studied, which were those staffed mainly by women, these supervisors were usually women. The supervisors in the packing departments were assisted by women trainers who trained employees new to the departments and supervised the work of particular sections. The paper work connected with the payment system was dealt with by checkers who also reported to the supervisor. The executive chain of command was supplemented by a small number of staff and service departments including the personnel department, a factory office, and a wages office.

Changes in the labour force

The changes in traditional organization dictated by technical developments and expanding markets were far less disruptive than

MARRIED WOMEN WORKING

those demanded by the dramatic reversal of traditional recruitment policies during and after the Second World War. When the population of Bermondsey was halved as a result of the war, employers found peacetime expansion hindered by severe labour shortage. Those who, like Peek Frean's, had a strong incentive to remain near to the docks, did their best to cope with the difficulties. As the post-war world took its unfamiliar course of full employment and rising prosperity, the shortage was further intensified by the general buoyancy of trade and commerce, and by the loss of juvenile workers—particularly the local girls—to office desks in the City and to department-store counters in the West End. In 1955 the local Employment Exchange had many more vacancies than applicants for work, so that any person wanting employment normally had a number of possible employers from whom to choose.

For Peek Frean's this period of severe labour shortage was a particularly serious challenge since it was also a time of expanding markets and of unprecedented trading opportunities. Under these circumstances there was no room for hidebound employment policies. The limiting factor in expansion was the inadequate supply of the women workers who form the major part of the labour force in the biscuit industry. The firm's policy governing the employment of women clearly demanded review.

In pre-war days Peek Frean's, enjoying a good reputation in a neighbourhood harassed by casual labour and unemployment, had been able to select their workers carefully and to lay down rigid employment conditions. In common with many other firms in Southern England, no married women were employed and single girls had to leave on marriage. The first break with this custom came in 1937, when a register of women prepared to do seasonal work was compiled; employees who had left the firm to get married were given the option of going onto this register. At the outbreak of war some of these seasonal workers had already been approached to meet the Christmas rush. These women were retained, many of them replacing men who joined the forces. From these small beginnings married women have come to form an increasingly vital part of the firm's labour force.

As the war went on the employment position became more difficult, and married women were engaged on a new basis as part-time workers. This, however, was regarded as a temporary measure only, and when the war ended the expected move was made to replace these part-time workers by full-time ones. But Bermondsey's diminished popuation and highly-competitive labour market inevitably frustrated the firm's desire for a wholly full-time labour force. By the

66

THE PEEK FREAN FACTORY

middle fifties 82 per cent of Peek Frean's factory women employees were married, and of all operatives 46 per cent were women engaged on a part-time basis.

The growing inevitability of part-time work led to a second radical departure from traditional employment policy, the introduction of a variety of shifts. The firm offered a choice of hours to attempt to meet the varying domestic circumstances of married women who were only prepared to work part-time. The full-time working day continued to be from 7.30 a.m.–5.30 p.m., but over a period of time four shorter shifts were eventually introduced.

TABLE 3

Women employees at Peek Frean's by % in shift; and average age of shift, 1955

Shift	Hours of work	Total time worked (hours)	% of all women employees by shift	Average age (in years to nearest year) by shift
Full-time	7.30 a.m.–5.30 p.m.	9	26	38
Part-time a.m.	7.30 a.m.–12.30 p.m.	5	30	45
Part-time p.m.	1.30 p.m.–5.30 p.m.	4	26	43
9.30 a.m.–4.00 p.m	9.30 a.m.–4.00 p.m.	5½	5	38
Evening	5.45 p.m.–9.30 p.m.	3¾	13	36

Of these shifts, the first three were integrated into the normal working day. The evening shift, which dates from 1951, was organized rather differently. Like the original register for married workers, this shift was introduced in order to give greater flexibility in seasonal rush periods. At first its workers were engaged for a limited period of time, and during the first three years their employment was terminated when the seasonal pressure was over. With continued expansion, however, the evening shift, though still officially 'temporary', came to be worked all round the year. By the time of the study, evening-shift workers had become as much an established part of the labour force as any other of the women employed at Peek Frean's.

The reaction of management

Within a few years fundamental changes had taken place in the recruitment and in the organization of the labour force. Traditional management policies were set aside, and for the first time Peek Frean's when setting hours of work took closely into account the domestic circumstances of its employees. In the reappraisal which inevitably followed there was, not surprisingly, controversy and contradiction among members of management as they re-defined the problems facing them in the factory.

During the early stages of the study, members of the team interviewed eighteen managers of different ages and levels of responsibility to discover their experiences and views with regard to married women workers. Since only one in four of the women employees worked full-time the views expressed by the managers were, in fact, mostly concerned with the problems of the part-time women workers, practically *all* of whom were married. The information provided by those interviews is used here to supplement the description of the factory already given.

When asked to mention ways in which the part-time employee was to be preferred to the full-timer, the immediate reaction of most of the managers was to declare that in their view there were no advantages; nor could they readily think of jobs which part-timers could fill more satisfactorily than full-timers. However, several said on reflection that the employment of part-time labour was the easiest way of dealing with rushes of work and of getting workers to take on overtime. A few considered that part-timers were probably quicker workers than full-timers; and another small minority commented that women working only part-time could tackle work that was physically heavier.

These first impressions of the part-timer were not particularly favourable to her; but more detailed discussion usually modified them. The managers did not feel that higher labour turnover was an inevitable characteristic of the part-timer. Some held that she tended to work faster than the full-timer; and it was occasionally suggested that she learned new operations more quickly. No manager considered problems of factory discipline to be difficult, either among the full-timers or the part-timers; and they believed that unwillingness to accept responsibility was common to both. This view, reflecting an opinion widely held in industry, was qualified by the comment that the woman with home ties was reluctant to take on a responsible job for fear she would not be able to see it through in the event of a domestic crisis.

A number of managers also suggested that the married woman did not seek responsibility because the difference in pay did not make it worth her while. To reach the first rung on the promotion ladder, by becoming a trainer, meant a considerable financial sacrifice for the skilled pieceworker. The managers also pointed out that the tradition of Peek Frean's was against married women supervisors, though a limited number were employed.

While the managers could not find many advantages connected

THE PEEK FREAN FACTORY

with part-time labour, they had little difficulty in listing its deficiencies. Those most frequently given were the lack of continuity in personnel, and the need for more time to be spent on training in relation to the total amount of work carried out. It was difficult, they argued, to develop group loyalty when the membership of work teams suffered frequent changes. The fact that overlapping and complementary shifts were worked presented the supervisors with the formidable problem of balancing the different sections of the work force, compelling them to move women frequently from job to job, a practice which led to friction.

A less frequent but nonetheless important criticism was directed at the married woman who threw up her job for what management regarded as insignificant reasons. Some felt this to be a general disadvantage of married women employees. The difficulties of production control created by a shifting labour force were also mentioned. Planning was said to be complicated by the inclusion of part-time workers, and bad feeling between full- and part-timer was not unknown. Jobs where continuity was essential, such as that of trainer or supervisor, were considered quite unsuitable for part-time work. Asked whether part-timers created extra work for other people, the managers pointed out that they added to the load laid on supervisors, checkers, and trainers; and on the wages, medical, and personnel departments.

There was no strong preference among managers for any of the five shifts, although a few thought the morning shift was definitely the best. Comments on the 9.30 a.m.–4.00 p.m. shift ranged from 'Sheer waste . . . as the machinery would be idle from 7.30 a.m.– 9.30 a.m. and from 4.00 p.m.–5.30 p.m.'; and 'The first shift I would abolish' to 'The most dependable shift, outstandingly the best, employees most willing to be changed round.'

Considerable importance must be attached to these views, since the strongly-held personal opinions of those in authority can often determine the success or failure of any scheme. Managers' views matter whether they are supported by facts or are merely impressions coloured by the speaker's outlook and background. Their strong and often conflicting opinions indicated still further the need for an objective appraisal of the problems indicated.

The implications for recruitment were obvious enough. If it was true that very little chance existed that married women—and especially those working part-time—would ever become long-term employees, then management would have little incentive to regard them as an investment and it would probably choose to employ them only for jobs in which a frequent turnover was relatively unimportant.

MARRIED WOMEN WORKING

If it were not true, such policies could only be damaging both to the firm and to the worker. In the vast majority of cases these women were not the sole breadwinners in their households, so that paid employment was not essential to them on economic grounds. If, at an early stage, their hope of a satisfactory job was disappointed because of management's indifference to them, they were likely to leave, thus confirming management's belief about the instability of the part-time workers. In view of this, there was plainly need for a detailed examination of the married woman's performance as an employee, and of her reaction to the personnel policies of the firm.

CHAPTER VI

Married Women as Employees at Peek Frean's

Recruitment–Labour turnover and labour stability–Absence–Training–Output–Supervision–Administrative complications–Relative merits of different shifts–How the married woman worker saw it–Manager and worker at Peek Frean's

ENOUGH has been said to show that at Peek Frean's the acute labour shortage of the post-war years provided something akin to a laboratory situation in which to study the problems posed for management by the great increase in the number of married women working, and by the rising proportion of part-timers. Though this chapter deals mainly with such problems, the viewpoint is not confined to that of management; the attitude of the women themselves to their work and to the policies of the firm are also considered. The chapter begins with an analysis of the problems as management defined them, together with the findings of the various studies made in the factory. It concludes by presenting the attitudes of the women themselves.

Recruitment

The severe shortage of labour necessitated a radical reorganization of the factory's hours of work, and in the late 1940's had changed the female labour force to one in which more than half worked part-time. Of the new shifts offered, it was envisaged that the 9.30 a.m.–4.00 p.m. and the 5.45 p.m.–9.30 p.m. shifts would be particularly suitable for mothers who had children to look after. This proved to be the case as regards evening work. When the shift was first introduced it was unnecessary to advertise it and the mere announcement to the Works Committee produced a queue of prams and mothers outside the factory gates. An evening shift was obviously attractive to the mother of very small children unwilling or unable to leave the house until her husband came in from work. But despite these new incentives recruitment difficulties persisted, as the team's study of the Newcomers Sample illustrated. Of 100 women engaged in the late spring of 1955, there were twenty-five who never started work at all, either because they decided that they did not want to take paid employment or because they had found a more attractive job between the day they were interviewed and that on which they were due to start at Peek Frean's.

71

MARRIED WOMEN WORKING

Labour turnover and labour stability [1]

Once recruited, what likelihood was there that the married women—particularly part-timers—were here today and gone tomorrow? The managers at Peek Frean's were inclined to think that turnover rates did not vary greatly between full-time and part-time workers, but they did believe that leaving was affected by family responsibilities. To investigate this, a detailed analysis was made of labour turnover for the whole of the factory women employees on the basis of the figures compiled by the firm for the year 1955. When the figures were analysed by shift, the turnover rates were as follows:

TABLE 4

Women employees at Peek Frean's by shift; numbers leaving; turnover rate, 1955 (excluding evening shift and clerical staff)

Shift	Average No. employed	Nos. leaving	% turnover rate
Full-time	801	390	49
Part-time a.m.	721	359	50
Part-time p.m.	640	402	63
9.30 a.m.–4.00 p.m.	195	216	111

These rates were further broken down according to the cause of leaving given by the woman to the personnel department, though it was recognized that any classification so derived might not be particularly reliable. The leaver might be unwilling to give, or even be unaware of, the 'real' reason; there might often be several reasons, the one chosen to explain her departure being that uppermost in her mind, the last straw but not necessarily the underlying cause of her leaving. While not unaware of these limitations, the firm did however attempt to classify causes of leaving: the distribution of causes between shifts is of interest. The five categories used were as listed in Table 5.

The factory's own information on labour turnover was supplemented by two special studies. The first of these related to the Newcomers Sample referred to earlier. Of these 100 potential workers, 25 never started and 40 left within three months. Within six months a total of 57 had gone, leaving 18 survivors, or 24 per cent of those who actually began work with the firm.

[1] $\text{Labour turnover} = \dfrac{\text{No. of leavers} \times 100.}{\text{Average No. of employees.}}$

$\text{Labour stability} = \dfrac{\text{No. with service of one year or more} \times 100.}{\text{Average No. of employees.}}$

MARRIED WOMEN AS EMPLOYEES AT PEEK FREAN'S

TABLE 5

Women employees leaving Peek Frean's in 1955, by shift; and main reason for leaving

Reason for leaving	% of full-time shift leavers giving this reason	% of part-time a.m. shift leavers giving this reason	% of part-time p.m. shift leavers giving this reason	% of 9.30 a.m. -4.00 p.m. shift leavers giving this reason
Dissatisfaction with job	9	12	10	13
Personal betterment	28	15	14	11
Domestic responsibilities	16	30	44	36
Illness or accident	15	16	14	18
Move from district	11	7	4	5
All other reasons	21	20	14	17
	100%	100%	100%	100%

Was this heavy turnover attributable to a sudden discovery on the woman's part that she had underestimated the difficulty of carrying simultaneously the responsibilities of home and job? So far as the sixteen women with children under five were concerned (only two of whom were still at the firm after six months), this might well have been the position. Most of these particular mothers had, in any case, chosen the evening shift where it was understood that employment was normally of a temporary nature. It seemed likely, though no direct evidence was found, that many of these women had started work with the intention of continuing for a limited period only; or to meet some non-recurring need. Their high turnover rate was not at all surprising, and it supported the findings of the small earlier study of labour turnover already mentioned (page 27).

But if the women with very young children were disregarded, quite a different picture emerged. When re-interviewed, at the end of six months, it was found that most of the Newcomers had not left in order to stay at home, but had gone straight into other paid employment. It was the condition of the labour market, not the burden of domestic duties, that lay behind the high turnover. This explanation was substantiated by other evidence from the Newcomers Sample which showed that those who left included all the single women and all the married ones with no child to look after. On the other hand each of the part-time groups contained some Newcomers who stayed with the firm, the most stable being those on the afternoon shift.

A contrast with the Newcomers Sample was afforded by the Leavers, a group, not a sample, of twenty-eight women who had left after having been with the firm for three years or more. Of these twenty-eight, only fourteen had obtained other work; the remainder were staying at home indefinitely, chiefly for reasons of ill-health.

MARRIED WOMEN WORKING

Half of those who had gone to other jobs mentioned that the new work was physically lighter and that they found this a considerable advantage.

Taken by themselves, these labour turnover figures would tend to confirm, rather than refute, the common impression of high turnover among married women, and particularly among the part-timers, although the explanation commonly given was not, it seemed, the major issue at Peek Frean's. The figures must however be read in conjunction with the stability rates for the same period, which create a much more favourable picture. For 1955 these were as follows:

Shift	Stability rate
Full-time	80 per cent
Part-time a.m.	81 per cent
Part-time p.m.	83 per cent
9.30 a.m.–4.00 p.m.	56 per cent

If the figures for the 9.30 a.m.–4.00 p.m. shift are excluded they show that more than 80 per cent of these women had been with the firm for more than a year, proving that many could and did settle down into reliable and permanent employees. The turnover and stability figures indicated—as is often the case—that newly recruited workers were most vulnerable during the first three months of employment, and, to a lesser extent, during the second three months. But after six months the chances that a woman would stay for a long time became very good indeed. In fact, therefore, there was little in the company's experience to support the belief that part-timers were at best to be regarded as temporary employees.

Absence

Irregularity of attendance is probably the most frequent criticism levelled at the married woman employee. There is no doubt that at Peek Frean's they had a less favourable record of attendance than any other type of worker. Factory records showed that in the last half of 1955 the absence rate of women employees was 40 per cent higher than that of men, and its fluctuations from month to month were sharper, and therefore less predictable.

There were, in addition, important variations between the shifts. As might be expected, those composed mainly of the younger mothers—the 9.30 a.m.–4.00 p.m. and the evening shifts—had the highest absence rates: full-time workers, which included the 18 per cent of single women in the labour force, had the lowest. This is illustrated by the N.B.1 study which examined absence from work

74

MARRIED WOMEN AS EMPLOYEES AT PEEK FREAN'S

for all causes in one packing department over a three-week period. The 130 women employed on packing in this department lost 198 days in the period; but the full-time and morning women had a better record than those in the afternoon and the 9.30 a.m.–4.00 p.m. shifts. While the former averaged approximately one day's absence per worker during the three weeks, the latter averaged nearly two. In addition the absences were supplied from 60 per cent of the afternoon and 9.30 a.m. to 4.00 p.m. shifts as against 40 per cent of the morning and full-time workers. An average absence for all workers in this department of as much as one and a half out of eighteen possible working days created serious problems for management and supervision—and also for fellow employees, whose earnings were threatened by the break-up of work groups. Apprehensions on the score of high absence rates seemed to have foundation, though the incidence varied considerably with the differing domestic responsibilities of the women concerned.

Management seemed prepared to accept this problem as the inevitable result of employing women with heavy home commitments. Attempts were made to meet any reasonable requests for absence, and at the same time to take action which would minimize the disorganization that was caused by high absence rates. School holiday periods meant a drastic increase in absence. The firm, recognizing the genuine need for many women to be away during these times, had introduced a system of approved absence without pay, under which a woman personnel officer, in consultation with the supervisors affected, screened requests for time off. A similar situation was created by the natural desire of wives to take their annual leave at a date that coincided with that of their husbands. Since a family holiday was one of the objectives for which many of the women said they were working, it was important that requests for leave should be met, and considerable effort was made to do so. As, however, the leave required frequently did not coincide with the firm's regular holiday period the already high absence figure was still further increased.

To minimize the disruption caused by absence rates at such levels, the firm was careful to keep off key jobs those women whose domestic circumstances were likely to lead to considerable absence. Their work, too, was so arranged that the burden on regular workers of carrying on when absence was high was reduced to a minimum.

Training

All new women employees at Peek Frean's went through a short training programme before being given a job on the factory floor.

MARRIED WOMEN WORKING

This was the responsibility of a specially appointed trainer attached to each group of workers: she had been through the Job Instruction programme of the Ministry of Labour's Training Within Industry scheme. The trainers were responsible to the supervisors of their department.

This training provision would appear to be as adequate as is generally provided in much of British industry. The firm certainly did not take the attitude that part-timers were unlikely to stay and were therefore not worth training. The team came to the conclusion that effective training was even more important for part- than full-time workers. The married woman can afford to be far more critical about her new work than the single one who is dependent on a job for her livelihood. If, in the early days and weeks of employment, a worker feels the job is not coming up to expectations, either in terms of earnings or conditions, then, for the married woman, it is easy to quit. Thus, inadequate training may well increase general dissatisfaction and labour turnover.

At Peak Frean's two factors appeared to militate against effective training. In order to reach a high standard of performance a worker needs first the training and then the opportunity to settle down to her job. This, of course, is particularly important where payment is on a piecework basis or on a bonus system. It was, however, a common complaint that new workers were continually being moved from job to job, not to give them planned experience but to meet temporary production needs. Since this alleged movement was found to be a major cause of dissatisfaction in the early weeks of employment, its causes and frequency were examined in considerable detail in the N.B.1 study. For three weeks a daily record was kept of all transfers within or to and from this department, in which some 241 women were employed. A very considerable number of moves was recorded. But on close examination two points of importance emerged. First, although some transfers were due to sudden production needs, most resulted from high rates of absence. The more the firm tolerated absenteeism the more were temporary transfers inevitable if work was to be kept moving. Secondly, in most departments transfers were governed by a Works Council decision, which management had vainly tried to get rescinded, that the employee with the shortest service must be moved first. In a few departments, including the one specially studied, this ruling had been slightly modified to bear less hardly on the newcomer. Transfers in N.B.1 were made on a formula agreed between the supervisor and the women in the department: and if it was thought that these agree-

76

MARRIED WOMEN AS EMPLOYEES AT PEEK FREAN'S

ments had not been observed, the supervisor's decision could be challenged. The combined effect of these regulations and of the high absence rate was to distort, sometimes quite seriously, the intended policy of training newcomers to reach maximum performance, and therefore maximum earnings, in the shortest possible time.

A second doubt as to the effectiveness of training arose from observation of the variety of methods of work used by employees who, nominally, were already trained. These variations appeared to exceed the degree of flexibility demanded by the individual differences of operators, and suggested that in some cases at any rate, the techniques taught to the operator were not based on a thorough method study. To the extent that an improved method could reduce learning time and speed up the process of reaching and maintaining a high level of earnings, any inefficiency was an additional factor hindering the adjustment of the part-timers.

Some of the managers had suggested that training might be a field in which the part-time worker was positively superior to the full-timer. As she had a shorter working day than the full-timer, it was thought that she might progress faster since her learning would be concentrated into shorter periods. To establish the point, however, it would have been necessary to find exactly comparable groups of full- and of part-timers being taught identical jobs. Unfortunately, despite a great deal of help from management, it was not possible to discover cases sufficiently alike to draw valid conclusions.

Output

A similar suggestion was made about output. It seemed plausible to argue that the part-timer, in her shorter day, might be able to work with greater intensity, producing more per hour. Investigations into this problem proved inconclusive. There was no doubt that many of the part-timers were extremely effective at their job, getting through a great deal of work. In 1955, pieceworkers' average earnings for all shifts (excluding the evening shift) were 3s 3d per hour. The pieceworker with the highest earnings for the year averaged 3s 7½d per hour, at a time when average earnings in the biscuit trade were 2s 7d per hour and 2s 9d for women in manufacturing industry as a whole. While these figures in themselves prove nothing, and could, indeed, be evidence merely of loose rates, it was clear that the faster pieceworkers were turning out a considerable quantity of work. It was not, however, possible to establish any tendency for part-timers to produce at a higher hourly rate than full-timers, though they were among the fastest workers employed.

MARRIED WOMEN WORKING

Supervision

However much the policy of the firm and the terms of the contract of service affected the productivity of the married woman worker, her effective use depended as much as anything else upon the nature of the day-to-day supervision on the factory floor. To stress in yet another study the importance of the supervisor's job in industry and the need to select and train her might seem superfluous in view of the emphasis given to the subject in the past twenty years. But at Peek Frean's the employment of so many married women on a part-time basis placed an exceptionally heavy responsibility on supervisors. The Ministry of Labour's Training Within Industry scheme has accustomed industry to think of the supervisor's job as being made up of five elements: (1) technical questions; (2) administration; (3) instruction; (4) the improvement of working methods; and (5) the development and maintenance of good human relationships. This analysis provides a useful starting point in the study of a particular supervisor's job, but it suggests a uniformity in the work of the supervisor throughout British industry which may well be misleading. It is essential to know the differences between supervisors' jobs, and this requires a detailed study of the individual supervisor's work.

It also seems likely that success in supervision will vary both with the special requirements of particular posts and with the attitudes and expectations of the supervised. Simply to say that the supervisor is the formally appointed leader of the department or the section omits the all-important issue of the kind of leadership to be exercised.

Lewin[1] and his supporters argue that different circumstances may dictate the choice of one of Lewin's three styles of leadership, the democratic, the laissez-faire, or the autocratic. But circumstances of course differ, both as regards the problems to be tackled and the attitudes of the led: to understand what is the supervisor's proper function one must analyse the expectations of the supervised.

The team did this by making a detailed examination of the supervisor's job in their N.B.1 study. Two supervisors, assisted by checkers and trainers and reporting to the Packing Manager, shared responsibility for the day-time running of the department. The evening shift was under separate supervision. To gain insight into the actual job performed by these supervisors, two members of the team shadowed them for a week, recording their activities in considerable detail. Their work on one quite ordinary day was as follows:

[1] See N. R. F. Maier, *Principles of Human Relationships*, New York, Whitney, 1952.

MARRIED WOMEN AS EMPLOYEES AT PEEK FREAN'S

A day's supervision in N.B.1

7.30 a.m. saw the two supervisors at their desk in the middle of a long work-room where, in the course of the day, some 208 women were at work packing biscuits into tins, and performing other ancillary jobs. As the day started a number of routine but necessary queries had to be dealt with. Some protective material for special handling was required by one woman; an absentee was reported and had to be replaced by someone from the relief team; two girls asked for leave of absence and a note requesting leave had to be written and dispatched to the personnel department; it was discovered that a checker, a key worker without whom a whole team would be held up, was not coming in and an urgent note had to go to the personnel department for a replacement. These preliminaries over, the supervisors walked round the department to see that nothing was amiss and to be available to anyone, trainers, checkers, or operatives, who wanted a word with them. These 'words' varied from an exchange of views about work left over by the evening shift to a warning that tins were in short supply, and a query about the quality of an unusually palefaced batch of shortcake which finally went to swell the bags of broken biscuits sold at the factory shop.

Of a less routine nature was a short interview with four workers who were to be permanently transferred to another department—information not normally received well. The women concerned were then sent to the personnel department to get further details of their new work. Unfortunately, on this particular occasion, the department asking for help was not yet ready to receive them and within twenty minutes the four were back in the department in no mood to appreciate the problems of management. A supervisor had to keep them properly employed until the new department was ready for them. The completion of absentee figures, and a brief consultation with a representative from the Production Planning Department were two of several further jobs which had to be tackled before the 9.30 a.m. shift arrived. With the coming of this shift a number of matters had to be settled and as the morning continued further queries came in from other departments: from the wages office a pay claim; from the personnel department requests for the temporary loan of women to be sent to another production department. Considerable trouble arose from a fault in the conveyor belt carrying away tins—a matter which could not be left as it might cause a serious blockage. During the morning the manager of the department looked in to sign the special wages sheet which had to be prepared in readiness for him.

MARRIED WOMEN WORKING

It is easy to see how fully the day was filled and how failure to cope could soon lead to chaos. But hardly a day went by without special problems arising. On one occasion about an hour before the dinner break a message arrived from the planning department to say than an emergency order of 1,500 special tins had to be packed, wrapped, and parcelled by noon on the following day. This meant a complete change of programme in certain sections of the room. One supervisor abandoned her other work to plan the new operation. She decided which teams were to be switched to the new work; 'phoned the electricians for some necessary adjustments; 'phoned the tinshop for extra tins; 'phoned the stationery department for additional supplies; transferred a woman immediately to begin lining tins so that the women on the afternoon shift could get off to a flying start when they came in; transferred another girl to prepare the perforated tickets that were specially required for this particular order. When the afternoon women arrived all was prepared and the job went through without a hitch.

In the evening just before 5.30 p.m., as the day shift was leaving, an angry worker and an indignant checker, spoiling for a fight, surged up to the supervisor. In this particular storm in a teacup there were two possible danger points, either of which could have led to far more serious trouble. The worker might, with some justice, have felt she was unfairly treated: the checker, also with some justice, might have felt that the supervisor, her immediate boss, had failed to give her reasonable support. In retrospect it was easy to see that both these points must be satisfactorily met. At 5.25 p.m., at the end of a working day which had started ten hours earlier, it would not have been surprising if the supervisor, with many other matters on her mind, had not fully grasped the situation. But she listened to what both had to say, and then by a skilful but perfectly proper deflecting of responsibility from the checker to herself, she was able to meet the woman's justified complaint without in any way allowing the checker to lose face. This may seem a trivial incident, but the history of industrial disputes is strewn with situations intrinsically no more serious, but which mishandling has converted from an incident to a crisis.

The record of the supervisors' activities during the week studied was analysed in terms of the five elements recognized by the Training Within Industry scheme. By far the largest proportion of the supervisors' time was spent on administration, on planning and controlling the factors affecting the flow of work in contact with the

MARRIED WOMEN AS EMPLOYEES AT PEEK FREAN'S

outside departments, and on making adjustments within the department. In terms of time spent, the problems arising from human relations came a poor second. The remaining elements were scarcely touched at all; instruction, for instance, was relegated to the trainers, though they reported to the supervisors. The final analysis suggested that these two supervisors were department managers in all but name, and might indeed have been accorded this title had they been men.

Such was the nature of the job: what of the other factor suggested as vital in supervision, the attitudes of the supervised? Questions on attitudes towards supervision were included both in the Peek Frean Shifts Sample and in the N.B.1 study where a sample of fifty-three employees was interviewed.

Replying to the questions 'Would you take on a supervisor's job?' an overwhelming majority of the Peek Frean Shifts Sample made it clear that they had no desire to do so. As some of the managers suggested, they were possibly influenced by financial considerations. To become a supervisor it was necessary first to be a trainer, and a skilful pieceworker could earn considerably more than a trainer. It was also clear that many women appreciated the heavy responsibilities a supervisor carried, and had no wish to shoulder these burdens. This was not only because it would have added to her personal load but also because, in some cases, the woman feared she would not be able to meet the obligations of a responsible post.

This impression was confirmed by the interviews in N.B.1. Asked for suggestions about improving the running of the department, few of the women had constructive comments to make. Their answers to an open-ended question regarding the quality of supervision in the department were more fruitful, producing results which, in their own phrases, are shown in Table 6.

This generally high level of appreciation of the supervisors' work on the part of the women was frequently reinforced by such remarks as 'I shouldn't like to be a supervisor—no pleasing some of the girls'; or, an understanding rider to a complaint about breaking up work teams, 'But I can't see what can be done, with so many leaving and absent'. Unfavourable general comments on supervision concentrated mainly on any failures to maintain a steady flow of work, on disturbances on a regular job in a familiar working group, or, infrequently, on petty disciplinary requirements.

In short, what these married women expected of a competent supervisor was a steady flow of work enabling them to make the

MARRIED WOMEN WORKING

TABLE 6

Views of women employees at Peek Frean's on quality of supervision

	Full-time shift	Part-time shift a.m.	Part-time shift p.m.	9.30 a.m.– 4.00 p.m.	Total
Likes					
(1) Supervisors. Very fair in arranging work—no favouritism	6	8	9	13	36
(2) Trainers. Good	3	1	1	5	10
(3) Checkers. Good	1	1	2	5	9
Dislikes					
(4) Supervisors can't take decisions—have to refer to someone else	3				3
(5) Supervisors can be hard-hearted		2			2
(6) Would rather take questions to a committee girl than to supervisors	1				1
(7) Too many trainers—always someone over you	2	1	2	2	7
(8) Trainers bossy and officious	2	1	4	2	9
(9) Trainers don't train properly	2		3		5
(10) Work inspected when off at tea			3		3

best use of their limited hours in the factory. A really well organized department was what they wanted. Though it may sound heretical, there was very little evidence that they aspired to 'opportunities for participation'; or took much account of the life of the factory as a whole. They were no more interested in the organizational problems of the firm which provided them with the opportunity to earn a useful wage, than they were in the marketing problems of the greengrocer who supplied their vegetables, always provided both job and vegetables were up to standard. On the other hand, they did expect to be treated with the respect and consideration due to married women who were successfully carrying a heavy load and making a useful contribution to industry as well as looking after a home. Their outlook makes a vivid contrast with that of the male worker, and of the single woman of pre-war days. Their conception of the good supervisor was not in terms of a 'democratic leader', essential though she might be with a different type of labour. Rather they looked for an efficient organizer whose skilful management was

MARRIED WOMEN AS EMPLOYEES AT PEEK FREAN'S

their direct gain and who would be considerate and flexible in meeting their individual needs.

From this analysis, a job specification for the supervisor of part-time married women workers can be seen to emerge. It includes the ability to plan ahead, to co-ordinate a number of continuously changing factors, and to make quick decisions—qualities more frequently associated with a higher level in the management hierarchy than that of the supervisor. In addition the supervisor needs the personal characteristics which enable her to establish and maintain good relationships with workers who are under no pressing need to stay. It would seem that for a firm to take the employment of married women seriously, the proper recruitment, training, status, and pay of supervisors is a first essential.

Administrative complications

The problems created by the employment of married women were not limited to the departments in which they actually worked. For production purposes, two half-timers equalled one full-timer; but the recruitment of two part-timers called for as much care and attention by the personnel and medical departments as if these women had been full-timers. The burden carried by the wages office, too, was the same for every woman, irrespective of the number of hours worked; while the time and effort needed in training was not noticeably reduced. Rather more paper work was involved: since the great majority of workers were only at the factory for part of the day, queries could not always be dealt with as they arose, but had to be recorded as needing attention when the part-timer next appeared. As a result, time was wasted, effort duplicated, and the risk of muddles increased.

A consideration of more general importance arose out of the requirements of the National Insurance Act of 1946. Under this Act, insurance has to be paid for the part-time worker at the same rate as for the full-timer, thus proportionately increasing the size of the employer's contribution relative to the amount of work produced.

Another problem arose from the application of the Disabled Persons (Employment) Act of 1944 under which the firm was required to employ the prescribed quota of 3 per cent registered disabled people. In a count taken shortly after this study was completed, it was found that in Peek Frean's main manufacturing and service departments only 2 of the 1,433 part-timers were registered disabled persons, and only 9 of the 816 full-timers. In order to meet the requirements of the Act, however, 66 registered disabled men were

MARRIED WOMEN WORKING

being employed out of the 1,233 men, or 5·35 per cent; while in the main manufacturing section, which employed 574 men, the percentage rose to 6·62.

Relative merits of different shifts

The findings of the study indicate important differences between the shifts in absenteeism, labour turnover, labour stability, and average earnings. The morning shift had the best record. The full reasons for this were not clear, but it was certainly related to the high proportion of women on this shift who had no children of school age or under. Some of the afternoon workers would have preferred to work on this shift, but their domestic responsibilities prevented them from doing so. It is possible that morning workers are able to put more effort into factory work than those who come to work having already expended a good deal of energy on domestic chores. The 9.30 a.m.–4.00 p.m. shift, so helpful to the mother of the school child, was difficult to incorporate in the factory routine and wasteful from the point of view of machine-utilization. Management often resorted to a completely separate organization of this shift, putting the women together in small groups away from the main body of workers. One set of the mechanical packing tables in N.B.1 was operated exclusively by women on the 9.30 a.m.–4.00 p.m. shift so as to reduce the disruption caused by absence during part of the morning and of the afternoon.

How the married woman worker saw it

Management's views and problems are only part of the story. What of the woman herself? What did factory work have to offer her, and what were her responses to the incentives and disincentives of the industrial job? Paid employment, even on a part-time basis, involves loss of freedom and leisure and at times almost inevitably causes conflict between loyalty to family and loyalty to firm. Nonetheless, the high stability rates found among the Peek Frean part-time workers suggests that even for the woman working only four or five hours a day, there must have been very strong attractions to keep her at work and at one firm. Was the pull that of money alone, or were there other satisfactions in the work at Peek Frean's which brought the married woman out of her home and which deterred her from drifting from job to job?

To obtain more detailed information on the women's views on particular jobs, the N.B.1 study included an analysis of the organization of the work of the department and of the women's attitudes.

MARRIED WOMEN AS EMPLOYEES AT PEEK FREAN'S

The labour force in N.B.1 was divided between the shifts as follows:

			9.30 a.m.–4.00	5.45 p.m.–9.30	
Full-time	Part-time a.m.	Part-time p.m.	p.m.	p.m.	Total
23[a]	68	49	69	32	241

[a] 23 at date of analysis, not the 26 normally present in department.

It was decided to focus attention on the first four shifts, the evening one being excluded because it worked at different tasks under different supervisors. These 209 day-time workers had to be effectively united into a series of teams, despite the fact that their personnel might change twice in the course of the day: and this was a major task of the two women supervisors whose work has already been discussed. To collect their views on working in this department, fifty-three women were interviewed from a sample of sixty.

The room in which the women worked was large and well lit, with windows around three sides. It was divided into three main areas by the T-shaped pattern of gangways shown below:

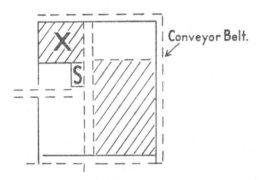

The supervisors worked from a table raised on a platform so as to enable them to see the whole of the room; though their view was sometimes impeded by the piles of tins and trays. The gangway marked off not only areas of work but also, to some extent, categories of workers. In the diagram's shaded areas women worked in teams on mechanical packing tables (known as MTs), and in the areas left blank they worked individually, packing from trays into 7-lb. tins. In the shaded area marked X, the mechanical tables were staffed wholly by the 9.30 a.m.–4.00 p.m. shift: this group was in effect segregated from the rest of the department. The shaded area

MARRIED WOMEN WORKING

opposite the supervisors' table included a few mechanical tables staffed entirely by full-timers; the rest being staffed by both morning and afternoon workers. Around three of the outside walls of the room ran a conveyor belt which carried away the fully-packed tins.

The continual flow of work and the rotating movement of the mechanical tables gave the impression of continuous activity at a brisk pace, interrupted by occasional breakdowns of the conveyor belt. On the mechanical tables the principal task was the packing into fancy tins of assorted biscuits, plain, cream, chocolate, etc. The tins were placed on a moving belt and as they passed an individual worker she packed into them the range of biscuits for which she was responsible. When the tin had completed a full circuit of the table, it was check-weighed and placed on the conveyor. The speed of the belt was regulated by the women themselves. Successful, speedy packing depended on quick co-operation, and called for teams of workers approximately equal in speed and skill. An observer walking round the room would be struck by the contrast between the essentially co-operative character of work at the mechanical tables, and the isolated individualism of that among the packers elsewhere.

Interviews with the women were carried out on a comprehensive schedule which included many open-ended questions and covered the following main points: why the woman came to Peek Frean's; her length of service; the nature of her job; what she liked and disliked about it; why she found her shift suitable or otherwise; any suggestions for improvement; her views on part-time work. A good deal had been discovered from the Peek Frean Shifts Sample about attitudes to work in general: what was wanted from the N.B.1 women was as full an expression of opinion as possible on particular topics. Attention was paid to the frequency with which these topics were mentioned: e.g. when asking about likes and dislikes check points were listed, such as pay, hours, supervision, movement on the job. Her comments were recorded in full since it was felt that at this stage of the research illustrative material should be collected and no attempt made to compress shades of opinion into narrow categories.

The method of sampling adopted meant that the full-time workers were over-represented. Their attitudes and outlook were valuable as they provided a sharp contrast with those of the three other groups. Broadly speaking, the part-timers gave far more positive approval than the full-timers to management's policies. They were certainly much less critical, particularly those on the 9.30 a.m.–4.00 p.m. shift. This shift had fewer comments in general than the other ones except as regards the workings of the relief system, a matter of considerable importance to a shift with a high absentee rate. Asked whether in the future more women were likely to work part-time, the women held varying views. The 9.30 a.m.–4.00 p.m. shift was almost unanimous that the practice would spread: it was the full-timers who had most reservations. Of all the part-time workers interviewed in this phase of the investigation, only two said that they would not continue to work part-time while the opportunity lasted.

The 9.30 a.m.–4.00 p.m. shift more than any other stressed the great advantage of part-time work, that it allowed the mother to be at home before and after school: this confirmed the findings from the main Shifts Sample. None of the full-timers thought it worth mentioning that a particular shift was specially suited to the mother with young children. Both morning and afternoon shifts mentioned their husband's working hours as an important factor in determining their own choice of shift.

In general, differences between the full-time and the part-time worker in N.B.1 seemed to arise out of their views on management, and also on the suitability of the Peek Frean working hours for the woman with domestic responsibilities. These apart, full-timers and part-timers agreed on many points.

Information on length of service in the factory showed the department to be a remarkably stable one—in fact more stable than the factory as a whole. This is particularly interesting in view of the fact that it was so dominated by part-time workers. Only four of the fifty-three women interviewed had been at Peek Frean's for less than a year, and nearly half had more than five years' service. The bulk of these were part-timers who had always worked in the one department.

The need for money was the woman's most frequent explanation for choosing to work at Peak Frean's, and it is a reasonable assumption that she was attracted by the prospect of high piecework earnings. Comments on the unfavourable aspects of their jobs showed that these hopes about high earnings were not always realized; once again it was the full- rather than the part-timers who were critical. Twenty-four women mentioned the convenience of a choice of shifts as a reason for working at Peek Frean's. Eleven said that they had relatives or friends working there, an advantage illustrated by a woman who took turns with her sister in looking after the children. The speaker worked in the morning, her sister in the afternoon. The reason for coming to work in a factory is not necessarily what prompts the employee to stay; these women, when asked why they continued at Peek Frean's, mentioned only one point with any frequency—the opportunity to work with friends. Eleven referred to

MARRIED WOMEN WORKING

this, and the somewhat resentful attitude to the disruption of work groups suggested that social ties constituted an important work satisfaction.

There was no doubt whatever that it was the high level of earnings which attracted most of the women to Peek Frean's, and kept them there. All part-timers interviewed commented favourably on the pay. Piecework was liked, some preferring a group, some an individual basis. There were certain reservations to this general approval. The piecework rates set for certain jobs were thought to be too tight, making it difficult to earn your money. Some kinds of biscuits were hard on the fingers and troublesome to handle; others were brittle and liable to break when the operator exceeded a certain speed. Several of the women paid on a group basis stressed the importance of an even standard of skill among all the members of the group if good earnings were to be obtained.

Hours of work were also considered satisfactory; thirty-four of the women were positively content, the part-timers being particularly appreciative. All the facts indicated the general approval of the wide range of hours offered, and the consequent ability of part-timers to choose the shift best suited to their home ties. These hours were closely influenced by their domestic circumstances. Six of the afternoon workers with a personal preference for the morning shift nevertheless chose the afternoon one in order to meet their family's needs. Of the 13 full-timers interviewed, 10 made complaints, as compared with only 8 complainers among the 40 part-timers interviewed. It seemed likely that unfavourable comparisons with the shorter hours enjoyed by the part-time workers made the full-timers feel that their working day was unduly long.

The relative advantages and disadvantages of group and individual work provoked interesting comments. Though twenty-nine women preferred group work, a sizeable minority (seventeen) expressed a preference for working on their own. This preference was based on a belief that more could be earned this way, though there was no conclusive evidence that this was so. Full-time group workers were irked by the change of shifts which required them to co-operate with a different set of workmates before and after the dinner hour. Turnover and absenteeism were also felt to upset the effective operation of the group, even though, in N.B.1, workers had co-operated with supervisors to devise a system of reliefs which minimized the disruptive effects of heavy absenteeism on work groups.

Unusual appreciation was shown of supervisors' problems. This was especially true of the 9.30 a.m.–4.00 p.m. shift. Minor criticisms came from the full-timers, and, to a lesser degree, from the afternoon

MARRIED WOMEN AS EMPLOYEES AT PEEK FREAN'S

shift. In N.B.1 the customary criticism of supervision seemed to be deflected on to the trainers, the link between the employees and the supervisors.

A major cause of general criticism, especially from the full-timers, concerned delays in coping with interruptions to the work flow. On the vexed question of movement of worker from job to job, N.B.1 expressed less dissatisfaction than had been voiced by the women in the main Shifts Sample. In N.B.1, however, supervisors and workers had together devised a roster method which largely controlled internal transfers, thus reducing the disruption of work groups. This appears to explain why as many as twenty-four of the women commented tolerantly on the problem of job movement. The ten who did mention it as an unsettling factor stressed the daily uncertainty that it caused as to one's place of work and companions. Only four mentioned that it tended to separate the worker from her particular friends.

Comments on working conditions were generally tolerant. Absence of criticism was again noticeable among the 9.30 a.m.–4.00 p.m. shift. Such discontent as there was came from the full-timers and the afternoon workers, and centred on overcrowding, excessive heat and inefficiencies of physical layout.

Manager and worker at Peek Frean's

The impressions gained from the study of management problems may be summarized as follows. Despite a remarkably high proportion of part-timers, the firm still had considerable difficulty in recruiting suitable workers. It had, however, managed to establish a core of stable and efficient part-time employees. The problem of labour turnover seemed to be confined, as is usually the case, to the first six months of employment; from then on part-timers would stay with the firm as long as anyone. There was no evidence to suggest that they were any more or less efficient than the full-time workers, and all married women were undoubtedly prone to stay away from work if a crisis developed at home. Management had come to accept high absence rates as an inevitable characteristic of this kind of labour, and, although experimenting, had yet to devise effective means of minimizing the disruption inevitable at a firm with a complex system of production. In all this, a heavy burden was placed on the supervisor, who had to deal with an increased number of women and an unstable pattern of work groups.

On the employees' side, the conventional criticism of management was mild. As this tolerance was an outstanding characteristic of the part-timers, it could be concluded that the efforts made by Peek

MARRIED WOMEN WORKING

Frean's to attract women with domestic responsibilities led to favourable comparisons with other employers in the district. Another more comprehensive explanation would be the attraction of piecework earnings, and the evidence that women at Peek Frean's found part-time work well-worth-while financially. It seemed that the part-time worker valued above all the opportunity to earn 'good money'; conditions and supervision which maximized her earning power; tolerance by management of her domestic situation and temporary difficulties. The contrast with the attitudes of full-time workers, particularly as shown from the N.B.1 study, is striking. Was the fact that criticism came almost wholly from the full-timers a reflection of their status as a minority group in the department? Were they resentful of the concessions made to the part-time worker? And were the part-timers, on their side, more prepared to accept deficiencies in their conditions of work and relations with management because, for them, their paid job was not the most significant part of their life?

A study of this kind inevitably raises more questions than it answers. Although at Peek Frean's the more alarmist view of the deficiencies of the married woman worker—and particularly of the part-timer—did not stand the test of objective enquiry, nonetheless a rising proportion of part-time workers in the total labour force does demand drastic readjustments in the policies and practice of management.

CHAPTER VII

The Bermondsey Wives who Worked

*The Bermondsey Household Sample–Types of work–Age
in relation to work–Number of children: age of youngest
child–Husband's occupation–Why they worked–Financial
motives–A family holiday–Status–'It makes a change'
–The wife who did not go out to work*

WHEN the factory study came to an end, the research was extended
to enquire into the significance of married women's employment for
family life in the borough of Bermondsey. As the team's contacts
with the locality and with Peek Frean's developed, a growing need
was felt to compare the married women who worked at the factory
with other married women in Bermondsey—a representative local
sample in fact. In the Peek Frean study, Bermondsey's closely-knit
and distinctive community seemed an unexpectedly important influence on the wives' attitudes to work, on the methods devised to
reconcile employment with home duties, and on how the children
were affected. But were the women who worked at Peek Frean's
representative? They gave the impression from their interviews of
being energetic and resourceful individuals, living the busiest of
lives, much helped in their domestic affairs by co-operative husbands,
and by sensibly-brought-up children. They appeared to devote their
extra income largely to their well-kept and efficient-looking homes,
to more ample meals, better clothes and shoes, and a holiday away.
In all this they kept the children's welfare very closely in mind. Going out to work was trying physically, of course, but it was worth it.
There was little evidence of feelings of guilt, and the practical difficulties were not insuperable. Often these women seemed to have laid
hold on a new lease of life through their work, and relatively few
showed signs of the problems generally associated with married
women's employment. By extending the study to Bermondsey as a
whole, certain facts could be established about the local wife who
worked in terms of the age groups from which she was drawn; her
type of work and earnings; the effect of the structure of her family
on her ability to leave home at all; and whether she was making her
first return to work at any particular stage in her life. To these basic
facts more tenuous matters could be related, viz. what the women
themselves revealed of their motives for working; the satisfactions

MARRIED WOMEN WORKING

afforded by a job and an income of their own; as well as the sacrifices in terms of hard work and lost leisure.

The Peek Frean study had demonstrated beyond question the significance of a planned timetable and a co-operative family in making it possible for the wife to undertake a dual role. The Bermondsey interviews sought further information on the impact of a job on domestic life, and on the attitudes of the woman's household to her own extra load: little was known about either. How the children fared in all this was obviously a matter of vital importance. Much of the team's work in the second stage of the study was spent on the children's progress and on the many related problems. In this and the following chapters the topics dealt with have been grouped thus. This chapter analyses the general characteristics of the Bermondsey wife who worked, and why she chose to do so. Chapter VIII describes how she coped with the practical problems, and Chapter IX tries to assess the effects on the children. Though the Bermondsey study provided most of the material relating to these issues, many of the points which arose in the Peek Frean study have been used for illustrative purposes.

The Bermondsey Household Sample [1]

The survey of Bermondsey households undertaken between September 1957—September 1958 consisted of interviews with a one in twenty-five sample of addresses for the entire borough. These, drawn from the Electoral Register for 1957, gave a list of 770 addresses. At each household living at an address (and an address might, of course, contain more than one household) an interview was requested. Sufficiently full information was obtained from 517 households for the interviews to be regarded as satisfactorily 'accepted'. Nine of these accepted interviews were discarded because a vital point, the work situation, if any, of the woman responsible for the housekeeping was not recorded. Of the accepters, 380 households contained a married couple; the bulk of the material in this chapter relates to these, the 'normal' households who are known in the study as the Husbands and Wives. A further eighty-five households contained no wife, but their domestic affairs were organized either by a widow or a woman separated or divorced from her husband. These two household types were grouped together for certain purposes into 465 Wives and Widows households. (Of the remaining forty-three

[1] Appendix I, Method; and Appendix II, Table 27.
[2] For brevity's sake Tables 26 to 43 have been put into Appendix II.

THE BERMONDSEY WIVES WHO WORKED

accepting households, eighteen were run by spinsters, and twenty-five had no woman in charge.)

The woman's work situation in the 465 Wives and Widows households was as follows:

TABLE 7   *'Wives and Widows'*

Woman's marital status in relation to her work situation.

| Marital status | Total | Workers | | All workers | Not at | Home worker or self- |
		F.T.	P.T.	F.T. & P.T.	work	employed[3]
Wife living with husband	380	84	114	198	172	10
Widow	72	9	16	25	46	1
Separated or divorced	13	10	0	10	3	0
Total	465	103	130	233	221	11

[3] Included with housewife in all future tables.

This table shows that slightly more than half of the Wives and Widows went out to work. Since these figures related only to women who carried the main domestic burden of a home, and since they related to women of all ages, they suggest that married women's employment was more extensive in Bermondsey than the one in three of Dr Klein's national study.[4]

A second point to note is the large number of Bermondsey women working part- rather than full-time. The table shows that 56 per cent of those at work were employed part-time. This is far in excess of the Ministry of Labour's latest (1960) estimate of 13·2 per cent of the women in Great Britain in manufacturing industries being part-timers,[4] and shows, as did Dr Klein's survey, that in Bermondsey married women are undertaking a great deal of part-time work of a non-industrial type which is excluded from the official figures. Moreover, since the team followed the Ministry's definition of part-time as 'under thirty hours a week', many of the Bermondsey jobs classified as full-time were, in fact, considerably shorter than the normal industrial week of over forty hours. In the Bermondsey study, as many as 28 per cent of all those who worked, did so for less than twenty hours a week (Table 28).[5] The 'just a little job' they so often mentioned, might not be more than two or three hours a day. By London standards, too, the time spent on travelling was short, not more than forty minutes of their day for 61 per cent of these workers (Table 30). As Table 29 shows, they worked at many different times of day. Eight sets of times are recorded in the table, in addition to the normal industrial day of 8 a.m.–5 p.m. This

[4] Klein, *op. cit.*   [5] *Ministry of Labour Gazette*, February 1961.

MARRIED WOMEN WORKING

variety in the hours at which they worked also meant that many were spared the intolerable strains of London rush hour travel. In Bermondsey, despite the fact that more married women than usual did work, they had often settled for much less than the full working day. On the other hand, they were prepared to work early or late or indeed at pretty well any time of day if this suited their domestic needs. Their earnings, discussed in relation to spending patterns, are referred to in Chapter VIII.

Types of work

The variety of hours was not matched by variety in the type of work undertaken. Indeed, the jobs of these women with an almost uniform social background and a minimum education tended to be so similar in type that a special classification was devised to emphasize the smallness of the differences found.

TABLE 8   *'Wives and Widows'*

Woman's type of occupation—Percentage Distribution.

Types of Occupation	
Doctor, teacher, nurse, etc.	2
Supervisory level (e.g. manageress of shop, book-keeper)	7
Secretary, typist, student nurse, etc.	8
Office clerk, shop assistant, medical orderly, etc.	12
Skilled trade (e.g. sewing machine operator)	7
Semi-skilled manual (e.g. factory operative)	29
Unskilled (e.g. office cleaning, misc. domestic work)	35
	100

There was an almost complete absence of professional workers, and a marked preponderance of women in semi-skilled and un-skilled jobs. About a third were in some type of domestic work; this corresponds with the national figures given by Dr Klein.[6] Most of the 'unskilled' were cleaners in offices, schools, pubs, and cafés, since domestic work in private houses is rare in this part of London. The general picture of these Bermondsey wives is that they had not strayed outside the traditional fields of feminine employment—a fact which may well ease the strains of the dual role.

It proved difficult to get any accurate record of the woman's jobs since she had married—a complex pattern in many cases. Little more can be said than that factory work occupied an important place. Their pre-marriage jobs, however, were more consistent as to type, factory work predominating. Fifty-four per cent of those whose work before marriage was known had been factory workers (Table 31).

[6] Klein, *op. cit.*

94

THE BERMONDSEY WIVES WHO WORKED

Age in relation to going out to work

Analysis of the ages and work situation of the 'Wives and Widows' gave the following results:

TABLE 9   *'Wives and Widows'*

Woman's age in relation to her work situation.

Age of woman	F.T.	Worker P.T.	Total	House-wife	Total	Workers as % of total	P.T. workers as % of total at work	P.T. workers as % of all wives and widows
Under 20 years	2	0	2	0	2	100	0	0
20–29 ,,	15	11	26	37	63	24	43	17
30–39 ,,	28	33	61	61	122	50	54	27
40–49 ,,	26	38	64	24	88	73	59	43
50–59 ,,	25	28	53	27	80	66	53	35
60 & over	5	20	25	81	106	23	80	19
Age not known	2	0	2	2	4	50	0	2
Total	103	130	233	232	465	50	56	28

Leaving aside the two wives under twenty, the women most likely to work were in the age group 40–49, of whom 73 per cent worked. This group was followed by that of women in their fifties. As was to be expected the groups who worked least were women in their twenties who probably had a small child, and, of course, the elderly. But even among the older women, those aged sixty and over, nearly a quarter were still working. Although the main stage for work was early middle age, it is worth noting that half of those still in their thirties, and therefore likely to have a dependent child, were in employment.

The age at which the first main return to work was made proved impossible to establish with any accuracy because few of these women had had anything like a consistent, easily recalled career. From what they could remember, it seemed that the age at which they were returning to work was falling. An attempt was made to ascertain the work situation of mothers (in the Wives and Widows sample) at the time when they had a child in a specific age group (Table 10). This was ascertained at four dates, 1943 (a war year), 1948, 1953, and 1958. The high proportion of workers in 1953 among mothers of the younger children is puzzling; but apart from this the figures, far from showing an increase in the numbers of workers among these mothers with children at or under Junior School age, show some decline.

MARRIED WOMEN WORKING

TABLE 10   *'Wives and Widows'*

Mothers (with a child in age groups 0–4 and 5–10) who worked,
as a % of all mothers with a child in these age groups

Year	Mothers with child 0–4 % working	Mothers with child 5–10 % working
1943	29·3	61·1
1948	28·4	50·0
1953	35·6	52·3
1958	21·4	49·5

There appeared to be some correspondence between age and type of work. Whereas just over half of those who worked (including the self-employed) were aged under forty-five, only a third were as young as this in the unskilled jobs like office cleaning. Of the twenty-nine who were younger still—under thirty—as many as eleven were in shop or office work (Table 32). This was in line with the current tendency of the young girls in Bermondsey to move out of the industrial and unskilled jobs traditionally followed by the women of the district, into clerical and shop work. A small illustration of this was provided by a comparison between the job held by mother and daughter in ten households. This showed that, on leaving school, six of the girls had taken work in an office or in a skilled trade like that of a dress cutter; whereas eight of their mothers had, as girls, gone into factories. Their mother's current job, too, if any, was in factory or domestic work. The Youth Employment Bureau figures for 1958–59 (though these included Southwark as well as Bermondsey) showed that 25 per cent of the local girls had gone to jobs outside Bermondsey.[7]

	Boys	Girls
Local children placed locally	1054	591
Local children placed in other districts of London	216	193
Local children placed outside London	1	1
Non-local children placed in Bermondsey from other districts in London	72	101
Non-local children placed in Bermondsey from districts outside London	10	2

Children at home

The Peek Frean interviews had pointed out two features of the household structure as being highly relevant to the wife's ability to go out to work. The first was the number of children living in the home: the second was the age of the youngest child. Both points were examined further in the Bermondsey study.

[7] *Placings for year ended 31.8.59: Southwark & Bermondsey Y.E.B.*

THE BERMONDSEY WIVES WHO WORKED

TABLE 11   'Husbands and Wives'

Number of children (all ages) living in household in relation to woman's work situation

Number of children	F.T.	Worker P.T.	Total	House-wife	Total	All workers as % of total	P.T. workers as % of all workers
0	42	30	72	44	116	62	42
1	27	34	61	53	114	54	56
2	8	31	39	45	84	46	79
3	7	14	21	27	48	44	67
4	—	3	3	10	13	23	100
5 & over	—	2	2	3	5	40	100
Total	84	114	198	182	380	52	58

The table shows the number of children (including grown-up sons and daughters living at home) in relation to the mother's work situation in the normal family, i.e. that containing both parents. The number of households with more than three children was too small for any firm conclusion to be drawn. In general, however, as the number of children increased, the mother was less prone to work: but at the same time, there was a rise in the proportion of those who worked part-time.

Possibly the number of children in the home might restrict the mother less than the age of her youngest child. Table 12, relating the youngest child's age to the mother's work situation, shows a close correspondence between the child's age and the mother's work situation. Part-, not full-time work was much preferred when the child first started school: mothers whose youngest child had reached the secondary school stage showed a greater tendency to work full-time. The fact that this group of mothers also contained the highest percentage of those who worked at all, supports the claim made in both the Peek Frean and the Bermondsey interviews, that the mothers were going out to work for the sake of the children, since this is usually a time of increasing expenditure.

The habit of working, however, continued after the last child had left school. Possibly it was the mother's wages which enabled the adolescent to stay on at school, or to take the low paid apprentice's job; or possibly she was proud to keep up Bermondsey's tradition of the good mother who took only a minimum of board-money from a young earner and supplemented wages by generous presents, especially in the form of clothes.

In view of the concern so often expressed about the risks to very young children if their mother works, the figures showing the employment situation of the ninety-eight women whose youngest child was still under five were examined closely. Only twenty-one of these

MARRIED WOMEN WORKING

TABLE 12   *'Wives and Widows'*

Age of youngest child at home in relation to his mother's work situation

Age of youngest child	F.T.	Worker P.T.	Total	House-wife	Total	All workers as % of total	P.T. workers as % of total
Under 1 year	0	4	4	26	30	13	13
1–4 years	7	10	17	51	68	25	15
5–10 years	13	32	45	24	69	65	46
11–14 years	15	20	35	10	45	78	44
15–20 years	9	14	23	8	31	74	45
21 and over	7	12	19	37	56	32	21
No child or no information on child's age	52	38	90	76	166	54	23
Total	103	130	233	232	465		

mothers worked, a low proportion in comparison with the other groups shown in Table 12, especially when it is remembered that the women in this sample of Wives and Widows included those who had no husband at home and might therefore have heavy financial responsibilities. Of the ninety-eight workers with a child under five, only seven worked full-time, and none of the seven had a baby under one. Moreover, as will be shown in the chapter on the children, full-time work until the child was about eleven was closely related to exceptionally safe minding, usually by a relative. The belief that married women's employment means large numbers of mothers leaving little children for long hours was certainly not borne out in Bermondsey.

Husband's occupation

The analysis of husbands' occupations did not show that the wives of any one particular category of worker were markedly more, or markedly less, prone to work than the wives of any other category. Those wives whose husbands were professional men and in clerical jobs worked least; those whose men were skilled manual workers, most. It was interesting that the incidence of full-, as compared to part-time work, was high among the wives of skilled manual and highly paid unskilled workers (who would include the newly prospering dockers); while part-time, rather than full-, was characteristic of the women whose husbands were in semi-skilled and low paid unskilled work. The higher incidence of shift work may have had some influence here: or possibly the poorer type of household had a combination of low-earning husband and larger-sized family.

The basic characteristic of the women who worked can be summarized as follows. Among the Wives and Widows the great majority

98

THE BERMONDSEY WIVES WHO WORKED

TABLE 13   'Husbands and Wives'

Husband's occupation in relation to his wife's work situation

Husband's occupation	Worker F.T.	Worker P.T.	Total	House-wife	Total	Workers as % of total
Professional:						
doctors, managerial, owner shopkeepers, publicans, police superintendents	5	5	10	15	25	40
Supervisory level:						
foremen, policemen	2	7	9	8	17	53
Clerical:						
office workers, salesmen, railway checkers	4	10	14	20	34	41
Skilled manual:						
craftsmen, drivers	29	26	55	39	94	59
Highly paid unskilled manual:						
dockers, stevedores, steel erectors	16	11	27	24	51	53
Semi-skilled manual:						
postmen, bus conductors, ticket collectors	8	17	25	21	46	54
Bottom category unskilled:						
general labourers, night watchmen	17	35	52	49	101	51
No information	3	3	6	6	12	50
Total	84	114	198	182	380	

were in semi-skilled and unskilled manual work. Leaving out women over pensionable age, the Wives and Widows who worked most were in their forties and fifties--i.e. women whose family responsibilities were lessening. They were least likely to be in their twenties —i.e. mothers with a baby. Though this, the expected pattern, was found, it is worth noting that half of those still in their thirties went out to work. Another characteristic was the extent not merely of part-time employment but of the quite small, part-time job. Rather more of the Wives and Widows worked part-time than full-time: and considerably less than a quarter of this group of workers had as long as a forty-hour week or more. As regards family size, in those households containing both husband and wife, the preference for part- rather than full-time employment increased as the number of children in the home rose.

Why they worked

The reasons why it has become physically easier for the married woman to go out to work have already been discussed. The personal history of very many of the families met with in Bermondsey illustrated vividly the demographic and social changes which have led

MARRIED WOMEN WORKING

these families to consider the possibility of the mother going out to work. It is less easy to state with any conviction why, especially in an area like Bermondsey, an increasing number of wives are choosing to do so. These homes have never been so well off as they are now: and it is undoubtedly the wives themselves who carry the extra load, however generously they credited what they called 'being able to get by' to their husbands and relatives.

The reasons which the women gave, complex, overlapping, and sometimes contradictory, were on the whole less stereotyped than those commonly advanced as to why a married woman ought *not* to work. Their job history and the level of their current work did not indicate that they were pursuing any idea of a career; nor that they were seeking 'fulfilment' by holding positions of responsibility. Little indicated that their job was an essential ingredient of their life: rather, as the Peek Frean study had suggested, going out to work had to fit into the existing pattern of their life and day. The strong preference for part- as opposed to full-time work confirmed their claim that they put the family first. Though they were clearly seeking, and appreciative of, the improved status that going out to work made possible, nevertheless this new role was in every sense subsidiary to the traditional one of wife and mother.

The fact that they worked in order to earn seemed too obvious to most of these wives to need further comment. Few could put into words the satisfaction they may have felt in contributing to the world's work in a second field. On the other hand, that they themselves recognized the inadequacy of economic motives as their sole reason for work, was hinted at by the clinching 'anyway' they so continually brought in at the end of a discussion—'Anyway, what is there to keep me from working?'

In trying to extricate some of the wife's deeper reasons the team encouraged her to discuss the obvious, themselves interpreting what she said in the light of their own knowledge of local patterns and values and, when possible, of the family's history. No statistical analysis of 'reasons' was attempted, except in the case of such things as holidays and consumer durables which it was possible to check.

The team was interested to find that the reasons (interpreted in this broad way) which the Bermondsey families talked about confirmed those given by the Peek Frean employees. Nor did these reasons seem markedly different from those put forward by women drawn from a variety of social classes.[*] The implication is obvious—

[*] Klein, *op. cit.*

THE BERMONDSEY WIVES WHO WORKED

that employment outside the home is meeting deep-seated needs which are now felt by women in general in our society.

Financial motives

Bermondsey, like other working-class districts, has a strong tradition of being on the lookout for any chance to make the odd bit of extra money, from the old man on the street selling a single box of daffodils he has bought up cheap, to the man who is prepared to do a friend's decorating at the weekend. The best bet of the local married woman who wants some extra money, even if only for a short-term objective, is a regular job, however small and however brief. The odd job is less easy for a woman to come by than it is for a man; home work is badly paid and difficult to get; and lodgers, even should the house have room for them, are normally friends or relatives and expect to pay accordingly.

Bermondsey is one of the great centres of dock labour, and certain characteristics of dock work probably generate particular pressure on the Bermondsey wife to earn. The influence is not confined to the household of the docker, since dock work has for so long dominated the life of the area. In the past, and to some extent this holds good even today, an alternative source of income in the house was a highly desirable safeguard against the hazards of casual labour and of an industry where strikes are endemic. Even now, the 'docker's bumper', his 12s 6d day's pay when no work is available, represents a very considerable drop in his £12–£13 average weekly earnings. Though overtime may step up earnings, it cannot be relied on, so that the desirability of a second income, however small, is self-evident. The fall in earnings is also likely to be sudden, so sudden that it has affected next week's housekeeping before the wife has had time to save. Possibly, too, the man's traditional uncertainty as to what next week's wages will amount to make it difficult for him to appreciate the steady rise in housekeeping costs that face his wife, and over tart with his 'You kept home on that before, why can't you now?'

The team was told, by those very familiar with Bermondsey, that most families were still living fully up to the week's income, apart from any short-term savings. Few appeared to have any capital, wills were unknown, and no one expected to inherit anything that could conceivably be mortgaged. This absence of expectations, together with the unpredictability of the weekly income, was reflected in spending habits. It helped to explain the intensive spending at the weekend, or the seeming improvidence of the couple who argued

101

MARRIED WOMEN WORKING

'I've made ten quid, you've made eight, so that's £18 we've got to spend this week.'

In the past Bermondsey's way of getting by in a financial crisis was to borrow. The good husband was the one who, in a bad week, himself took on the responsibility for borrowing the bare essentials to cover food and fuel. When most men were in precarious work, little stigma attached to this; the difficulty was to find a source of credit. Today people try to keep their money troubles to themselves. In any case, the personal loan has largely been replaced by 'tick buying', said to have come into use in the 1930's, when the new homes that slum clearance provided led to a need for more ample furnishings. This was the date when the local press advertised such aids as 'Brass bed complete with bedding, 2s a week.' Today, of course, hosts of credit methods and ways of instalment buying are available; provided too much debt is not involved most are regarded as sound. They include the Co-operative or Provident cheques by which (at a cost of 1s in the £) the customer gets the goods at once and pays off weekly; the £20 club where the member pays down £1 per week for twenty weeks and draws lots as to which week the full £20 worth of goods are hers; the 'pay-off', popular for children's clothes, where the shop holds the article until the full cost is met. A less reputable method is that of the tallyman. He calls, makes no enquiries as to the home's finances, leaves the goods, demands no signature, and no cash until next week. Bermondsey is inclined to think that this particular method tempts the wife unfairly, especially since the tallyman's wares are poor in quality. Finally, there is hire purchase proper, which itself can be worked towards by cash credit —pay what you like, when you like, till enough is put down to go into HP itself. That so much of the buying is done on a weekly basis probably aggravates the worries of the home where the husband's earnings are liable to sudden fluctuations. Even if the wife's wages are small, they represent a measure of insurance and, furthermore, the money is under her own control.

It is difficult to say how far this desire for a second income was a reflection of economic necessity measured in an objective sense. Though the women underlined financial aspects with statements like 'It's no good stopping at home if the children have to do without,' and 'We couldn't do what we do on just his money,' there was no hint whatever that husbands were urging their wives to work. Certainly by the standards even of the immediate past, levels of living were vastly improved; and in general the spur was the determination to improve on the improvements.

THE BERMONDSEY WIVES WHO WORKED

However, some husbands earned less than others: might not this be an incentive for the wife to work, and level out the difference? This proved an extremely difficult matter on which to reach firm conclusions. Accurate information about husbands' earnings came from only 61 per cent of the Husbands and Wives interviewed.

TABLE 14   *'Husbands and Wives'*

Husband's earnings in relation to his wife's work situation [9]

Husband's net weekly earnings	F.T.	Worker P.T.	Total	Housewife	Total	Workers as % of total
Under £10	13	36	49	27	76	64
£10–£12.19.0	35	33	68	40	108	63
£13–£15.19.0	5	10	15	16	31	48
£16 and over	3	3	6	6	12	50
Total	56	82	138	89	227	
Husbands did not work/no information					160	
All husbands					387[1]	

Last week's earnings less P.A.Y.E. and National Insurance.
[1] Total of 387, not the 380 of the 'Husbands and Wives' Sample, is probably due to the fact that O.A.P.s pension was in some cases given as earnings. Cf. also Table 17.

The figures in Table 14 suggest a connection between the husband's low earnings and the wife's going out to work. A difference in the proportions at work at different income levels can be brought out by drawing a line between husbands who earned less than £13, and all those who earned more, i.e. between those who were generally earning below, or just up to, the national average weekly earnings for a man[2] at the time of the study, and those who were earning more. If this is done, then 64 per cent of the wives with husbands whose earnings fell below this line went out to work. But the large number of cases in which the husband did not work, or in which no information could be obtained on the husband's earnings, makes it impossible to arrive at firm conclusions. The proportion of women unwilling to give information as to what their husband earned was highest among those not at work, especially the older ones: this may well understate the proportion not at work whose husbands had low earnings, and thus exaggerate the difference between the two groups. An attempt was made to relate whether or not a woman worked to the adequacy of her husband's earnings. 'Adequacy' was assessed

[2] Adult male industrial workers' average weekly earnings October 1958— £12 16s 8d. *Ministry of Labour Gazette,* Feb. 1959.

103

MARRIED WOMEN WORKING

by measuring his earnings against the National Assistance Board's basic subsistence scale, which relates income to family size.[3]

TABLE 15   *'Husbands and Wives'*

Husband's income (as % of N.A.B. figure) in relation to his wife's work situation

Husband's income as % of N.A.B. figure		Worker				Workers as % of
	F.T.	P.T.	Total	Housewife	Total	total
Over 200%	41	38	79	55	134	59
200% or less	15	39	54	45	99	55
Not known	28	37	65	82	147	44
Total	84	114	198	182	380	

An arbitrary division was made at twice the N.A.B. figure appropriate for each family. It emerged that wives whose husbands' incomes were well above subsistence were slightly more prone to work. This may appear to contradict the figures in Table 14, but there is a possible explanation. Table 15 shows that, among the women at work whose husbands were relatively low-earners on the N.A.B. scale, there was a higher proportion working part-time than among those women workers who, as Table 14 shows, had low-earning husbands according to the national average (59 per cent). This suggests that a higher proportion in the former group had children at home, since this would affect the 'adequacy' of earnings according to the N.A.B. scale: while it has already been established that the woman with children at home is more likely to work part-than full-time (Table 38). What can safely be inferred from these figures is that low earnings on the part of the husband (in relation to the national average) was a factor in the wife seeking work outside the home; but it also seems to be the case that relatively high earnings by her husband did not discourage her from doing so, particularly if she had no children at home.

A family holiday

In discussing financial questions with the families interviewed, the team tried to relate the extra earnings to certain fields of expenditure,

---

[3] N.A.B. scale for needs other than rent (January 1958)

		s.	d.
(a) for a married couple		76	0
(b) i. for a person living alone or a householder		45	0
ii. for any other person			
aged 21 years and over		41	0
aged 18 years and over but less than 21 years		31	0
aged 16 years and over but less than 18 years		26	0
aged 11 years and over but less than 16 years		20	0
aged 5 years and over but less than 11 years		17	0
Under 5 years		14	0

THE BERMONDSEY WIVES WHO WORKED

partly to help verify the women's reasons for working. This raised further difficulties, which are discussed in Chapter VIII. Holidays, however, proved such a word to conjure with in Bermondsey and were so often mentioned as a reason for working, that they deserve separate consideration in any discussion of motives. Despite the importance attached to them, a family holiday of even one week, still less one of a fortnight, was in no way a universal practice for Bermondsey families. Thirty-six per cent of the Peek Frean Shifts Sample and 47 per cent of the factory Newcomers Sample had no holiday away in 1954: and 39 per cent of the Bermondsey Husbands and Wives whose holiday position was known had no family holiday in 1957 (Table 34). Had the figure related to Wives and Widows it would almost certainly have been lower still.

Holidays were still so much of a novelty that, illustrated by quantities of snapshots, they formed a major topic of talk throughout the year. The elderly postman would linger on his round to describe the tour he and his wife had just been on—'49 counties, 2,341 miles, 49½ guineas'. At the factory excitement mounted in the pre-holiday weeks—'Miss H. in the packing room going to Austria. Mrs B. on our bench and her hubby touring in their car; Mr and Mrs W. flying to Yugoslavia'. In this last case the mantle descended on to the speaker herself since, for the two weeks in question, she would be 'spelling out' Mrs W.'s job. Most families, however, took their holidays much nearer home, usually no farther north than Yarmouth, or west than Bournemouth; while one in five still opted for one or other of the Cockney's favourite resorts along the Thames estuary (Table 34). Parents made much of the fact that today's holiday is a united, family affair which gives old and young time to enjoy each other's company. In the past those children who were lucky enough to get away at all, went off separately; one to a convalescent home, another to a boys' club camp, a third to a Country Holiday Fund hostel. Still earlier generations had known no more than the Sunday School trip. The one exception, and here Bermondsey was fortunate, was the hopping holiday; but its pleasures were very dependent on the weather, and it was hardly a holiday for the adults as it gave no respite from work. Today the chalet or caravan type of holiday, usually at a fairly unsophisticated type of holiday camp, has largely replaced hopping and the children's solo holidays. A chalet is cheap, perhaps six guineas for six sleepers, allows the children freedom, and imposes fewer social constraints than boarding house or landlady. It does not give the mother a break from housekeeping of course, but to get away at all is such a novelty that there was seldom a hint that the week was, perhaps, not much of a holiday

105

for Mum. Even in the late 1950's, seven days in a caravan at Southend was the first holiday one forty-five-year-old wife had had since she married twenty-one years ago. The effort so many of these families put into their holidays, and their extravagant-sounding spending on just this one week, was perhaps Bermondsey's way of emphasizing the sheer contrast of the holiday with the rest of their life—an unconscious protest against the noisy, clock-ridden, money-getting background of so much of the other fifty-one weeks. Compared with the grime and drabness of inner London, the sea's freshness, the pretty gardens, and the gay holiday shops made a tremendous impact. So did the new acquaintances for families whose social life has been largely confined to a circle of relations, most of them known since birth, and to a very limited number of neighbours. Making new friends was held to enrich the holiday almost as much as the change of scene. All told, therefore, the wife's job and the extra work that it entailed for the whole household was felt to be abundantly justified if it made a holiday possible.

Status

Work so far has been discussed as a means of supplementing the income of the home, of raising standards, and of achieving specific objectives such as holidays. At the surface level, these were the principal motives and satisfactions. But it has always been acknowledged that work brings its own satisfactions. Was this the case with the Bermondsey wives who worked?

The first point noted was that these working-class wives rode no feminist band-wagon. They seldom mentioned frustration over wasted talents, while few would think of claiming that their job was of any particular value to society. Nor did they reject domesticity. Too hard-headed to see this as 'drudgerie divine', they appeared to be less in revolt against pots and pans, than not quite sure how to fill in their day.

Secondly, they were acutely aware of the ease of today's lot, constantly offering instances of the lightness of their own housekeeping compared with what they had seen of the life of their mother and grandmother. They did not confine the comparison to their own side of the family, but often brought in examples from the husband's side, indicating that the improvement in women's life were matters that they thought over and talked about in the family circle. The younger wives in particular had often been the first generation of girls to grow up in the smaller-sized family, and the first not to be involved in helping to bring up a succession of younger fry. That this traditional role of the older sister had vanished was shown by

THE BERMONDSEY WIVES WHO WORKED

the fact that, in the Wives and Widows households, only three contained both a child too young for school and one old enough to have left it. As teenage girls, therefore, today's wives have not had nearly so much experience of child care, housework, and minor illness, as was the case with their mothers when girls: housework alone would no longer have appeared to them, when girls, as their inevitable lot. The younger wives, too, had received a better education, and had earned far more than their mothers had done at the same age. This vast improvement in their status as girls probably made it that much harder for them to adapt to the drop in standards that, even today, they were likely to experience when they came to raise a family themselves.

While their life as girls had improved, as mothers it somehow seemed to have declined. Their mother's hand, whether tender or bullying, had been a confident one; whereas they themselves had hardly got the hang of child-rearing before the task was over. The Peek Frean Shifts Sample and the Newcomers, when asked for information about the number of children their mothers had borne and the number they had had themselves, gave this picture. Two hundred and thirty-nine of those who were mothers provided information. This showed that 34 per cent had been born into families of 4, 5 or 6 children; while only 12 per cent of the informants had themselves had this number of children. Indeed, only one of the 239 had more than six children herself, whereas nearly half their mothers (118) had had seven children or more. In the Bermondsey Husbands and Wives households, only 17 per cent had as many as three children or more (though this sample of course included women whose families were not completed). The sheer number of babies the old-time mother gave birth to, and her own survival of the great dangers of child-birth, in a way justified her as a woman in her own eyes. That she had managed to rear a child at all by her rule of thumb methods proved her personal competence, while no one questioned the hardness of her life. As late as the 1930's, a national survey of working-class wives noted how often 'the exhaustion both of funds and of strength does not proceed in equal stages with the arrival of each child, but by a terrible geometric progression'.[4] On the other hand, despite the strains, the mother of the big family had spent her time on a supremely rewarding job—that of raising living creatures: while the very frequency of her contact with birth and with death gave her dignity. Today's wives, facing progressively fewer of the traditional hazards and hardships of motherhood, and with more

[4] M. Spring Rice, *Working Class Wives*, London, Pelican Books, 1937.

MARRIED WOMEN WORKING

efficient tools with which to do their housework, may well feel some doubt as to whether they are really pulling their weight.

Some of this decline in status could be regained by going out to work. The paid job implies physical effort, which always commands respect in working-class circles. In this case, too, the effort was for the most laudable of reasons—'Here's one who'll put herself out for the kids' sake.' To add to the family's income showed that she cared about the proper things, like a lovely, modern home. The extra money meant she could dress better, wear her good clothes for part of every day, and be more of a credit to her husband when he took her out, a point often mentioned. To be able to hold down a job at all in the competitive outside world was reassuring and something that not every married woman would dare to tackle. How important it sounded to say you '*must go in tomorrow*', to talk of 'my mates', and to refer to rush jobs and overseas orders. Certainly the purposeful walk of the twos and threes of women going to and from work through the Park contrasted strongly with the bored looks of the mothers sitting about with a single child. Merely to be moving in a wider circle than the domestic one was a mark of some distinction since, in a place like Bermondsey, housewives lead a very uniform existence. For certain wives, too, the paid job helped to compensate for the exasperating traveller's tales spun by husbands who had been in the Forces. When the man had lived 'all over Persia, Egypt, the Levantine States', it made the wife's life look pretty thin. Why should she always be the one to stay at home? All these vague exhilarations which work provided were, of course, reinforced by the pride and pleasure of having an income of one's own. They put it modestly enough—just that 'You do feel nice when you get your bit of money on a Friday and know that you've earned it.'

Besides giving status, work could be a genuine relief; a measure of anodyne for the mother who had lost her baby, or for the suddenly-emptied world of the widow. It also eased the strain on the woman who had the sole care of an invalid, and helped give some perspective to the wife whose marital relations were unhappy. Even when her domestic life was contented enough, a smaller disability, the cramped size of most of these working-class homes, was relieved by getting out into another environment. Some Bermondsey homes are structurally dreary. At one such place, in Victorian 'buildings', the interviewer noted that the light had to be on at midday and on Midsummer's Day. The mothers on the evening shift at Peek Frean's often spoke of the relief given by the adult world of the factory after a day alone with small children in a confined home of this type;

108

THE BERMONDSEY WIVES WHO WORKED

especially in those high blocks of flats where the little ones could never go out to play alone, because the yard was out of the mother's eye and ear-shot.

'It makes a change'

Certain wives said that their doctors had recommended them to get a job as a remedy for what they called their 'nerves', and that the prescription had worked. The phrases used, 'I felt so heavy,' 'I got morbid,' 'I worried so over little things,' suggested that the speaker, like the Victorian lady with her vapours, was probably suffering from a psychosomatic condition due as much to under-occupation as to life's normal slings and arrows. Finally, to go out to work often gave exercise, fresh air, and a healthy tiredness to the physically robust woman who tended to get in the doldrums because her domain was so restricted, her housekeeping so simple, and her daily shopping done within five minutes' walk. The number of youngish women who seemed to be obsessed with the family's health possibly indicated lack of both physical and mental occupation.

The uneventfulness of the lives of many of these women was also suggested by such phrases as 'Nothing to look at but these four walls'; 'I used to turn the room round just for something to do'; and, the idiom regularly used for anything remotely pleasurable, 'It makes a change, don't it?' Even the families with cars mostly used them only at the weekend, and then for riding around locally. Though the family might start Sunday off by going over to Petticoat Lane, or begin their Christmas buying (in September) in Peckham, their most important shopping rarely took them to the West End. Many of the women seldom left Bermondsey except for an occasional day with a relation (mostly in another part of South-East London); or for an odd coach trip; or for the annual holidays.

Leisure time pursuits in the middle class sense meant almost nothing to them. One woman said, quite seriously, that her main hobby was checking her husband's pools for him; another, rising to the occasion, that her hobby was 'nagging the old man'. The women had far fewer activities than the men and they were narrower in range. Nor, unlike the middle class mother, did they reckon to spend much of their time in teaching and playing with the small children. This was not to say they found them boring, but that 'care' of this kind was not regarded as necessary. Nor had their education given them much taste for books or enabled them to turn to the arts for refreshment or consolation. The sympathetic but avid way in which they followed other people's personal stories in the press, suggested that their own life was probably short of interests and of drama.

MARRIED WOMEN WORKING

Very little in the way of novelty could mean a great deal. 'Letters, I love them; they make the day for me,' said a wife in her thirties, with three children, a car, a radiogram, TV, and all the gadgets.

Local societies—religious, political, or social—had little attraction for most of the women. Even if the Mothers' Meeting of earlier generations was no great intellectual feast, it provided an excuse for the wife to get out, while its link with the church drew the women's attention to a world other than the visible and perhaps trivial. The numbers attracted by these societies of the past proved a striking contrast to the total number (under 300 members) found among twelve Bermondsey societies open to women studied by the team.[5] In 1901, for example, there were 656 recorded members of the Bermondsey Mothers' Meetings of the Wesleyan Mission;[6] in 1900 there were '80 on the books and an average attendance of nearly 40' at one of three such women's meetings organized by the Bermondsey Settlement;[7] and 'seldom less than a hundred (men and women) present' at Mrs Colby's Sunday Bible Class at St James' Mission, a class which ran for years.[8] Nothing comparable exists today.

Loneliness was another of the reasons given for going out to work. Compared with the bustling homes in which so many had grown up, today's domestic life was often solitary. Moving house, as so many have done, has added to this problem. Even if the new neighbours are agreeable enough, one needs to be cautious, since over-hasty friendships can imperil privacy and hard-won standards. The neighbours appeared to fall into three groups: those with whom the contact was limited to mutual services—'She'll pay the rent for me but we don't speak'; those with whom one chatted but did not ask in; and the bosom friend with whom one swapped keys. The post-prandial doorstep talk, standing up, rarely blossomed into anything beyond this encounter on neutral ground, nor had these working-class wives developed anything akin to the suburban housewife's morning coffee, friends to tea, or gossipy 'phone call. And they had nothing that corresponded with the pub friends that their husbands made. If the wives ate out at all, it was with the children or a friend and, in front of strangers, a silent, rapid meal.

Flat life, too, greatly on the increase in Bermondsey, tends to cut one off audibly and visibly from the outside world. Fewer folk pass one's window and the engrossing details of street life can no longer be seen, let alone participated in. The street has become

[5] See p. 132.   [6] *South London Wesleyan Mission Report*, 1901.
[7] *Bermondsey Settlement Annual Report*, 1900.
[8] *Faithful unto Death*, Memorial of Rose Colby, St James' Mission.

110

THE BERMONDSEY WIVES WHO WORKED

less interesting than formerly since nowadays people keep their troubles to themselves: also there are fewer eccentrics at large in the community. The mothers with small children who lived in old and liftless blocks of flats were particularly lonely. One, whose home was on the fifth floor, never got down to earth until she could find someone to help with transportation (pram, baby, toddler, four-year-old and self); another, with three children and eighty-five steps, said she took on a (night) job partly because she found her daily life was so isolated. The shared yard, the garden cheek-by-jowl with its neighbour, and the chair on the front, all gave opportunities for contact that are denied the flat dweller. Flat life, too, increases the potential annoyances from the neighbours. The interviewers noticed how often the music from someone else's TV, and the crying of someone else's baby, sounded across the narrow passages and through the thin floors.

Going out to work did more than dispel loneliness. It enlarged one's social contacts beyond the set of related households and the one or two trusted neighbours. At work, new friends were to hand ready made; furthermore, these friends at work did not create complications since they could be kept apart from one's private life. To claim many such friends, to be able to exchange your 'Tat-ah-love, see you tomorrow' with a heap of people, was a mark of status worth having. There was also the special friend one made at work. Half the Peek Frean Shifts Sample said they had this particular friend. The value placed on 'my mate' and on their own small circle at work was indicated by the high incidence of complaints at the factory about the frequency of job transfer. It will be remembered that the N.B.I workers had done their best to minimize disruption by developing a relief system in which established groups were broken up infrequently, and in strict order. Those who went out to work also made much of the fact that 'You get a laugh mixing with the girls,' saying that it reminded them of the carefree existence of their girlhood. Small-talk about each other's affairs was another of the minor pleasures connected with going out to work. The domestic staff with whom the senior research worker was employed at the hospital derived much entertainment from the regular exchange of information about each other's daily meals. One woman, for example, who had given her family bread pudding for dinner brought five fat slices for inspection; another, the group's medical authority, handed round a new brand of cough lozenge she was finding efficacious for her boy; a third regaled the group with a daily instalment of a serial about the marital troubles of one of her daughters. And then of course there were the occasional highlights that workers organize

MARRIED WOMEN WORKING

among themselves from time to time. At Peek Frean's it might be dinner in the West End and a Dave King show for 112 of the bake-house ladies, or a pre-Christmas drink at a pub with the dozen girls on one's own machine—paper hats, false noses, and bursting spirits.

The wife who did not go out to work

This study is concerned with married women's employment, but since almost half the Bermondsey Wives and Widows responsible for running a home did not go out to work (Table 7), a brief account is appended of those who stayed at home. The following day's diary kept by a mother with young children was fairly typical of the life led by many such Bermondsey wives.

May 28 1957

a.m.

6.30 Linda, aged five, and Morris, aged two, wake up.

7.30 Rise—wash and dress. Make tea. Dress Morris. Cook break-fast, oats, marmite, buttered toast and vitawheat. Open beds. Feed dog and cat.

8.30 Clear breakfast dishes, prepare veg. for dinner. Wash up. Boy locks himself in bedroom at 9. Girl goes to school 9.15. At 9.20 finally manage to persuade boy to throw key out of bed-room window. Order restored. Make custard for children's after-dinner sweet.

9.30 Make beds. One double, two single. Vacuum and dust bed-rooms and landing, sweep and dust stairs and front lobby. Sort and put away yesterday's washing.

10.30 Make morning coffee. Start on living-room, vacuum, dust, etc. This room is the one that is most used and therefore takes the longest to clean up.

11.30 Put meat in oven for dinner, wash up odds and ends. Cook meat for animals. Also prepare and cook meat for tomorrow's pie.

p.m.

12.15 Start to tidy sitting-room.

12.30 Dish up dinner. Linda arrives home from school at 12.40.

1.00 Put dishes to soak, cigarette, and look at paper. See Linda off to school.

1.30 Wash up dinner dishes. Finish off ironing left over from Mon-day's wash. Clean up kitchen and back lobby.

2.30 Three visitors arrive—make tea. Visitors leave at 3. Pop round local shop for few odds and ends.

112

THE BERMONDSEY WIVES WHO WORKED

p.m.

3.30 Make pastry ready for tomorrow's pie—put in 'fridge. Make ginger cakes and jam tarts topped with almond sponge. Also for tomorrow. Mother and friend coming for a day. Wash up.

4.30 Prepare children's tea. Spaghetti on toast. Jelly and blancmange. Cake. Orange juice. Have a bath and change.

5.30 Prepare tea for husband and self. Eggs, bacon, and tomatoes. Husband washes up!

6.30 Bath children. Give them apple and biscuit and put to bed. Feed cat and dog. Sort out mending.

7.30 Do mending. Finish off dress for Linda—nine buttonholes and sew on buttons.

8.30 Change over to knitting to watch film on TV.

9.30 Still knitting and watching TV.

10.30 Make meat and salad sandwiches for supper.

11.30 Retire.

The non-workers included such obvious categories as the elderly; those whose home ties prevented them being away at regular hours; and those with ill-health themselves. There were also the wives on whom their husbands had imposed the ban absolute, 'When you start work I stop.' Among the older couples this by no means implied an unhappy marriage; the wife was of her generation, and accepted her role. In the case of the younger couples, the mother who was made to stay at home against her inclinations seemed in certain cases to be a slap-happy individual whose husband was enforcing what appeared to the onlooker to be only reasonable. On the whole, those mothers who deliberately chose to stay at home were perhaps somewhat below or above Bermondsey's general social level. They included women who had had an unusually comfortable childhood; and those who, marrying well, had acquired middle-class norms of the wife not having to rough it, and of the children needing training as well as physical care. A case in point was a mother with three small children who had had a Grammar School education and was married to a West End salesman. Apart from the wife's obvious domestic ties, this couple believed in the mother having time to enjoy the children and to teach them. At the other end of Bermondsey's shortish social scale was the slow-witted, untidily dressed woman, poor at housekeeping and probably living a semi-communal life with her mother's household. Possibly she lacked the intelligence to make use of the new domestic aids that speed up housework; possibly she was physically below par. Her house often indicated that she was no planner; and the interview suggested that any attempt

MARRIED WOMEN WORKING

she made to go out to work would be short-lived, indeed doomed to failure. Though the neighbours excused her as probably never having known a house with a regular wage coming in, they also classed her as a 'right muddler, just sits around, gossips on the corner, doesn't really get any more time off than us'. There was also the bone-idle individual, not short of brains but, in Bermondsey's view, too selfish to give up her freedom for the family's sake. Just a few of the wives who stayed at home appeared to be near-neurotics who made a fetish of housework. Finally there was the wife whom the health visitors classed as 'a real Mum'. This woman's domain had none of the glossy smartness and immaculate tidiness of so many homes, the furniture was more old-fashioned and fewer expensive toys were in evidence. She even took a certain pride in contriving, in hunting down the shop where things were a few coppers cheaper, in trying out an inexpensive but tasty recipe, and in devising clothes and curtains from remnants. Nor was she ashamed of using any services going. She would get one of her children away through the Country Holiday Fund, though this had low prestige compared with the family holiday. She was 'creative' in a homely way: *liked* spending time on making, not just the essentials but the child's party-dress that she could not afford to buy ready-made; enjoyed having plenty of living things about the place; encouraged other people's children to come in and out besides her own; and was willing to house a more interesting assortment of pets than the ubiquitous budgie. The families of these real Mums gave the impression of having rather more hobbies than most homes, and the children were perhaps rather more likely to be linked with the churches and youth groups. The mother herself, a leisurely individual, was possibly the personality type who takes life easily. The door of her home tended to be on the jar and she was a pleasantly forthcoming person to interview. One could not see her being bully-ragged into going out to work because everyone said it was easy done, or even just for the sake of being in the swim. These wives stood outside the general movement towards work and all that it implied. Whatever the reason for their attitude, in a district like Bermondsey they showed considerable independence of outlook in deliberately choosing to stay at home.

CHAPTER VIII

Home Making

Earning and spending–Running the house: methods and efficiency–The personal strains–Time off in Bermondsey

ALL the evidence from the Peek Frean study had emphasized that the wives who worked continued to centre their life on their homes. But did they, in fact, maintain their housekeeping standards, look after the family's welfare, and allow themselves a modicum of leisure? This chapter discusses the methods which these Bermondsey wives had evolved to cope with their extra domestic load, and it tries to assess the effectiveness of their endeavours. The next chapter deals with a still more controversial subject—did the children suffer?

Earning and spending

The first point examined was the effect that the wife's wages had on the home's total income and its material standards. Since, as has been shown, a low-earning husband tended to act as a spur to the wife to work, while the fact that she had a high-earning one did not deter her from doing so, it might be that the two sets of families evinced markedly different patterns of expenditure. Was there, for example, at one end of the scale, the family who only managed to 'get by', as they called it, because of the help provided by the wife's earnings; and at the other, the family 'living it up', and surrounded by the status symbols of the affluent society? To answer such questions accurately requires the collection of two particularly troublesome types of data—how much people earn, and how they spend what they earn. Some of the difficulties involved have already been described when discussing the relation between the wife's employment and the husband's earnings. Six questions on earnings were included in the Bermondsey schedules. The two basic ones, asked of the husband and wife separately, were 'How much did you earn *last week* (after deducting P.A.Y.E. and N.I.)?'; and 'How much do you *usually* earn (after deducting P.A.Y.E. and N.I.)?'. By issuing separate cards for husband and wife, and code numbers for their replies, it was often possible to ease some of the tension. Even so the number of people who would not provide information was considerable; but what replies were given were believed to be reasonably accurate,

115

MARRIED WOMEN WORKING

the figures relating to various weeks within the year ended September 1958.

TABLE 16   '*Wives and Widows*'

Woman's earnings (in week previous to interview) in relation to her work situation[1]

	Workers		
	F.T.	P.T.	Total
Under £1	—	4	4
£1 and under £3	2	50	52
£3 and under £5	15	42	57
£5 and under £7	47	5	52
£7 and under £9	17	1	18
£9 and over	8	—	8
No information on earnings	14	28	42
Total	103	130	233

[1] After deducting P.A.Y.E. and National Insurance.

Information was obtained on the earnings of eighty-nine of the 103 full-time women workers. Forty-seven earned between £5 and £7 which was comparable with the £6 1s 8d [2] which was the national average at that date for women industrial workers. Fifty-six of the 191 workers (part-time and full-time) whose earnings were known made under £3. Only eight women earned £9 or more, all, needless to say, full-time workers. Part-time work rarely brought in more than £5, usually much less. In view of the emphasis the women themselves laid on the money as their reason for working, these earnings may appear small when compared with their home's total income. On the other hand, they could hardly have hoped to earn more in view of their educational limitations, lack of technical training, and the limits they themselves imposed as to the number of hours and time of day at which they were prepared to work. Some examples of actual earnings are given on p. 117.

It will be remembered that use of the N.A.B. subsistence scale indicated that the wives of the better off husbands were slightly more prone to work than the wives as a whole (Table 15). Further analysis (Table 33) showed that in the families with the highest spendable incomes—for example in those with at least two and a half times that of the N.A.B.'s subsistence income for a family of this type—the wife was almost invariably at work. Of the twenty-five whose spendable income was more than three times the N.A.B. figure, twenty-four were working, twenty-two of them full-time. Only five of these had a child or children in the house. Quite clearly, the Bermondsey families at the top of the income scale were those

[2] *Ministry of Labour Gazette*, August 1958.

116

HOME MAKING

Examples of earnings

(from ten consecutive interviews in households where the wife was a worker)

		Normal hours per week	Woman's age	Last week's earnings (week previous to interview)
Cardboard box maker	F.T.	45	30	£6—£6.19.0
Dress machinist	F.T.	40	59	£4—£4.19.0
Machine hand (Pickle Mfr.)	F.T.	40	29	£5—£5.19.0
Trainee (Biscuit Mfr.)	F.T.	45	40	£6—£6.19.0
Receptionist (Photographer's studio)	F.T.	40	36	£7—£8
Packer (Box Mfr.)	P.T.	23½	39	£3—£3.19.0
Cleaner (Public House)	P.T.	24	49	£3—£3.19.0
Cleaner (Office)	P.T.	14½	58	£2—£2.19.0
Cleaner (Fur Importers)	P.T.	28	39	£4—£4.19.0
Solderer (Tin Box Mfr.)	P.T.	22	59	£2—£2.19.0

whose wives were in full-time work. Adequate provision (in terms of the N.A.B. scale), seemed, if anything, to act as an incentive to add a little more.

Questions on earning and spending had gained poor response among the Peek Frean employees. In the Bermondsey study it proved possible to ask the kind of questions that might show up obvious differences in the spending patterns of workers and housewives, and determine whether any such differences really affected the wife's decision to work. They might also throw some light on the delicate question as to whether the fact that the wife herself was an earner created difficulties between husband and wife. But even where the basic facts about earnings and housekeeping money were fairly firmly established, spending was a very different matter. This was partly because, in homes like the docker's where the men's earnings still show such frequent, sudden, and steep fluctuations, the pattern of family finance is exceptionally interwoven. Indeed, in all types of home, there was much variation as to who paid for what each week, especially as regards contributions towards the special 'buys', items like the £21 cycle for a son, or the £30 carpet for a living-room.

One of the claims the Peek Frean women made was that their wage enabled them to stock up the home with better furniture and bedding, with labour-saving devices, radiograms, and the many big buys they considered benefited the family as a whole. The Bermondsey interviews examined this claim in relation to four of the items frequently mentioned, refrigerator, washing machine, TV, and car. (Since the car was so often a very second-hand affair, its cost might not differ greatly from that of the other three items.) For the purpose of these figures the goods had to represent a permanent addition to the home, to have been not only bought, but kept.

MARRIED WOMEN WORKING

TABLE 17   *'Husbands and Wives'*

Amenities in household in relation to wife's work situation

		F.T.	Worker P.T.	Total	House-wife	Total
No. of families which have bought:	Car	17	21	38	15	53
	W/machine	8	15	23	16	39
	Refrigerator	5	10	15	17	32
	TV	42	71	113	86	199
No. of families which have bought:	one of above items	35	48	83	70	153
	two or more items	17	31	48	27	75
No. of families not known to have bought any of the items		32	35	67	85	152
Totals of families with wife's work situation as described		84	114	198	182	380

The relative popularity of these acquisitions was: TV (199); car (53); washing machine (39); refrigerator (32). In only 57 per cent of the cases where one or more items had been bought was the wife out at work: while of those who (as far as was ascertained) had acquired none of the items, only 44 per cent were workers. To put it another way, 53 per cent of the housewives had acquired one or more of the items, as compared with 66 per cent of the workers; and 15 per cent of the houswives two or more of the items, as compared with 24 per cent of the workers.

It was by no means evident that these particular goods were an incentive for the majority. The wife did not work in six of the sixteen homes known to have bought three of the four items; nor did she do so in the two which had acquired all four of them. In the case of TV, the part-time worker had more often acquired one than the woman doing the better paid, full-time job. Bearing in mind that the 'no information' figures were high (i.e. those relating to the number of families not known to have acquired any of the selected items), nevertheless Table 17 does not appear to support the view that the wife decides to work largely for the sake of consumer goods. The interviews gave the impression that though some women started to work with a particular short-term aim in mind, they tended to continue working after the original objective had been reached.

Since the above figures took no account of household structure and financial obligation, a further comparison was made in the case of two of the selected items, car and washing machine. When the home was less adequately provided for (on the N.A.B. scale) by the husband, the wife who worked did not acquire either a car or washing machine any more often than did the housewife; when the home had a higher-earning husband, the worker's home was more likely

HOME MAKING

to have one or other of the articles in question. The part-time worker in the better off home was more likely to possess a car or washing machine than the part-timer in the poorer home (Table 35). The four items referred to were, of course, arbitrarily selected; and they represent only a fraction of the range of goods being acquired. It is also fair to add that the worker's home gave the impression of more lavish spending than the housewife's as far as durable consumer goods in general were concerned.

The wife's earnings might, of course, be used for saving towards a long-term objective. The interviewers failed to get precise information on this point, but long distance saving appeared to be unusual, except on a small scale, e.g. an endowment policy against an only daughter's 21st birthday, 3s to a loan club, or a weekly 5s 9d death insurance. Such pipe dreams as the possibility of 'setting up a public', or of buying a caravan, were not particularly common, and did not lead to much action. Indeed, any questions on saving on a large and longish scale, for such things as house purchase or education, or against the possibility of widespread unemployment, tended to be dismissed, not as impertinent but as almost outside the conception of these families who had never handled big sums and had always lived on a weekly or even daily wage. One of the Visiting Families, who were spending perhaps £100 per annum on smartening up their house, nevertheless felt that to save the £400 for which they could have bought the place would have involved an impossible effort. The very idea of handling so much money alarmed them. As regards unemployment, people certainly did not dismiss its possibility, but there was a kind of fatalism about it—a waiting for things to happen rather than an attempt to stave them off.

The attitude to short-term saving for a concrete objective was very different. Any type of saving for an objective well within grasp (and as has been said earlier many people hardly distinguished between straight saving and the hosts of methods used for tick buying) was regarded as an obvious justification for the husband to do overtime, and the wife to take on a job. The interviews gave the impression that a great deal of this type of saving was taking place, a view confirmed by such people as the Town Clerk of Bermondsey and the officials of the local National Savings Committee and London Trustee Savings Bank. These knowledgeable people thought there had probably been little increase in long-term saving since before the war: but, as regards saving for quick use, they pointed out that Bermondsey was ninth of the fifty-three London boroughs for savings through the National Savings Committee, and they drew attention to the following pre- and post-war figures:

119

MARRIED WOMEN WORKING

Growth in number of Bermondsey Savings Groups (including P.O. deposits) of N.S.C.

Half-yearly return	Total of groups	Industrial	Schools	Social	Street
March 1939	103	49	50	4	0
March 1955	231	123	26	11	71

Another possible use to which the wife's wages might be put was for personal spending on herself. The Peak Frean employees had, by implication, refuted this idea when they claimed that they worked for the sake of the family. The Bermondsey interviews certainly did not give the impression that the women were putting the bulk of their earnings into spending on their personal appearance. Nor, according to the uninhibited chat that the senior research worker met with when working on the domestic staff of the local hospital, did this play much part in the reason why these particular married women went out to work. Indeed, they disparaged any of their contemporaries who were held to dress over-smartly. Pin money spending in general seemed to be almost confined to cigarettes, nylons, and the hairdresser, a point illustrated in the accounts which nineteen families kept for the team of the weekly finances of each member of the household. The families in question contained 12 wives who worked (whose homes had 17 children under 16); the 7 where the wife did not work (whose homes had 14 children under 16). In the worker's household the husband's earnings tended to be lower than in the housewife's, so that the figures should not be used for comparative purposes.

Wives' spending on selected items in nineteen households for one week in spring of 1958

	Cigarettes, tobacco, etc.	Personal appearance	Sweets—apart from those specifically for the children	Entertainments	Household—laundry, etc.	Printed matter	Children—sweets and pocket money	Food regarded as 'extras'	No. of tins of food bought	House furnishings	Animals—food and care
	s d	s d	s d	s d	s d	s d	s d	s d		s d	s d
Housewife's spending	9 2	4 3	7 9	1 5	1 0	2 3	3 3½	7 9	3	1 9	2 4
Worker's spending	11 5½	5 7	1 4	8 3	3 8	4 0	4 1	6 11	5½	1 2	10

The wife who worked appeared to derive her chief financial return for working by having money of her own, and by her ability to spend more freely on her daily shopping, on food, and on the smaller

HOME MAKING

articles of clothing and household goods. She could be what she called 'more choosy'—buy steak instead of mince, the best quality bacon, tulips at 4s a bunch for the front window, and give her child 'milk not water when he wants a drink'.

One of the part-time workers at Peek Frean's, a wife of thirty-seven with three children, made this comment on how the extra money was used: 'When you start to earn you buy now what tempts you—a second pair of curtains instead of washing out the only pair; red salmon as you fancy; oranges *and* a pound of apples; and you begin to pay on a bedroom suite in a sixteen weeks' club.' The mothers also pointed out that, however lavish the parental spending from the home's joint income on big items for the children, for example £10 for doll's pram, or a camera, or a watch, this kind of present might be less important to the child itself than the small daily treats the mother had no qualms about providing if she had earned the money herself. Though certain parents felt that perhaps the children were getting more than the lion's share of the new wealth, and admitted that some of all this spending was for the adult's own pleasure, nevertheless the mothers' claim that their earnings went largely on the children was undoubtedly true.

Spending did not appear to be unduly competitive and any signs of particularly daft buying tended to be disparaged. The husband in the family living next door to the senior research worker was a case in point. He thought it ridiculous of all his brothers to be buying cocktail cabinets just because our Fred had gone in for one. The older people shrugged off a lot of this type of spending with 'everyone's so posh today'. In any case, aspirations to subtopian standards are not particularly powerful in Bermondsey, since few except the girls have jobs that take them into suburban or West End circles, and even the most up and coming families live in the same sort of housing as their neighbour's, have been at the same schools, and can make a shrewd estimate of each other's incomes.

Though there was a very great variety in how families controlled their income, it appeared that the wife normally paid the food bills, bought her own and the children's clothes, and, if an earner, did as she pleased with her own wages. No instance was met of a wife being expected to hand over her money to her husband. One change frequently remarked on was that today families are more open about money than in the past, and more ready to treat earning and spending as matters which should be jointly controlled. A couple in their thirties compared their own share-and-share-alike method with the carping attitude of the wife's parents. 'My father,' said this wife, 'used to bark at my mother "I've put 2d in the light—you owe me

MARRIED WOMEN WORKING

2d".' At another household, that of a window cleaner, the thirty-five-year-old wife contrasted the way in which she and her husband shared their earnings, with what she had seen of her parents' usage even in a family where the father was in a 'pretty good', meaning a regular, job. The speaker's father never let her mother know what he earned and her mother's allowance never varied: if on a 'low work' week making, say, £5, he would give her £4 10s; if on a full week making £7 he would still give her the same, though he would perhaps buy some additional food. But, as the speaker pointed out, this was not necessarily how her mother would have used the extra money. Although a generous gesture it was not a regular sharing of the luck, good or bad, as the speaker and her husband tried to do.

The team could see little evidence that if the wife had money of her own it was a bone of contention. Unhappy situations existed, of course, ranging from tiffs, 'You can be a bit independent if you go out', via soreness, 'He'd give me more but I'm too proud to ask', to downright defiance, 'I *won't* take his money.' In general, however, the concrete advantages appeared to outweigh even such questions of prestige as that to have the wife working reflected on the man's earning capacity, or on his personal generosity. Husbands and wives themselves certainly talked far more of the solid financial benefits derived from the second income than they did of such nebulous matters as less leisure together when the wife was a worker. It was also pointed out that if the wife earned too, this allowed the husband more money for his personal pleasures, a definite sweetener of relationships. So did the joint planning and sharing of a new range of common interests like the car, the family holiday, and, above all, the home.

In the typical husband-and-wife families the home, whether modern council flat or shared Victorian terrace house, was mostly furnished by middle-class standards. Paint and paper were immaculate and it was most common for local authority tenants to decorate at their own expense, rather than wait for the council's periodical servicing, which anyhow might not be up to the family's own tastes and standards. In the old type of housing a modern unit had practically always replaced the yellow $7\frac{1}{2}$ inch deep 'London sink' at which the women have been used to spend so many laborious hours. Whether the house was old or new, nearly all the Husband and Wife homes, except those of pensioners, seemed to have acquired some of such things as a modern cooking stove, sink unit, washing machine, refrigerator, electric dryer, and kitchen cabinet. Centre-piece lighting was supplemented by standard lamps and wall brackets. Rooms were comfortably warmed by modern stoves, carpets had

HOME MAKING

replaced lino, and there was an easy chair for each adult. Bedding was new, and, an enormous change in these homes, bedrooms as smartly furnished as the sitting-room. To the essentials were added fancy cushions, satin bedspreads, ivy-leaved mirrors, smoker stands, wall plaques, 'jardinaire boats', trinket sets, ding-dong bells, and occasionally a framed picture. Although practically no one owned their home, the refurbishing was not confined to the interior. Modern front doors were replacing old-fashioned ones, and many tenants were doing their own external painting. The noticeable feature in all this was that it was a comparatively recent effort, and that, except in the case of pensioners, it was not confined to any one age group.

It was also largely a do-it-yourself affair, demanding considerable ingenuity since, in the old-fashioned terrace house, the premises were often structurally poor. But, whether the place was ancient or modern, it entailed the family in hours of weekend and evening activity. Since wood is easy to come by in Bermondsey, and since most families have craftsmen relations and neighbours, all this carpentry was very much a family affair. There were family consultations about the modernization of a cupboard, the boarding in of old-fashioned banisters, and the contemporary wallpapers and gay paint that were used with uninhibited boldness. Sunday morning's shopping down Blue Anchor Lane, and the family shopping spree to Deptford or Peckham on Saturday afternoons, more often than not centred on something new for the house. Once back home parents, children, and neighbours shared in the excitement of seeing how this week's buy set off the rest of the house. These families were proud of quality too, and proud to claim that they would have nothing but the best for *their* house. No mock modesty deflated all this. The home's latest acquisition formed a standard subject of talk in the buses and 'What's new since last time I was here?' was always a well-received opening gambit by any member of the team.

There seemed to be four main reasons why these Bermondsey families placed so much emphasis on the appearance of their home. The increasing number of households who now live in a structurally separate dwelling encourages a higher standard of furnishing and of housekeeping. Couples of all ages have had to set up home again since the war; and the mere sight of freshly decorated walls jerks the couple, however long married, into stepping up the furniture. Thirdly, the new building and the dust and clatter of demolition taking place in almost every street, are bracing reminders that past standards no longer obtain. Moreover, in Bermondsey, few people control where and in what manner they are housed. The shortage is

MARRIED WOMEN WORKING

such that most people accept that they will probably spend their lives in whatever type of dwelling, street, and neighbourhood is decided for them. What they can control is the inside of their home; and they now have the means to order this as they like.

Today's emphasis on the most up-to-date, on band-box new, on matching sets (from toilet fittings to the schoolgirl's nine-piece outfit) is very understandable. It is plainly a revolt against the days when only the 'wealthy' home, where the father was in regular work, ever expected to buy furniture that was whole; and when, in the average home, nothing ever matched because even the pots and pans were bought secondhand. The change in standards may of course be carried to an extreme, as in the case of the small girl's Sunday clothes which are frilled and beribboned to a degree. But all of this is very understandable. One aspect of the many changes that these working-class homes have seen within a single generation is epitomized in today's attitude to curtains and to the parlour. The traditional 'store' curtain was a standardized, solid affair, effectively screening off not only the room's occupants but any deficiencies in the furniture; today's curtains, a great feature of the home, are as much for show as for privacy; indeed they may be drawn apart at night just to show the street how smart we are. The old 'parlour', too, has vanished, since nowadays anyone can be invited into any room in the house.

This passionate concern with the looks of the home is so widespread that it would seem to be meeting deep-seated needs. There is first of all the glaring contrast between past and present. Compare today's typical home with what one sixty-year-old man remembered of his childhood. At the time of which he was speaking, his parents and his seven brothers and sisters (all aged under fifteen) lived in a one-up-one-down house in a street so narrow that carts could not enter. The cooking was done on a gas grill in the living-room. He himself always slept on a settee. He remembered that when a corpse lay in the house the one main bed had to be dismantled. Moreover, this man's home was no exception: in his own street there were fourteen other families living under much the same conditions. Perhaps the mere fact that today's house contains fewer people makes the occupants more sensitive to its inanimate contents; or perhaps these families have for generations been aesthetically starved. Whatever the reasons, a pleasant place to live in is regarded as so reputable an aim that it more than justifies overtime for the man, an outside job for the wife, and extra effort for the whole family. 'A lovely home' would seem to be a major step towards that better life which,

124

HOME MAKING

in the eyes of the team, was the ultimate objective of many of the Bermondsey families they met.

Running the house—methods and efficiency

Those wives who worked made the substantial claim that they could do so without neglecting, or even inconveniencing their families, and without lowering their housekeeping standards. The part-timers, half of all the Wives and Widows who worked, were helped to do this by the fact that the part-time job, if available at a range of times, enabled them to fit their working day to the needs of their family. The great variety in the hours at which they did in fact work, lent support to this claim.

Both part- and full-time workers stressed the importance of routine, e.g. of doing the essentials daily; of allocating one particular job to each of the five working days; and of having a blitz at the weekend. They pointed out that those women who, poor things, were born muddlers and only did their housework when in the mood, were not the ones who consistently went out to work. The irregularity of the men's working hours, and complicated systems of inter-family aid in connection with meals and minding, made it essential that one person at least should have a fixed timetable. The interlocking character of the wife's day and the need for order and punctuality is shown in the case of a mother with two children, one at school and one a toddler. This wife included in her daily chores a midday meal for the four people in her own family; she housekept for her mother and a sister, both of whom worked; and she did 'just a little' job (1-5 p.m.) herself. The diaries which certain of the Peek Frean Visiting Families kept for the team, and the informal contact over five years with certain of these households, indicated that if the wife was to make a success of going out to work she needed the intelligence to plan a routine and the character to stick to it.

This impression of the capability of the wife who elected to go out to work was confirmed in various ways. When the school careers of the children in the Bermondsey sample households were analysed, they showed a much larger proportion attending a grammar school when the mother was a worker than when she was a housewife (Table 22): and in the limited number of cases where the school provided information on specific aspects of the children's progress, the worker's child also showed up better.

Those wives who had to pack a job into their day used the time-honoured expedient of getting up earlier. To be down by 6 o'clock instead of 7.30 does, of course, produce the equivalent of one eight-hour day in the week. In the Peek Frean Shifts Sample, 45 per cent

125

MARRIED WOMEN WORKING

were up by 6 a.m. on the day before the interview; and this was the normal rising time for 30 per cent of the Bermondsey Wives and Widows who were workers. Of all the Wives and Widows, workers or not, about 10 per cent (presumably the office cleaners) were up by 5.30 a.m.

The domestic aids which the busy wife regarded most highly were those associated with labour-saving, heating and the washing. Anything that eased the drying problem was particularly helpful in these confined, and mostly gardenless homes. Some type of outside laundry service (bag-wash, launderette, municipal wash house, etc.) was used by more than half the Peek Frean Shifts Sample. No comparative figures were obtained from the Bermondsey study, but the psychological significance of all the new domestic aids, from the £90 washing machine to the sliced loaf, was much in evidence. Whether the wife worked or not she constantly compared the ease of her own household jobs with the load her mother had carried—'all that scrubbing, coal carrying, and blackleading'.

The wife's most valued source of help, however, came neither from labour-saving devices nor from the services of relations and friends, but from her husband. This help was not measurable; but the team's long contacts with certain of the Visiting Families confirmed that husbands did far more than lend a hand during a crisis, or than the occasional job of re-decorating or window cleaning. Typical examples of solid, reliable help was one husband who always did the major part of the week's wash, another who, while his wife did the ironing, always polished the lino.

The children helped too; but the wives attached less importance to their aid than to that of the husband. There was a strong feeling that children still at the Junior School stage should not be put upon. Whether their mother worked or not, any help asked of small children was not more than errand running and looking after still smaller children. Nor was much dependence placed on adolescents, though families showed much variety about this. Of the children aged 15, 16, and 17 about whom anything on this point was known, about half did not appear to give domestic help at all—and this was irrespective of the mother's work situation. Those on whom most calls were made appeared to be the 12- and 13-year-olds.

One interesting feature of local life was the intensive mutual servicing that went on between related households and between very close friends. Its importance in relation to child minding will be discussed later; but it also included a great deal of repairing, plumbing, gas and electrical fitting, decorating, furniture moving, and, of course, car repairing. Most of the work was done at cost price. Then,

HOME MAKING

too, shopkeepers and customers were so well acquainted that things were often 'traded in': indeed a good deal of the buying was on the principle of 'Half a quid less to *you*, mate', or 'I'll see you're all right.' Much of this type of help, springing from and cementing Bermondsey's local ties, certainly stepped up real income.

Though Bermondsey now has a high proportion of unshared homes, space is one of the middle-class luxuries that few families have as yet acquired. Three main rooms or less probably represent the typical home, and these rooms are small. The total floor space of the terrace house (see illustration 'A Bermondsey home', facing p. 128) is about 900 sq. ft.; that of a council flat occupied by a childless couple, under 500 sq. ft. Low windows and narrow passages, and in many homes the absence of stairs, yard, shed, or garden, all reduced housework. Despite all the new purchases, by middle-class standards, these homes still possessed relatively few goods. They had no stocks of bed linen, china, cutlery, sports gear, trunks, etc., stored away. This lessened the housewife's work, as did the fact that they seldom had visitors to stay, and did little of the kind of entertaining that involved a cooked meal.

Cooking was simple: the fact that meals were expected to meet capricious tastes, meant that their preparation tended to be a last-minute affair. The after-work meal might consist of 'a steak for Him, a fried egg for Betty, and I think I fancy a salad'. The wife who worked was able to afford more fresh fruit, more tinned and processed foods, and could buy the more expensive cuts of meat, which also tended to lighten the amount of time she spent on cooking.

One change in eating habits, the shift of the main meal from midday to after work, appeared to be of importance to the whole question of going out to work. It not only reduces the number of meals the housewife has to provide, but gives her a sufficient span of time free from cooking and serving meals to make an outside job worth while. Less than half the Peek Frean Shifts Sample prepared a midday dinner for anyone but themselves. For the children, school dinners were available if wanted: while those of the family who were at work could get their midday meal at a works canteen or at one of the many 'dining-rooms' numerous in this dock area. Quite often dinner was taken at a relative's house, which kept cost to a minimum. One wife, for example, working an evening shift herself, cooked a midday dinner for her own family of four and for three others, her sister-in-law and two nieces. About half the school children were estimated to have their dinners at school; it was difficult to get exact information since there was unexpected flexibility in many homes as to whether the child came back at midday or not. That this particular service did not seem to be closely related to the mother's work situation was itself a reflection of the variety of times at which the mother who worked was absent from home.

An attempt was made to compare housewives' and workers' homes as regards one week's standard of feeding in the nineteen households referred to earlier. Two types of feeding were noted, on the one hand 'good' and/or 'good home-cooked' food, which implied balanced meals, e.g. as regards proteins; and on the other hand starchy meals, or those reheated, or those that were really no more than solid snacks. When the week's meals were examined on these lines, the adults of the two sets of households were found to be equally well fed; though the children of the mother who worked eat slightly less well than those of the housewife.

Though no attempt was made to draw more than a very rough comparison between housewife and worker as regards the cleanliness and orderliness of the house, it could hardly have escaped notice if sluttish housekeeping had been common. On the contrary, the interviewers were struck by the well-kept appearance of the great majority of houses, a testimony confirmed by health visitors and other people who saw much of the inside of the Bermondsey home. All told, the wife's claim that in going out to work she neither put the family to serious inconvenience, nor lowered her domestic standards, was more than substantiated. Given reasonably sound bricks and mortar, and a high enough income to provide more than the bare necessities, it was plain that these couples were prepared to pour skill and energy into creating a comfortable, efficient, and attractive-looking home. Today's levels are particularly striking in such a district as Bermondsey which, within the memory of its older residents, used to be ranked with Poplar as one of London's most notorious slums.

The personal strains

A Victorian street ballad has as its refrain—

> 'There's no man can imagine
> What a woman has to do';

and the tag seems to remain apposite in Bermondsey even though the wife's tasks are now partly self-imposed. Snatches of bus talk support this view, as between a couple of youngish wives on their way home from morning jobs in the City:

A. 'Wish I could cut myself in half there's such a lot . . . Sunday afternoon I nearly knocked myself up with washing.'
B. 'You can't do nothing till he's had his tea and it's cleared away.'

3
A BERMONDSEY HOME

Right: Old type housing - exterior. *Photo: Bermondsey Central Library*

Below: Interior of second house from right. A corner of the front room (also used as a bedroom). Decorated by husband and wife

4. FIVE GENERATIONS OF BERMONDSEY WOMEN
Above left: Emma, aged about 70. Born *c.* 1802. Died *c.* 1892
Above right: Annie, aged about 60. Born *c.* 1848. Died *c.* 1935

Mabel, aged about 20
Born 1892.

Pat, aged
Born 194

Rosie, aged 24
Born 1914

HOME MAKING

A. 'I managed to scrub my scullery last night—10 o'clock it was when I went into the sitting-room to do the carpet. He may come in any time, you never know.'
B. (Of a schoolgirl daughter) 'I left her coppers and all and she never even put the sweeper over the carpet so I said, "Now I'm telling you—today you've *got* to do it".'
A. 'Work-tired I am . . . nothing won't shift it. No, not sickness. Something grips you there, like cramp it is. I can feel it now. I'm always frightened . . . just as if something's screwing up.'
B. 'I got a bloody headache.' (As clock strikes) 'Gone 10 again. This gets you down don't it . . . Got to rush around now.'

The attempt to assess actual ill-health met with little success, although the questions were kept as simple as possible. Four points asked of the Peek Frean Shifts Sample were: 'Do you yourself have any trouble with (*a*) feet, (*b*) nerves, (*c*) tiredness, (*d*) any other?' The replies were unsatisfactory, as were those to the one question on health included in the Bermondsey interviews: 'Which of the family suffers from any chronic (long-lasting) illness or physical disability?' The answers to this certainly gave no indication of the 10 to 15 per cent of serious disability believed to exist in the population as a whole. It was also noted that menstrual troubles were rarely mentioned, possibly because they are a topic on which the working-class woman tends to be reticent. All that could be inferred from the answers to any of the health questions was that any troubles which did come to light were not concentrated in the worker's or in the housewife's home. If mere looks are any indication of health, then the team's own comment was that, compared with the middle-class London woman, the Bermondsey wife gave the impression of being thin, having a poor posture, and a rather taut expression. Nor should one dismiss out of hand the commonly held local view (perhaps true of any working-class population) that wives look older for their age than their husbands.

Some of the strain was inherent in the manual work which many of the wives were engaged in, and which itself implies higher occupational and accident risks than that of the black-coated worker. Their jobs might involve lifting and trundling considerable weights, and long bouts of standing, all possibly undertaken in heat and noise. Such strains were in addition to the complications of group work, and the self-inflicted drive of certain of the pieceworkers. At Peek Frean's their frenetic activity was found distasteful by the other employees—'They watch each other's output all day', and 'They've no time to say hello even'. It was felt to be a dehumanizing

MARRIED WOMEN WORKING

attitude. There was also criticism of the alleged increasing pace of the factory as a whole.

The busyness of the Bermondsey streets, and the bus queues from 6 a.m. onwards, show that an early start is still the pattern in a working-class area. It meant that the wives dismissed as irrelevant another potential source of strain, the long day that their early rising denoted. As far as personal convenience went, they preferred to have a morning rather than an evening job. If Table 29 is studied, it shows twenty-eight women working 6 a.m.–9 a.m., compared with ten working 5.30 p.m.–8.30 p.m. Since the fifty-four women working 'other hours' did not include many industrial workers, one can infer that not many of them were on evening work. The few women who worked at night undoubtedly had a hard life. One such was a thirty-nine-year-old mother with children of eleven and four, who was employed from Sunday to Thursday for an office cleaning agency. She started work at 8 p.m., finished at 7 a.m., and had a forty-minute journey. Her only real rest was about four hours in the afternoon, when she lay down with the younger child. Though she got some domestic help from a daughter-in-law living nearby, the physical strain must have been heavy; and the interviewer made a special note that she looked much older than her years.

One noticeable feature of these workers' lives was the lack of any rest period longer than time for just the odd cigarette. The following diary of the wife of one of the Visiting Families is fairly typical. The woman had four children aged 15, 13, 12, and 7 and worked on a little domestic job in the morning, and on the evening shift at Peek Frean's.

7 a.m.	Got up, got breakfast for three.
7.30	Got children up.
7.30	Got Jean off to work.
7.30–8.00	Tidying up, rushing around in general.
8.15–10.15	Out to work across the road.
10.15	Home. Out again for shopping. Brought back bag-wash.
11.00	Started potatoes for dinner.
11.30	Started cooking dinner.
	Hung bag-wash washing out with husband's help.
	Made bed upstairs.
12.30 p.m.	Children come in.
12.45	All have lunch (five people).
1.45	Wash up.
	Folding washing, taking it in. TV for tennis, but husband was painting.

HOME MAKING

3.45 p.m.   Out to shop to buy something for tea.
            Came back, got tea, had tea.
4.30   Children home from school.
Just after 5 Left for work (biscuit night so left early).
9.45   Back from work.
            Husband leaves for work.
            Cleared up husband's painting.

Another typical record was that of the wife whose day ran as follows:

'Yesterday up 6.45; cup of tea; cigarette; no breakfast; walk to work 15 minutes; shop on way home; turn water heater on; vegetables ready to put on; started cooking for three; tidy up; washed up; H. helped dry; ironed two shirts; got boy to bed; sat down; read; bed 11.'

The first of the above women had a fairly light weekend by local standards. Her weekend diary (ten days after the one recorded above) showed that she had been at work on Saturday morning; shopped at Deptford and visited her mother on Saturday afternoon; got the family's tea at six; saw to the children's baths; and then sat down to TV. On Sunday morning she did housework; got the dinner; and turned out a bedroom. She read the paper in the afternoon; and looked at TV at night. Most of those who worked probably eased off less at the weekend than did this woman: indeed some felt that Saturday and Sunday were the heaviest part of the week. The more time-consuming domestic jobs had to be undertaken then, any special shopping that could not be done in Bermondsey, and, above all, the family expected good meals. The conscientious mother did her best to meet such expectations as that of one schoolboy son who, in an essay on vegetarianism, thought 'some nice lean slices of meat placed on a plate with brown gravy trickling over it' was a sight worth seeing. One potential source of rest, the occasional weekend away, rarely came the way of these wives. Even the treasured yearly holiday seldom freed them from housekeeping, as this holiday was so often in a bungalow or caravan. In any case 39 per cent of the Husbands and Wives of those whose holiday position was known did not get away, and of those who did, 44 per cent went for one week only.

Another source of strain, that connected with getting the children properly minded, is discussed later. Here the best laid schemes, if they should go wrong, might have serious consequences: moreover, they were not always in the mother's own control. Would the minder really be at her appointed corner to take over the toddler so that the

131

MARRIED WOMEN WORKING

mother could clock in sharp by 1.25 p.m.? Anxiety of this kind could add to the day's load on the mother.

When all is said and done, the fact remains that the wife who works inevitably carries a heavy load. Though many of her domestic tasks may be trivial, they are of the kind that demand constant attention. Moreover, when the inevitable emergency within the family circle does arise, its solution mostly depends on the woman of working age whether she is in a job or not. The real risk probably lies not so much in the occasional emergency as in the daily strain inflicted by a timetable which allows practically no slack in a routine that is arduous.

Time off in Bermondsey

A criticism levelled against married women's employment is that women, instead of using their new freedoms to benefit themselves and society, are being sidetracked into a life of mere getting and spending. Even taking into account the fall in the borough's population, it is probable that the local membership of social groups connected with the churches, settlements, and political parties, has fallen in the last twenty-five years; and nothing appears to have directly replaced such organizations. Homes, of course, are nowadays vastly more comfortable places in which to spend one's free time; and people have more money for entertainment, and to pursue hobbies. Car maintenance, family car-riding, and do-it-yourself activities connected with the house, are today's obvious alternatives to some of the pursuits formerly engaged in through an organization. More wealth has diminished the peripheral attractions of the old-time societies. Jumble sales, free outings, and cheap holidays for the children are much less in demand. The decline in membership may be specially evident in a place like Bermondsey where so many of the leading spirits of these societies used to be known to almost everyone.

An attempt was made to see whether the current women's membership of organizations appeared to be adversely affected by the fact that women go to work. A study of twelve such societies showed that their members were drawn almost equally from workers and housewives. The societies chosen included Church and Settlement groups, a Parents' Association, two Community Centre Classes, Civil Defence, the Labour Party Women's Section, and one Oddfellows group called the 'Pride of Bermondsey' Female Lodge. All but three of these organizations estimated the average age of their members as under fifty, so they were in no sense old folks groups. Of the total membership, i.e. of those the society counted as its live members,

HOME MAKING

136 were found to be housewives and 139 went out to work. The interviews of the whole sample also gave the impression that having a job did not affect membership of a society adversely. There sometimes seemed to be a family predeliction towards joining, a socially active household in which the wife, irrespective of whether she worked, was a joiner herself. It was also plain that many of today's wives did not regard these societies as providing anything positive. They were, rather, compensation for an unsatisfactory life—'I don't need one, I'm happy with my husband'; or, 'Why join if you've a nice home?'

Social life in general was family-centred, perhaps because of the high number of inter-related households. Six households, drawn at random from the anthropologist's [1] case book, showed them as having respectively 19, 15, 3, 7, 25, and 30 relations other than those in the family, living actually in Bermondsey. And at another home, an old lady of eighty-one said she had 8 children, 58 grandchildren, and 22 great-grandchildren, all alive. Half of those adults who, when interviewed, said they were in contact with relations, added that they met them 'very regularly', as distinct from those speakers who did so 'quite a lot' or 'a little' (Table 37). Since mutual service was frequently involved in these regular meetings, going to work might actually increase the contact. Both worker and housewife of course reckoned to take part in family occasions. The wife in the family beside the research worker's home counted on meeting about thirty of her blood relations at a certain pub near her mother's home on New Year's Eve, a custom her grandfather had inaugurated.

Although Bermondsey was said to spend far more on entertainment now than formerly, neither cinema, sport, nor pub occupied much of the wives' leisure. There is only one cinema in the borough so that, by London standards, going to the pictures takes time and effort. None of the younger wives, the sixty-five who were still under thirty, appeared to play any outdoor game, just one was known to be keen on swimming. Nor did any appear to be able to drive the car which one in seven of the Husband and Wife households possessed.

Their indoor interests, too, were limited. In only a third of a run of fifty households (interviewed by a member of the team who took a special interest in reading habits) did the wife say she was a reader of either books or magazines, those who were readers being equally divided between workers and housewives. The three main leisure-time interests were TV, refurbishing the house (which really amounted to a hobby), and knitting. The latter was constantly given

[1] See Method, Appendix I.

133

as the wife's sole hobby, and was the recognized time-killer if she happened to be off work—as in the case of one woman who turned out eighteen sweaters for her family in a matter of weeks. Circumscribed as their pursuits sounded, the women felt that they had wider interests than their mothers had had. They constantly referred to the new worlds which TV was opening to them, and pointed out that their embellishing of the house, the holiday away, and the car, were all interests unknown in their mother's day, and, moreover, ones in which the whole family now shared.

In a very poor area like Bermondsey, the women have always expected to be over-occupied. It is still a novelty to have any regular stretch of free time, and they hardly know what to do with it. Leisure is still equated with physical rest, work with physical effort. 'Just sit', 'put your feet up', 'drop off', 'have a lay down', were phrases used to describe how the wife used her leisure. One woman's reply to what she did when she had a bit of spare time was 'nothing always', and she saw no need to defend it. Today's increased leisure plainly presents quite a new type of problem to these women. Going out to work, which is difficult to stop once the new pattern of spending has been established, is the first solution that springs to mind.

To sum up. The evidence did not suggest that standards as regards care of the family and household management were adversely affected by the wife working. The extra earnings were used primarily to raise the physical level of the home and to give the children what their parents were so conscious of having themselves lacked in childhood. General objectives of this type rather than specific material acquisitions such as TV sets and washing machines were pursued as a primary aim by these working wives. But of course most wives, whether working or not, tried to acquire goods of this type as part of their move towards higher standards.

Going out to work undoubtedly made more demands on the family as a co-operative organization. Though relatives regularly played an important part in children minding, the wife's major domestic help came from her husband. Husbands and wives were aware of, and welcomed, a closer partnership. This new sharing of life found its expression in joint action about improving and 'beautifying' the home, and in more sharing of other interests. The area of joint decision-making, too, was expanding, especially as regards the children's upbringing. One factor in all this was the status and independence conferred on the wife by participating in affairs outside the home, and that given by becoming an earner herself. On the other hand the cost to the wife was heavy—for some in physical strain, for almost all in loss of leisure.

HOME MAKING

Married women's employment can be seen as one of the social changes resulting from smaller families, better health, improved services, and lighter domestic chores. These Bermondsey wives had developed an attitude in which they viewed going out to work not as neglect of their family, but as a sign of their concern for it.

CHAPTER IX

The Children

*The bearings of the child's age on his mother's work situa-
tion–The time of day at which the mother worked–Minding–The progress of the children as assessed by outside
agencies; The children aged under five; The children of
school age–Children involved with the Children's Department and the Probation Service; (a) The children of the
sample; (b) Bermondsey children in general–Local provision for children's leisure–Local norms of child care*

To decide what constitutes child neglect is always a formidable
exercise. In the past it was held to consist in such immediately
recognizable things as hunger and rags, sores and vermin. When
accompanied by blows, the picture was unmistakable. Today, though
the mother who knocks her child about is almost extinct, less obvious
forms of ill-treatment are said to be increasing. A case in point is
the 'latchkey child'. Blamed on the mother who works, he seems to
be the current equivalent of the Victorian waif outside the pub, and
still to be pitied even if his mother's motive is not gin but a job.
Another example of lack of care is that of the mother who 'couldn't
stay off work just for his holiday, could I—so I give him ten bob and
told him to hop it for the day'. This particular case happens to be
true, but is it typical? The team were less concerned with gross
neglect of this type than to see whether the mother's absence harmed
the day-to-day life of the child. The reproaches are a commonplace
—empty house and over-strained mother, mischief unchecked, and
spending money unlimited. The Peek Frean employees had vigor-
ously repudiated any such charges of neglect, asserting that it was
primarily the children who benefited from their mother working.
In view of these divergent claims the team tried to test a hypothesis
which, at its simplest, was that the children of the Bermondsey households whose mother went out to work 'fared worse' than those whose
mother was a housewife. Was the worker's child subject to more serious illness than the other children in the sample? Did he display more
behaviour problems than his school thought normal? Had he been involved with the Juvenile Court? An attempt was made, when the parents gave permission, to obtain a progress report for each of the 424
children under eighteen in the Wives and Widows households, and

136

THE CHILDREN

it was obtained for 80 per cent of those children who were still dependent. One risk, foreseen but unavoidable, was that the parents of the less satisfactory home were likely to be among those who refused the team permission for a progress report. This difficulty was, however, overcome as regards one particular set of children who had 'fared worse', those who had been involved with the Juvenile Court.

The parents themselves at the interview supplied certain information relevant to the child's progress, but the main assessors were outside agencies; for the child under five, the health visitor who had had this child in her particular care; for the school child his headmaster or mistress, generally in consultation with his class teacher. Other assessors included the local Probation Office and Children's Department. The assessor, from his own official records and personal knowledge, filled in a form on the child's progress, and in most cases discussed this report later on with one of the team. All this information was then set against the mother's current work situation. In some cases her work history since the child's birth would have been more relevant; but, as has been said earlier, this past history was often inexact, revealing no more than whether she had in general been at work since the child was born, and whether the work had in general been part- or full-time.

When the material came to be analysed, certain groups of children appeared to call for further attention. The team, therefore, re-examined all the material on any child whose school record was markedly poorer than that of the rest of the sample: and because the toddler or junior school child who is separated from his mother all day is at special risk, the team also re-examined the records of each child under eleven whose mother worked full-time. Finally, there were the children who had been in trouble with the Court, and those for whom the Children's Department had had to be called in. Since these two sets of children might tend to come from homes which had refused the interview, in their case the 770 addresses of the total sample were combed through to see which of the children had been so involved.

The bearing of child's age on his mother's work situation

The child's chronological age was a first rough-and-ready indication of possible risk if the mother worked.

Table 18 shows that 46 per cent of the children under eighteen had a mother who worked. The mothers had a tendency not to work at all until the child was old enough for school. The proportion of

MARRIED WOMEN WORKING

TABLE 18

Children's age in relation to their mother's work situation

The Children's Age	Mother at Work			Mother a Housewife	Total of children	Workers as % of total
	F.T.	*P.T.*	*Total*			
0–4 years	8	17	25	102	127	20
5–10 ,,	17	54	71	82	153	46
11–14 ,,	26	43	69	32	101	68
15–17 ,,	8	23	31	12	43	72
Total	59	137	196	228	424[1]	46

[1] This total of 424 refers to all the children of the 465 Wives and Widows, aged under eighteen and living at home.

children who had a mother at work rose from 20 per cent for those under five to 34 per cent for those under eleven; and to 68 per cent for those of secondary school age. Since the primary school child is, in fact, in school for almost as many hours as the older child, the figures suggest care on the mother's part.

It was plainly important to discover how long in general the mother was away. If the home contained a child, 65 per cent of the mothers who worked, did so part-time: if there was no child, then the situation was altered, 58 per cent of those who worked doing so part time (Table 38).

When the work situation of the mothers of the 127 very young children, those under five, were analysed, it was found to be a full-time job for only 6 per cent; rising to not more than 11 per cent in the case of the child aged 5–10. And for the children as a whole, including those who had left school, the mother worked part-time in 32 per cent of the cases, compared with full-time in 14 per cent (Table 18). Moreover, the definition of full-time work used throughout this study, 'thirty hours and over', may mean considerably shorter hours than those normal in industry—the forty-five hours worked at Peek Frean's for example. Only 8 per cent of all the children had a mother working forty hours or over. A minor point made earlier, was that, for Londoners, the Bermondsey workers had a relatively short journey to work; and, since their jobs seldom involved responsibility, they left punctually and could be fairly certain of the time they would be home. All told there was little evidence that going out to work took these particular mothers away from their children for long spells each day.

The time of day at which the mother worked

Another line of defence used by Bermondsey working mothers was that the time of day when they were absent mattered more to the children than the actual hours they were out. They quoted two in-

TABLE 19

Children's age in relation to the times of day at which their mother worked

Age of Children	8 a.m.–5 p.m.	8 a.m.–12 noon	Monday to Friday (approx. working hours)			6 a.m.–9 a.m.	5.30 p.m.–8.30 p.m.	6 a.m.–9 a.m. & 5.30 p.m.–8.30 p.m.	Any other Hours	Works on[1] Sat.	Sun.	Mother does not work or no information on this point	Total of Children
			1 p.m.–5 p.m.	9.30 a.m.–3.30 p.m.	11 a.m.–2 p.m.								
0–4 years	5	1	1	—	4	2	2	2	5	8	2	105	127
5–10 ,,	8	4	5	12	2	4	5	6	23	25	6	84	153
11–14 ,,	18	8	4	8	1	4	3	5	18	23	5	32	101
15–17 ,,	7	3	2	1	1	5	1	5	6	12	1	12	43
Total	38	16	12	21	8	15	11	18	52	68	14	233	424

[1] All those shown working on Saturday and Sunday also worked during the week.

MARRIED WOMEN WORKING

stances. The early morning charring job, from 6.30 a.m. to 8.30 a.m., meant that the child hardly missed his Mum; and even if he did, this was kinder than dragging him out to a minder in the early morning and in all weathers, as was likely if the mother held an ordinary industrial job. An evening job was almost unnoticed by the toddler, since he was in bed most of the time, and his father likely to be at home. The figures supported the mother's argument; Table 29 shows the wide scatter of hours these women worked outside the normal industrial eight hours for five days a week. They also fitted their hours to the children's ages, particularly to that of the youngest child (Table 19). Only seven of twenty-two children under five about whom information on this point was available had a mother working four hours or more during the normal day-time hours of work, i.e. during the small child's own day.

The empty house was another danger that the mothers recognized. As regards leaving the children in the early morning, as did many of the office cleaners, the mother argued that the children were busy getting themselves up, and had the excitement of the school day ahead. The after-school period was a different matter. Few instances were found where the mother made no provision for this, and one in three of the mothers who worked were in jobs that allowed them to be home by at least 4 p.m. Perhaps the really significant point about the gap was less its physical hazards than that at this hour both mother and child had the day's strain on them. The first couple of hours after she got in were especially taxing ones for her: she had to cope with the children and get the family's evening meal ready for a fixed time. Pleased as she might be to see the children again, it was not the moment for expending sympathy on any except their more obvious needs. As regards work at the weekend, if the mother's work hours were examined for all the children, i.e. for those of both housewife and worker, as many as 16 per cent had a mother working on Saturday, only 3 per cent on Sunday. Though this 16 per cent would involve quite a high proportion of the mothers who worked, minding problems are, of course, less acute at the weekend.

The above findings from the Bermondsey study were broadly in keeping with those from the Peek Frean study where a generalized picture showed the mother as leaving full-time work on the birth of her first child; doing an evening job while her youngest child was under school age; changing to the 9.30 a.m.–4.00 p.m. short day shift when he started school; to the afternoon one when he moved on to a secondary school; and finally, as soon as he left, choosing according to her inclination between morning, afternoon, or full-time work.

140

THE CHILDREN

Minding as it had taken place in the last week preceding the interview and in the last long school holidays

It seemed to indicate responsible attitudes on the part of these mothers that so many did refer to the question of minding as one of their major difficulties. It would possibly clarify matters if certain of the team's working methods on this topic are noted here. They were anxious that the minding about which they asked should refer only to responsible care, not just to 'keeping an eye on' which may, or may not, be a sketchy business. The fact that relatively few of the children under eleven were said, at the interview, to have been minded, led the team to believe that the question had been interpreted as it was intended. Three of the team's arbitrary assumptions should also be made clear. The first was that the child of the mother who did 'home work' had no minding needs; the second, that father equated with mother for minding purposes; and the third (a considerable assumption) that once the child reached secondary school age he no longer needed direct adult supervision. Certain teachers and mothers thought that a capable child might be able to dispense with minding in the accepted sense even before he reached secondary school age; but they qualified this by pointing out that the psychological risks might be greater then than in the child's earlier years, since the time-scale of the little child is shorter than that of the ten-year-old, and he is less likely to store up emotional troubles.

Both the straightforward facts and the adequacy of minding proved difficult to establish. Minding is a highly charged subject emotionally, it is related to the individual child's own maturity, and to family and class interpretations of what constitute proper care. The seven-year-old not allowed to come home from his play centre till six o'clock was presumably being 'minded'; but did this hold good for the child deposited in and picked up from the playground half an hour before and after school? And how foolproof was the plan for odd holidays made by a mother who was away from home by 7.10 a.m.? She kept her two girls, aged ten and six, up late the previous night, so that they should not wake before their father called them on his way out at 7.30 a.m. They breakfasted off the milk and cereals their mother had left ready, told the lady in the next flat that they were up, and then went off to a nearby playground until their mother got in at half past twelve. The fact that this playground had a good shelter and a garden-keeper, and that the father worked across the road from home and could sometimes pop in, added to the parents' feelings of security. Minding was often an interlocking affair, as where a mother gave her sister's boy his dinner

MARRIED WOMEN WORKING

and then went to a 2–6 p.m. job herself while the sister minded *her* child. At this mother's home an aunt, too, was relied on for odd occasions, and the paternal grandmother for some evening minding. Topsy-turvy situations might arise, as where a young wife minded her mother's child because the latter was the worker. This household had living near by three other closely related families, all potential minders.

The school holidays, five or six weeks in the summer, nearly three at Christmas (when bad weather drives the children indoors), and nearly three at Easter, were a recurring difficulty to the mother who worked: and so were the London schools' half terms and their ten 'occasional' days. These latter hardly justified the bother of finding a minder and, in any case, some of the days were liable to be sprung on the mother at short notice.

Rather than generalized questions on minding the team pinned down two specific periods. First they asked what, if any, minding had taken place in the week before the interview. The figures were able to be analysed for 77 per cent of these children whose mothers worked, and these 155 included all but six of those aged under eleven. The number said to have been minded was thirty-three; a relation had done this minding in twenty-seven cases and in half of them she was the maternal grandmother (Table 39).

The second period asked about was whether any minding had taken place during the last long school holidays. The facts were obtained for 117 of the 171 children over five who had a mother working; and they included all but fifteen of the children aged five to ten. Forty-six children had been minded, a relation had done the minding in twenty-nine cases, the grannie again being the minder-in-chief (Table 40).

It may be relevant to add that though the grandmother played so important a part in minding, her presence did not appear to affect radically the wife's actual work situation unless the mother and her daughter lived under the same roof. In the twenty-three instances among Wives and Widows where this was the case, sixteen of the daughters worked.

Although it appeared from the interviews that many women helped other mothers by looking after their children, analysis of minding in general showed that the children were much more likely to be minded by a relative than by a friend of the home. This had been observed in the Peek Frean study too, though there, since so many of the women worked an evening shift and could not have done so unless the father had been at home, the latter shared with the grandmother pride of place in minding.

142

THE CHILDREN

Before going on to discuss the use made of an institution, as distinct from a personal minder, the following facts about the minding of children who appeared to be in an especially vulnerable position may be noted. The number of children under eleven was 280. Re-examination of the records of these children under eleven showed that only twenty-five had a mother working full-time (Table 18). Numerically the problem was small. Moreover, in most of the twenty-five cases there were what might be called extenuating circumstances. Four of the homes had no male wage earner; and in nine of the remainder the child, though under eleven, was old enough for school. The mothers, too, had made particularly careful arrangements about minding. A grandmother, an aunt, or the child's own married sister, was the minder in thirteen cases, and a grannie supplemented a day nursery for another child.

The use made of the official provision for minding has been left to the last because both the Peek Frean and Bermondsey studies showed that it played only a minor role, despite the area's long tradition of the mother going out to work. Though not officially a minding agency, the School Meals Service was, of course, a help to the mother who worked, but it was made less use of in this connection than had been expected. Under the L.C.C., the service is available in school holidays as well as term time though it may not be at the child's own school. Only two children were recorded as having been minded during the week preceding the interview by a professional minder. The same applied to the last long holidays. None was recorded as having been in a day nursery or a nursery school in these two periods. In reply to the question, 'When did any of your children use a Day Nursery or Nursery school?', the answers showed that thirty-five children had used the former, thirty the latter. A blank in the answer column could mean that none of the woman's children had used the provision, or that the question had not been answered. By reason of this, and also because of the time lag involved when the woman was referring to events long past, the figures are likely to be an understatement. Nevertheless they appear low in view of the fact that Bermondsey's official minding agencies are long-established and well regarded. The day nursery, of course, is not intended for, and does not meet the needs of, the part-time worker: it costs too much, and an eight to six day is far too long. Though planned to meet the requirements of the mother who works full-time, the long hours the child is required to be at the day nursery are held by many to impose an excessive strain on a small child. The nursery school's hours (9.30 a.m.–3.30 p.m.) though shorter, are still over-long for the needs of the great majority of part-time workers. That it keeps school terms

MARRIED WOMEN WORKING

is another disadvantage, presenting the mother with her standard worry, the school holidays, in an intensified form since the child at a nursery school is younger than the ordinary school-goer. The same holds for the nursery classes attached to six of the primary schools. Though Bermondsey's one nursery school had a waiting list of over 300 for its ninety places (which certainly suggested that more provision on these lines would have been welcomed) even this number was low for an area with perhaps 5,000 potential users. And at the date of the interviews one of the four day nurseries was about to be closed.

The chief practical advantage of the personal minder as compared with an institution was undoubtedly her flexibility. She could adapt herself better to the unpredictable changes of domestic life, a particularly important consideration in an area where the men's hours are often irregular. The best of institutions inevitably has its rules and above all makes yet another clock on which the mother must keep her eye. There was also the reaction observed at certain of the interviews, an almost shocked denial that the child might have been put into a nursery. This hinted that in Bermondsey the use of an institution, however admirable, was a reflection on the home, whereas to have the child minded by a known individual was not. The day nursery possibly did imply some stigma, since its children mostly came from disrupted or hard-case homes; moreover, the uncertainties about the future of the day nurseries, together with confusion and grievances about the charges they made, possibly lessened confidence. Perhaps there was an implied reproof merely in the dejected look of their battery of prams, with never a mum at the handle end.

One dominating aspect of all the minding was not so much the attention paid to the physical risks—(fires, gas taps, keys)—which worry any but the most irresponsible parent, but the general attitude to child care. Baby sitting, leaving a child just so that the parents could go out to enjoy themselves, was rare. It was regarded as rather selfish, and much less correct than having a child looked after so that the mother could work. Much of the minding was a mutual exchange of service. Where payment was made it appeared to play a less important role in the mother's consideration than did the minder's suitability, which supported the claim that these mothers were conscientious. Nor was there any hint that minding was a money-making racket. Rather it was a kindly service for little enough profit, 5s 0d a week perhaps, for two grandchildren's teas and twenty hours of their company, or 25s a week for the day-time care of a toddler. In all this, Bermondsey's network of related households was an enormous asset. It solved many of the mother's practical problems and

THE CHILDREN

gave the parents fewer misgivings. Relations' ways were 'like my Mum's, and even the toddler taken 'down my Nan's' would sense the family tie. If the minding by relations *had* a fault it was that of over-indulgence, which was anyhow in keeping with the permissive upbringing approved in these working-class homes.

The progress of the children as assessed by outside agencies

The babies and little children of the family were, of course, mostly at home when the interviewer called. What the parents themselves said of the children's progress was recorded on the schedule. In the case of the under fives, this was later supplemented by detailed information from whichever of Bermondsey's ten health visitors was responsible for the child, and, if he had been at a nursery school or day nursery, from its principal. For the school children the assessment came from the heads of the fifty-three schools they were attending. Finally the team examined all this material, testing, as was explained earlier, the validity of the assumption that the child of the mother who worked made markedly poorer progress than the housewife's child. Certain points should be stressed regarding these followup studies: (1) No attempt was made to include psychological material. (2) The child's progress was set against his mother's work situation at the time of the interview, which might, of course, have been different at earlier and more critical stages of his life. (3) No account was taken of the increased risk of infection should the child (under five) have had siblings at school or been at a nursery himself. (4) On the advice of a pediatric consultant, particular attention was paid to the type of illness (pneumonia, bronchial pneumonia, and bronchitis) which might have been caused by symptoms neglected because the mother was pressed for time.

The progress of the children under five

There were 127 children under five in the sample households interviewed; the parents gave consent for a follow-up study to be undertaken on 100 of these children and the team obtained it for ninety-two.

The figures in Table 20 relate to the children's general health as recorded by the health visitors. Since the figures did not indicate that the worker's child had had a poorer record than the housewife's, the work situations of the mothers of the fourteen 'not quite healthy' children were re-examined. Of these, three were cases of disability at birth: a mongol, with siblings aged two, thirteen, and fifteen, had a mother who worked on an evening shift, the father acting as minder. To go out to work may have been a welcome relief

MARRIED WOMEN WORKING

TABLE 20

General health from birth of children under five in relation to their mother's work situation at date of interview

| | Worker | | | | Total of |
	F.T.	P.T.	Total	Housewife	Children
Normal healthy child	5	10	15	63	78
'Not quite' healthy child	1	3	4	10	14
No information: or no health visitor's follow-up	2	4	6	29	35
Total	8	17	25	102	127

for this mother. The health visitor decribed the home as 'very affectionate'. The remaining cases were of serious illness. Most of them were respiratory troubles, two enteritis or dysentery, and one T.B. Six of these mothers had in general been out to work in the past. The health visitor had, incidentally, classed three of the families of these children who had a poor health record as below average in their general standards. A further point of interest was the small number of early deaths—one child had died at birth, the second at one week.

TABLE 21

Immunization and vaccination of children under five in relation to their mother's work situation

	Worker	Housewife	Total of Children[1]
Immunized	17	60	77
Not immunized	3	13	16
No information: or no health visitor's follow-up	5	29	34
Total	25	102	127
Vaccinated	13	40	53
Not vaccinated	6	28	34
No information: or no health visitor's follow-up	6	34	40
Total	25	102	127

Information received on one additional child from sources other than the health visitor.

In the case of the 20 per cent of children under five who had a mother working, these workers' children received as much clinical care as those of the housewife regarding immunization and vaccination: while the mother's regular use of a clinic, based on ten or more attendances during the child's first year, was higher for worker than housewife (Table 41). The comparisons were not extended to part- and full-time workers, since the number of mothers who worked full-time if they had a child under five was so low. And, of course, attendance was not an infallible indication of care, since it is normally

146

THE CHILDREN

higher for a first than subsequent babies, and indeed might have been due to a new pregnancy, not to the child in question.

Bearing in mind the caveats on all the material about these little children, there was no evidence obvious to the layman that the child whose mother worked made less progress than that of the housewife.

The progress of the children of school age

The school children were often at home when the team member called, since much of the interviewing was done in the evening and in school holidays. Here again, what the parents had to say on the child's progress was taken into account alongside the school's assessment, and, in the case of certain children, that of the Probation Office and Children's Department.

As with the children under five, it was necessary to get parental permission for the material connected with the child's progress at school; and it was obtained for 224 of the 297 children aged five to seventeen inclusive. Of the seventy-three for whom no follow-up study was made, about thirty[3] had already left school.

To obtain a general indication of progress the team examined the type of school attended by those of secondary school age; and also the regularity of attendance for those of all ages. Both were points on which it was thought the information would be readily available and dependable.

TABLE 22

Children aged 11 and over by type of school attended and mother's work situation

	F.T.	Worker P.T.	Total	Housewife	Total
Secondary Modern	17	15	32	20	52
Grammar	3	8	11	2	13
Technical	2	3	5	—	5
Comprehensive	2	6	8	3	11
Primary and all age	2	7	9	8	17
Total	26	39	65	33	98
No longer at school or no information	8	27	35	11	46
Total	34	66	100	44	144

Of the eighty-one children at a secondary school, eighteen were at a grammar or technical school, and sixteen of these had a mother who worked. It was noted that eleven of the thirteen grammar school children had a working mother; and that the children who attended

[3] Figures include one child aged sixteen (at secondary modern school), one aged seventeen (at grammar school).

147

MARRIED WOMEN WORKING

grammar and technical schools had the highest proportion of mothers working, those at secondary modern schools, the lowest. Again the figures certainly do not show the worker's child at any disadvantage in schooling, interpreting disadvantage as not having been offered or accepted a place at a grammar or technical school.

A self-evident risk in placing over-much reliance on the above findings is that any decisive influence exerted by the fact that the mother worked, has operated when the child was at his junior school and preparing for the secondary stage. On the other hand, what was known about the sample as a whole indicated that these Bermondsey mothers tended to be fairly consistent workers or non-workers throughout the whole of a child's school life provided other circumstances (e.g. a younger child) did not interfere. A second risk, relating to differences in the parents' own educational history, can probably be dismissed, since practically all these parents had left school at the minimum leaving age.

The child's attendance at school was obtained for 224 children.

TABLE 23

Children's attendance at school (children of all ages) in relation to their mother's work situation

| | Worker | | | | Total of |
	F.T.	P.T.	Total	Housewife	Children
(a) Good, very good, or regular	38	74	112	83	195
(b) Bad because of health	2	1	3	11	14
(c) Rather poor, or irregular	2	4	6	7	13
(d) Very bad	—	—	—	2	2
	42	79	121	103	224
Did not apply (e.g. not at school) or no information	17	58	75	125	200
Total	59	137	196	228	424

The table shows that of the workers' children, 93 per cent were good attenders and 81 per cent of those of the housewives. The teachers said most mothers stopped off work if the child was really ill, but that there was a strong temptation to chance it if he was 'just a bit roxy'; or even when the mother found it handy to have him at home. Certain of the heads had noted that their own registers dropped when the nearby primary school had a holiday. It should be pointed out that eleven of the fourteen children whose poor attendance was due to ill health, had a mother who was a housewife.

It was not possible to draw up a similar table on health, because a number of the schools did not provide sufficiently detailed information and in any case there was much risk attached to what was no more than a layman's attempt to interpret, at second-hand, medi-

148

THE CHILDREN

cal material. With this warning, the following figures are presented. Of the 224 children at school for whom follow-up permission was given, 133 had had no serious trouble, and 53 per cent of them had a mother working: only twenty-seven had had serious trouble and 55 per cent of these had a mother working, in ten cases part- and in five full-time (Table 42). These figures did not imply that the child's health suffered if his mother worked.

The matter was, however, pursued further by re-examining all the material on those forty-three children (of the 224 above) whose school record indicated any of the following kinds of trouble: poorer progress than the rest of the 224 in health; receiving special treatment; or having a poor attendance record. In the case of health it was thought desirable to withdraw those whose disability was unlikely to have been related to the mothers working or not; i.e. any mongols, those who had had childhood illnesses like measles or scarlet fever, and cases of minor accidents (no serious one was recorded). This left 9 children, 4 with respiratory trouble, 1 with enteritis and dysentery, 1 with polio, 2 with diphtheria, and 1 with otitis media. The mothers' current work situation showed that 4 were in work (3 part-time); that 5 were at home; and that only 3 had a fairly steady history of work since the child was born. The children who had received special treatment, 17 in number, with one exception were different from the above. Of them, 6 had had eye trouble, 2 bad feet, 1 a physical deformity, 1 was an eneuretic, and 7 had miscellaneous disabilities. The mothers' current work situation showed 10 working (5 part-time) and 7 had a past history of work. The poor attenders were 15 in number. Only 6 had a mother who worked; and the mother's past work history showed housewives and workers about equally distributed. Both the mothers were non-workers in the 2 cases where 'rather poor' was plainly an understatement, since the attendance officer and N.S.P.C.C. had been called in.

None of this evidence on the children at school indicated that the child was harmed if his mother worked. He did, in fact, do 'better' than the housewife's child as regards the type of school for which the 11 + had selected him; his attendance was slightly more regular; and his health did not appear to suffer. Nor was there any indication that those children whose progress had been below that of their peers were the children of the mother who worked.

Children of the sample involved with the Children's Department and the Probation Service

Another set of children from the sample households whose progress might be deemed below average were those who had been officially

MARRIED WOMEN WORKING

involved with the Children's Department and the Probation Service. As far as the Children's Department was concerned, low numbers were expected since the Department deals with only a tiny minority of children, and in any case the reason for the child's involvement may be no reflection on parental care. When the Department's live records at July 1958 were consulted, they were not found to contain any of the children under eighteen of the sample households nor, as far as could be ascertained, any child from the 770 addresses of the total sample, interviewed or not. This negative result was felt to support Bermondsey's general claim to stability.

The team's source of information from the Probation Office attached to the South-East London Juvenile Court was its card index of cases appearing in the last ten years. The names on the index were compared with those of all the children under eighteen in the households at the 770 addresses of the total sample, i.e. at addresses where the interview had been refused as well as those where it had been accepted. When the index was so compared it was found to contain the names of fourteen children, twelve boys and two girls. They lived at ten addresses, five of which were discovered to be households who had refused the full interview (though at that date the interviewers, of course, had known nothing of the family history). The fourteen children's ages ranged from ten to sixteen, with eight in the twelve to fourteen group. The Court's decision was 'absolute discharge' in 1 case; 'conditional discharge' in 5; 'probation order' in 4; 'supervision order' in 1; 'committed to Approved School' in 3.

TABLE 24

Children of sample households involved with Probation Office in relation to their mother's work situation

		Worker			*No information on mother's work*	*Total of*
	F.T.	*P.T.*	*Total*	*Housewife*	*situation*	*Children*
Mother's work at date of offence	4	7	11	1	2	14
At date of interview	4	8	12	2	—	14

If the seriousness or otherwise of the offence was examined in relation to the mother's work situation, it showed that all three of those sent to an Approved School or put under a supervision order had a mother who worked, but so, it should be added in fairness, had four of the six who were given absolute or conditional discharge. In general, however, the worker's child did less well than the housewife's. But since all these figures were so small (itself a satisfactory finding) the matter was examined from a second wider angle.

THE CHILDREN

Bermondsey children in general

Bermondsey is within the jurisdiction of the South-East London Juvenile Court and the team was advised that this was the Court at which all but a tiny minority of the juvenile offenders with a Bermondsey address would appear.

In 1958 the borough had a child population (aged eight to sixteen inclusive) of about 7,100. The total incidence of delinquency as dealt with at the above Court was examined for the year April 1957–58, and set against what could be ascertained of the work situation of the children's mothers. This was examined for *every* child who had a Bermondsey address (irrespective of where his offence had been committed) on the Probation Office's case load for the twelve months ended April 1, 1958. Sixty-three children were found to have been involved with the Court at least once, their more recent offence being the one which the team recorded. They comprised 54 boys and 9 girls whose ages were 8–10 (14 children); 11–14 (37); 15–17 (10); age unknown (2). The Court's decision was 'absolute discharge' —16 children; 'conditional discharge'—12; 'supervision order'—5; 'probation order'—23; 'fit person order'—2. In one other case the Education Act was invoked; in four the Court's decision was not known.

TABLE 25

Bermondsey children in general involved with Probation Office in relation to their mother's work situation

	Worker			Housewife	No information on mother's work situation	Total o Children
	F.T.	P.T.	Total			
Mother's work at date of offence	15	13	28	17	18	63

As the above table shows, these sixty-three Bermondsey children in general, like those of the sample households, probably had a mother more prone to work than usual for the sample, though the high proportion of cases in which the official records had no information on the mothers' work situation made it dangerous to deduce any conclusion.

The Probation Office records only showed the mother's past work history in the case of forty-four of the sixty-three children, and even so it was in a generalized way. She appeared to have worked regularly, or mostly, in the case of twenty-eight of the children, very occasionally or not at all in sixteen cases. Absolute or conditional discharge, or a two-year probation order, was rather more usual for the child of the housewife (14;17) than of the worker (20;28).

None of the team's material on delinquency took into account any-

151

MARRIED WOMEN WORKING

thing about the child's circumstances except the mother's employment or non-employment. This was a foreseen limitation. The team did not, on the other hand, expect that the number of the children of the sample in trouble, viz. fourteen, would be so small as to invalidate comparison between the child of housewife and that of worker. Nor did they envisage that the Probation Office records on the Bermondsey children in general would provide little about the mother's employment history.

In general what figures there were showed that the worker's child had a less good record than the housewife's. Another point that told against the worker's child was that the nature of his offence was on the whole more serious. However, since the Probation Office's card index was of cases appearing in the last ten years, a total of fourteen children from a sample of 770 addresses, cannot be considered high, even allowing for any errors that may have crept in. Neither did the total amount of real trouble appear to be heavy in the case of the Bermondsey children in general; twenty-eight of the sixty-three concerned in a year's cases were given an absolute or conditional discharge, and no one was sent to an Approved School. In view of Bermondsey's long traditions of the mother going out to work, the effects, as far as official trouble is concerned, do not sound very alarming.

Local provision for children's leisure

It was beyond the team's resources to draw any meaningful comparison between the leisure time habits of the worker's and the housewife's child. The reader might like to make his own guess, from the following extracts of diaries kept in the spring of 1957, as to whether the mothers of children concerned went out to work or not.

First Family. Diary of Norma (eleven) and Eileen (six) recorded by their sister Betty (sixteen)

A Tuesday in term time

8.10 a.m.	Children got up and got ready for school.
9.05 a.m.	They left for school. Norma took Eileen.
12.30 p.m.	Had school dinners.
4.30 p.m.	Norma got Eileen and took her home. Mother out shopping. Children lay the table for tea.
5.30 p.m.	Mum comes in. They have tea.
6.15 p.m.	Norma goes to play centre with her friends.
7.15 p.m.	Norma comes home and children go to bed.

THE CHILDREN

A Tuesday in the Easter Holidays

9.10 a.m. Children got up, had breakfast.
10.30 a.m. Norma went up park with her friends while Eileen went with her friends.
11.40 a.m. Came home. Norma went on some errands.
1.00 p.m. They had dinner. Norma went to the pictures with her friends. Eileen went again to the park.
5.00 p.m. Norma came home and had her tea.
5.45 p.m. Eileen came home and had her tea.
6.00 p.m. They played at painting and drawing and watched TV until bedtime.
8.30 p.m. Bedtime.

Second Family. Diary of Terry (eleven) written for him by his mother

A Tuesday in term time

7.45 a.m. Woke up, dressed and washed. Wished my mother a Happy Birthday.
8.00 a.m. Had my breakfast.
8.30 a.m. Gave my dog his water and meat. Took him for a run.
9.10 a.m. Went to school. Played in the playground.
12.30 p.m. Came home to dinner. Played in the garden till school time.
1.30 p.m. Went to school.
4.30 p.m. Came home, had my tea. Went out to play.
5.15 p.m. Came in for television. Saw Buffalo Bill.
5.45 p.m. Took my dog for a walk.
6.00 p.m. Played on my skates.
6.30 p.m. Washed, got ready for bed. Had my supper.
8.15 p.m. Went to bed.

A Monday in the Easter Holidays

Rose at 8.15. Washed, dressed, had breakfast. Read my comic. Left home to go to the lady who looks after me.
9.10 a.m. Waited till my friend was ready then went out on my bike with two other friends.
12.00 noon Had dinner.
12.30 p.m. Went out again on our bikes to Greenwich Park. Saw the Cutty Sark. Called in to see my Nanny Cook on my way there. Home just after 3.30.
3.45 p.m. My mother came home, had a cup of tea, biscuits and cake. Went out again on my bike for an errand. Played

153

MARRIED WOMEN WORKING

out till 5.15. Watched television till 6 o'clock. Had our tea, egg, chips and beans, bread and butter.

6.30 p.m.	I played with my bow and arrow.
7.00 p.m.	Watched television.
7.30 p.m.	Washed myself for bed. Had supper.
8.00 p.m.	Had to go to bed.[4]

In addition to day nurseries and a nursery school both the L.C.C. and Bermondsey borough make good provision for children's leisure, a point very relevant to the mother who works. Eighteen small gardens, many of them with seesaws, sandpits, climbing nets, and swings, are so well spaced throughout the borough that one or other is within easy reach of even the pram-pushing mother and the school child with a toddler in tow. There are organized open-air games during school holidays, with Punch and Judy shows and talent competitions at the peak traffic hours. Free cinema shows and a Thursday night theatre (adults 1s, children 3d) are available in the winter. Southwark Park, situated in the centre of Bermondsey, is an enormous asset. It has plenty of flat grass for informal games as well as cricket and football pitches, tennis courts and bowling and putting greens, the latter chiefly used by the élite of the male teenagers. In addition to covered swimming baths, Bermondsey has an excellent, tree-lined open-air pool to which children are admitted free on week-day mornings, and for 3d and 6d at other times. Apart from free admissions and school parties, 22,000 children used this pool even in the wet summer of 1958. The above facilities, ones that children can enjoy by themselves but where there is permanent adult staff in attendance, are of the greatest help to the mother who works.

At the time of the survey there were six L.C.C. play centres in Bermondsey open during term time on four days a week for at least a two-hour spell; during the school holidays there were usually two or three open in the borough all day. Students of the London School of Economics, temporary members of the team, attended two of the largest centres for a month in 1957 and again in 1958. They noted that the weekly (Monday to Thursday) attendance might be between 400 and 500 children, so that the centres must be a considerable help to any mother who wants to be temporarily relieved of her children, as well as providing them with a safe and large place in which to play. It was interesting that though the little children very often came in twos and threes from the same home, and that there was a family atmosphere about the centres, the staff could not, in general, associate any special characteristics with the children whose mothers worked.

[4] In both families the mother went out to work, part-time.

THE CHILDREN

Another indication of Bermondsey's care for its children, and of a facility that may help the mother who works, is the large number of long-established, well-regarded youth organizations. They have a higher than usual proportion of paid leaders and high membership figures. In a census taken by the Youth Committee in 1956–57, 23 per cent of the five- to eight-year-old population was estimated to belong to youth organizations; 55 per cent of the eight to eleven and as many as 72 per cent of the eleven to fifteen age group. Of the ninety-four actual leaders (not helpers), fifty-five live in Bermondsey.

The children have other facilities that appear to mitigate some of the disadvantages commonly associated with the mother being out at work. In the first place they do not lack playmates, as they have rather more siblings than the 'average' child. They also tend to have a good supply of relations living nearby. The three children living beside the research worker are a case in point. In 1959, when they were aged twelve, nine, and seven, and therefore fairly mobile as regards visiting, they had living in or just on the edge of the borough of Bermondsey, two maternal grandparents, twenty-two aunts and uncles, twenty-seven first cousins (four with spouses), and seven first cousins once removed. Even the only child normally has ready-made company since he is expected to play out. Nor, for London, are they short of playing space. The newer flats have surrounds that offer useful possibilities for chasing games and scooter riding; and even in the day-time the side streets are mostly quiet enough for ball games, hopscotch, and skipping. The great tarpaulin-covered lorries are a permitted substitute for tree climbing and make a fine playground at night; while the dangerous, slimy foreshore of the river offers such exciting pastimes as salvaging timber and catapulting pigeons. Identifying flags and cargoes is another possibility: with luck one may see anything from a skiff to a submarine, the *Magga Dan,* or the *Britannia.* Finally, there are 'the Ruins', the bombed sites which for the last sixteen years have been the undisputed, undisturbed territory of the adjacent households. These Bermondsey children, therefore, are not short of space or junk for the inventive play which their gardenless houses and tiny, tidy flats do not provide. Their games sound imaginative enough. Alleygobs, in its fourteen or so variations, includes 'Babies' Eyes', 'Electric Bank', 'A Child goes round the Mountain', 'Bang in the Hole', 'Nelson's Grave', and 'Ladies' Lavatory'. Of course television is in competition with much of this, but from the adults' point of view it has every merit, handy when the parents want to go out together, a solace to the lone minder, and a noise-stopper when the kids are driven indoors by wet days and cold nights. A small study made by a Primary School Headmaster on the leisure of sixteen of his children, showed TV occupying 36 per cent of their free time compared with about 12 per cent in 'playing out'. Of his two most ardent viewers, one had a mother who worked, one not.

Though all the above suggests that Bermondsey children have rather better provision for their leisure than is available in many towns, the children do, of course, face one major disability—that of growing up within a sprawling city. For them, living twelve miles from the nearest field, earth is 'dirt', wild flowers 'just weeds'; and toddlers may literally be afraid of the grass. Unlike middle-class urban children, who anyhow mostly live in the suburbs, these Bermondsey children seldom get away to stay in the country for the odd weekend or for weeks at a time in the school holidays, although an increasing number now go out for the day in the car. On the whole, however, their year is boringly uniform since their surroundings do not, like those of the country child or even of the town child who gets into the country fairly often, provide fresh sights and sounds with the changing seasons, birds' nests and the cuckoo, blackberries and conkers, brooks to dam and ponds to slide on. Moreover, such pleasures are free, whereas anything new that these city children see mostly has to be bought before they can enjoy it. Their budgies, and the occasional tortoise or frog from the pet store, are poor substitutes for handling and cuddling compared with backyard and farmyard pets, and less likely to provide the delight springing from the small child's capacity to identify with animals. These children rarely see cows and pigs or cocks and hens; and in some council flats even a cat is not officially countenanced. Dozens of toys, lashings of pocket money, and the most lush of coach trips to Southend are not the equal of 'nature's world of ready wealth'. Insofar as the great majority of these children see cowslips only in a lesson book and hear the skylark only on TV, they are still the deprived. Small wonder that Bermondsey parents claim that one of the justifications for the mother going out to work is that the children *ought* to have a country holiday, and that they *need* plenty of money for their day-to-day pleasures.

Local norms of child care

Bermondsey's fairly strong views on child care were illustrated by a small incident which took place just outside the team's window at Peek Frean's. A burst of wailing was found to come from two thirteen-month-old babies strapped into a large go-cart standing on the pavement. The crying continued, mounted in volume, and brought the factory gatekeeper over to eye the infants. Various

THE CHILDREN

housewives appeared enquiringly on their doorsteps, then two or three children gathered round, offering suitable distractions to the wailing babies. Finally one of the housewives started to wheel the go-cart up and down. The street's indignation mounted as word went round that the mother was in Peek Frean's employment office, seeing about a job. It was decided to despatch a messenger after her. No mother appeared so a second messenger was sent in. He eventually brought word out that the woman said these twins always did cry; that she knew what was best for her own kids, didn't she; and (presumably in justification of a prospective evening shift job) that her husband could manage them better than ever she could. The small drama lasted for half an hour and revealed something of the attitudes aroused when a mother was held to be going out to work in circumstances not approved by local standards.

A high child accident rate might have been expected in this district where the main roads bear extremely heavy day-time traffic. In fact the Bermondsey figures appear normal; and though so many mothers work there are many signs that the children's physical safety is not neglected. The younger ones are mostly delivered and collected from school by an adult, one particular bit of parental care that can hardly have been a feature of the big families of former days. Though no social stigma attaches to children playing in the street, one rarely sees, as is common in a slum area, toddlers scrabbling about on doorsteps. And the small child in the Park is practically always accompanied by an older one. A stable community like Bermondsey affords many safeguards for 'playing out'. If the child tumbles and cries in the street or in a flats' yard, several grown-ups come out on their balconies and can cope effectively because they know who the child is and where the various members of his family are to be found at that hour. People's movements are sufficiently regular for anything out of the ordinary to be spotted. Indeed, careful mothers sometimes think it safer for the junior school child to 'play out' than to be left alone in the house. The anthropologist who assisted the team commented on the amount of coming and going of children between households; it amounted to minding although no formal request was made.

Those mothers who worked were, of course, not blind to the many risks that had nothing to do with the child's physical safety. Such dangers are well known and are only referred to here because many of them were likely to be mitigated if the mother worked part- rather than full-time. The child whose mother worked was, it was said, liable to be over-compensated and bought off by presents. A blackmailing baby who traded on his mother's absence was one instance

157

quoted; a fourteen-guinea jeep presented to what the speaker called 'a little tiddy-dot-of-a-child' was another. Secondly, no clear-cut pattern of behaviour was set before the child. 'Slummicky' was the word used for this type of upbringing; examples quoted were the indulgence of an over-fond grandmother, and the bad manners caught off an ignorant, careless minder. One thirteen-year-old's remark on a friend of her own age whose mother had started work was that 'it makes Sandra more scatty, no happier though'. The friend had sensed the quick change in Sandra that had resulted from less consistent patterns at home. Thirdly, the mother was always pressed for time. This might mean no more than that a small boy had to abandon a messy hobby because his mother was too busy now to clear up after him; or that she didn't really enjoy his birthday herself although she still provided the treats; or that she was not at hand to give the quick trouncing that most children need on occasion. Or it might mean a more serious matter, that she never had time now to share the children's problems. Several adolescent girls who said their mother was always too busy to talk, half hinted that these particular mothers had missed the odd confidence that had needed to be made.

One thing that may have eased these mothers' anxieties about leaving home regularly was that in a working-class district the children are encouraged to grow up quickly. Peter Pan attitudes are rare. 'Don't mess my perm' snapped out by a three-year-old, and make-up on a girl of twelve, are thought rather bright on the child's part, laughed off perhaps but seldom frowned on. The children, too, are expected to make their own decisions. Christmas presents are not treated as a surprise. Mere infants decide exactly what they want weeks ahead and place their order, so to speak, with the parents. The widespread demand for earlier school admission also seems to stem not only from its convenience for Mum; school cuts the apron strings and prevents mollycoddling. The parents also pointed out that children are more capable now than formerly. They mature earlier, are physically stronger, and include fewer sickly children who need special care, and are liable to be victimized by other children. The one-family-one-home means that there are fewer adults about the place, and that the children have to shoulder more responsibility willy-nilly. School, too, places more emphasis on self-reliance now than formerly. This earlier maturity of children may well be one of the minor reasons that encourage mothers to come back into work sooner than did the older generation.

The children themselves were said to enjoy their improved status. It felt grown-up to have the key, the run of the home, and the chance

THE CHILDREN

to boss the younger ones about, while the material compensations were self-evident. Two boys of eight and eleven were quoted as highly approving of their mother working (at Peek Frean's) because it meant lots of biscuits and extra money, 2s 6d a day each with which to be seen off to school, and 3d for doing the washing up. This, of course, is strictly in keeping with the local custom of paying children for anything they do for an adult.

It was impossible to find out how the smaller children reacted to their mothers working: but the following points about the older children, made by grammar school girls in a school essay, are of interest. 'Working mothers,' wrote one fifteen-year-old girl, 'tend to be more broad-minded, more interesting people, because they are not bounded by the domestic circle. This gives the child greater confidence in its mother.' Another, aged sixteen, thought that 'Life at work is much more interesting for them (the mothers), and how much more interesting they are to talk to. They can chat about the things that happened at work and on the bus, and their family will be much more willing to listen than if they had sat at home and did nothing more exciting than sweeping and cleaning.' A third, aged fourteen, wrote: 'I believe going out to work can do the mother good because she gets away from the small, rather petty world of housekeeping and baby minding, where women soon begin gossiping and even conversing with themselves, to be among other people. My own mother recently took up a part-time job and I find that although she often feels tired and needs more help, she is much happier and has more interesting things to say.'

If these parents, themselves brought up in the free-for-all tussles of the big poor home, mistrusted over-mothering they had no doubt at all about the justice of sharing their own improved fortunes with the children. To treat them lavishly seemed only fair, and it had to be irrespective of the child's age. This resulted in some curious kindnesses, as in the case of the father who, debating a Christmas present for a year-old baby, decided to 'give her a quid and let her choose'. This sharing of the new wealth ranged from something to suck (for pretty well the asking); through a succession of toys on wheels and lethal weapons; to a £7 7s 0d toy typewriter for the nine year-old 'so she shan't go to a factory'; or a wristwatch for the boy who wrote 'Since I was eight I had always wanted a gold watch . . . I used to go to my junior school and the teacher would ask the time, and nearly everyone in the class put their hands up.' Even if the big presents went all to pieces in no time, it was felt that their price alone demonstrated proper parental attitudes. The same held for clothes. A father would contrast the single pair of shoes of his

159

MARRIED WOMEN WORKING

own boyhood with the sandals, bedroom slippers, Sunday pair, and 50s football boots of his ten-year-old son. Parents took much pride in being able to give the children a frequent change of outfit. Small girls' dresses and coats were frequently in the £5 to £6 range, although the mothers rarely paid beyond £10 for a garment for themselves. The itch for elegance noted in the furnishing of the home was shown again here. Dressed to kill, an eight-year-old might sport an elaborate nylon dress, cute hat and handbag, gold bracelet, socks, sandals and gloves in white, and a doll to match. She looked lovely even if it did cost an awful lot. The adolesecent wage-earners, too, had their full share in the adults' improved finances. They were given super presents and required to pay only the minimum board money. One mother who worked was proud to be able to say, of a son kept at school till sixteen and married at nineteen, that she had 'never made anything out of him'. It was in all probability as much the parents as the youngster who made possible the Christmas clothes of one adolescent boy—white shirt, grey pullover, flannels, snake-skin shoes, corduroy jacket, all brand new. A girl's rigout, worn at a youth club on fourteen evenings, was entirely different on at least ten of them.

Another feature of local upbringing was its permissive character. The same applied to behaviour. 'It's all right for him to shake his fist at me,' was the line taken, 'so long as he knows I'm there when he wants me.' Adults tried to close their eyes to naughtiness and to take peccadilloes lightly. The 'kind' (that is the acceptable) minder was not the disciplinarian but the one who let the child do as he liked within reason, gave generous meals, and made him a steady flow of small gifts. 'Now do it properly' was an instruction fairly often given to the small child in Bermondsey, but in general adults directed the children's manners, speech, and play less than in the middle-class home, so that in this respect the local mother who worked had less than the middle-class one to worry about.

Another common phrase, 'today's kids have jam on it', refers not only to improved material standards but to less harsh relationships between adults and children. The father in particular is a less feared and less distant figure than formerly. The team was told of a Deptford man, still living, who never did get the hang of all his children's names: he used to call them out by number. In the long family of the past the father's enormous age cut him off from the younger children. He was, anyhow, less in the home, more on his dignity about helping with domestic jobs and, a point often made, would have been ashamed to be seen in public with what was probably a shabby pram and a sickly-looking baby. A good many people had

160

THE CHILDREN

had rough treatment from their own parents, even though they mostly supposed there was a kind of affection behind it all. One recalled that 'if we was cheeky we got a thumping one across the mouth'; another, speaking of her mother ("Annie" of illustration, p. 80), said that though she had been a grand old stick, she did beat them unmercifully; and a third said that when she was a girl her father used to knock her from one end of the room to another. Not only is treatment kinder, but affection is said to be more openly expressed. The father's 'mind how you go' at the school gate is often accompanied by a kiss, and he will tuck the children into bed.

The parents were also asked about their ambitions for the children. The interest in the answers, as given at 152 homes, lay chiefly in the stereotypes used. Fantasy ambitions were infrequent and came from the wives who did not work; perhaps they knew less of the real world than their sisters. Two-thirds of those in homes where the wife worked hoped that the children would move up the social ladder but aspirations were realistic. They related the social rise to such things as the child speaking better, being able to talk to strangers, or going to different holiday places every two years or so. Except in a negative sense ('no factory work for my girl') the child's job did not come into the picture as much as his education and even this was not markedly competitive. The dull child producing an unexpectedly apt remark might be twitted with a 'he'll get to St Olave's yet', but the parents often seemed less disappointed than the child himself when he failed to get a grammar school place. They tended to leave academic issues and long-term plans to fate and the teachers, though making sure that their child did not fall below his peers in things like blazers and the school's foreign journeys, or in such essentials—all knowledge in a nutshell— as the £23 encyclopaedia, bought on H.P. and, at one home, thumbed through for weeks until someone cottoned on to the point of an index. These were commonly accepted reasons for the good mother to try to earn, whereas many of the parents had little conception of the educational ladder as a whole. Unlike the schools of newer areas, the local ones are mostly gaunt, nineteenth-century London School Board buildings, often war damaged; they do not proclaim in any obvious terms the recent advances in education. Nor are long-term plans about the children's future encouraged by the short-term pattern of these manual workers' earnings, with job termination at a week's notice.

While Bermondsey on the whole appeared to be satisfied that married women's employment did no harm to the children, nevertheless there was a good deal of uneasiness about today's children

MARRIED WOMEN WORKING

in general. They were said to be less contented now than formerly. Instancing some children's never-ending demand for 'things', the parents used such a phrase as 'they don't half expect a lot off of you today'. The children were thought to come by money and its temptations too easily, and were over-reluctant to take the rough with the smooth. Very many parents were bothered, to say the least of it, by the younger generation's unwillingness to accept external authority, though few saw this as a possible reflection on the new freedoms that the adults themselves are enjoying. One mother in a 'typical' family, living in a quiet block of old flats, said a disturbing thing—that she found today's children had 'more hate in them now than formerly'. Though the increasing tendency of mothers to go out of their homes may be a contributing factor to the troubles hinted at above, these problems are, of course, related to many other of the radical changes in our society.

The findings on the children may be summarized as follows: Bermondsey did not approve of the mother working if her child was under school age. From this stage on, the decision was hers, provided the minding was satisfactory. The stage at which minding needs were held to decrease markedly was when the child moved up into a secondary school. The more children the mother had, the less was it correct for her to work, partly because several children were held to be too much to ask of a minder, who was generally a relation or a friend. The mothers in both studies were emphatic that they worked largely for the children's sake, and their claim seemed to be justified in that the Bermondsey material did not show the worker's child to be at any disadvantage, while his material benefits were undisputed. Certainly nothing grossly abnormal was found in the children whose mother was a worker.

The unexpectedly satisfactory nature of these findings was thought to be so closely related to certain characteristics of the locality that they are repeated here.

1. The risks and strains so often associated with the mother's absence from home were lessened by the good opportunities the area afforded for part- rather than full-time work.
2. Bermondsey's industries and its closeness to the City provided that variety of working hours which permitted the capable mother to adjust her job to the demands of the individual home.
3. Local provision for the leisure-time activities of children was unusually generous.
4. The inter-related, stable history of the population eased the practical problems and lessened the physical dangers.

THE CHILDREN

5. The long tradition of the mother going out to work meant that the techniques for coping with the dual job had been tested by time.

6. Family lore about grandmothers and great-grandmothers who, when times were worse than usual, had more than pulled their weight by taking any paid job they could find, brought today's mother who worked into line with these good mothers of the past.

7. So many Bermondsey children had a mother who worked that the child's own anxieties were assuaged—'It's not just *my* Mum who leaves me.'

CHAPTER X

Conclusions

*Who went out to work?–Why did they work?–How did
they manage the dual job?–Did their families suffer?–
What enabled them to find work?–How did Peek Frean's
adapt itself to the new type of labour?–How satisfactory
was the married woman as an employee?–Some implications of married women's employment among working-
class-wives*

THE study which has been described in the preceding pages was
undertaken to clarify in a single locality and in a single factory
some of the social and industrial questions raised by the employment
of married women. It does not provide a basis for wide generaliza-
tions, but it may perhaps give greater insight into the problems discussed. In this concluding chapter an attempt is made to summarize
these questions as the team has come to understand them in
Bermondsey.

Who went out to work?

In view of the conflicting views on the wife who works, it was important for the team to establish who these wives were and the
extent of their family responsibilities. In the families living at the
770 addresses which formed the borough of Bermondsey sample,
just over half the Wives and Widows responsible for running a home
went out to work. Rather more than half of these workers were
employed part-time only, and of the part-timers over half worked
under twenty hours a week. The woman most likely to work was
aged forty to forty-nine. No less than 73 per cent of those interviewed in this age group were in employment, and 66 per cent of
those aged fifty to fifty-nine. These figures contrast sharply with the
24 per cent of workers in the twenty to twenty-nine age group and
the 50 per cent of those aged thirty to thirty-nine.

The working wife was not, typically, the mother of very young
children. Only twenty-one of the ninety-eight mothers with a child
under five were at work, including those who had no husband at
home; and only seven of them worked full-time. The mothers whose
youngest child had reached school age presented a different picture.
Seventy-eight per cent of those whose youngest child was aged
eleven to fourteen worked and 65 per cent whose youngest child

164

CONCLUSIONS

was aged five to ten; in both cases part-time work was much more common than full-time. The fewer the children the more the wife tended to work, though this was less marked than might have been expected. In the Husband and Wife home with no children, 62 per cent of the wives worked, 58 per cent of them full-time. Where there was only one child, 54 per cent of the wives were in employment, but the figure dropped only to 40 per cent in the few homes which had as many as three or more children.

In relation to the type of employment of the husband of the working wife, it was the skilled manual worker whose wife had the most marked tendency to work—59 per cent with husbands in this category were in employment, followed by 54 per cent for semi-skilled workers and 53 per cent for supervisory grades. While the low level of the husband's earnings, as compared with the national figure, was a factor which led the wife to go out to work, she was not deterred from working by the relatively high earnings of her husband, especially where there were children in the family.

Why did they work?

In the great majority of cases the wives studied were not driven out to work in order to keep the wolf from the door. The reason for working most frequently expressed was the desire for more money. The earnings of the Wives and Widows in full-time employment mostly ranged from £5 to £7 per week, which was in line with the national average for women industrial workers at the time of the study. Part-time work seldom brought in as much as £5, usually far less. The way in which her wages were spent showed that the woman worked neither to meet basic economic needs nor to provide personal pleasures for herself. Money was wanted as a means of raising the family's standard of living. It was used to build up, on a do-it-yourself basis, a more modern and attractive home, to provide more generous food, better footwear, and larger wardrobes, to buy durable consumer goods, to give the family a seaside holiday, and to acquire a cheap second-hand car. In addition, the wife's earnings eased her housekeeping. Many women referred to the relief of being able to shop more freely, and to the pleasure of exercising some choice instead of accepting 'the cheapest always'. A pay packet of her own provided both extra notes for her purse and an easy conscience in spending them. In deciding how the money was to be used the parents stressed the paramount importance of the children's welfare. They were determined that their children should not suffer the deprivations of their own poverty-ridden childhood. Any extra

165

MARRIED WOMEN WORKING

money was to be shared with the children in a way that would bring the child immediate happiness.

Money, however, was not the only reason for working. Demographic and social changes have dramatically altered the daily life of the Bermondsey housewife. The marked fall in family size and in the age at which the woman has her last child, better health, improved housing, and labour-saving devices have all made her physical load lighter than that of any previous generation. For the first time large numbers of working-class wives have found themselves with time on their hands. These changes, however, have meant not only an easier but a lonelier life. To Bermondsey women increasingly aware of the world beyond their own four walls, taking a job seemed the obvious way to use the time and energy no longer absorbed by the demands of home. It also enabled them to meet new people and to overcome some of the isolation and restlessness created by women's new situation. It was alleged, too, that the status of the Bermondsey mother had declined, speakers pointing out that, in contrast with today, 'it *used* to be Mums as was the bosses round here'. If this is a fact, going out to work may well provide a welcome challenge to competence. Moreover, as these changes affected the great majority of Bermondsey families, the wife who worked was not exposing herself to the criticism of her neighbours. Provided that the arrangements she made about her children were considered adequate by local standards, her decision to work was socially approved.

How did they manage the dual job?

Alterations and adjustments in both domestic and industrial life have made the dual job possible, but housekeeping still has to be undertaken and the family cared for. How did these wives manage to cope with the demands of both work and home?

By middle-class standards the Bermondsey wives had small and compact homes with few goods and chattels. Nor had they hidebound housekeeping traditions. They were ready to take full advantage of laundry aids outside the home; they made extensive use of labour-saving devices; and they did not scruple to throw away anything past its prime. Housekeeping was done to a plan, entertaining was negligible, cooking simple and stereotyped. Communal feeding, in the school meals' service, in works canteens, and through the use of luncheon vouchers, reduced the time and effort the woman was obliged to spend on feeding the family. Indeed, the shift of the main meal eaten at home from midday to the evening appeared to be an important factor in enabling the wife to go out to work.

CONCLUSIONS

In dealing with her daily chores the wife who worked felt free to ask for regular help from her relations. Though she did not employ a paid domestic worker, a good deal of her washing, shopping, etc., was done for her by relations at a low cost. The older children were expected to give some help with the housework, though they were rarely exploited. The husband, on the other hand, assisted on the grand scale. He not only undertook the traditional man's jobs of house-decorating and repairs, but gave a very considerable hand in the daily round of washing up and cleaning grates. In addition he frequently made himself responsible for such regular tasks as window cleaning, floor polishing, ironing, and turning out a room. His domestic help was not only extensive: even more important from the wife's point of view, it was dependable.

The major problem of the working mother was not, however, her housekeeping but the proper care of the children while she was out. Public opinion, strong in Bermondsey, discouraged her from work as long as she had a child below school age. Of the relatively small number of such mothers who were working at all, nearly all were employed part-time and those children whose mothers did work full-time were looked after by a close relative. The problem of minding was, therefore, primarily the problem of supervising children before and after school and during school holidays. Again it was to a great extent relatives, and particularly the wife's mother, who took on this job. In this the wife was undoubtedly helped by the close family links in Bermondsey, where the team's own sample indicated that about half the adults were born in the borough. The other minder of great importance was the husband. The Peek Frean study showed that, when the wife worked on the evening shift, it was the husband who regularly undertook the care of the children— an act of partnership which tied him for five evenings a week. Regular minding of this type presented fewer difficulties than the short-term needs arising from school holidays, illness, or the sudden, unforeseeable emergency. These were the situations in which the clash between the claims of work and home were most apparent. Recognizing the mother's obligations to her children, at Peek Frean's management often allowed her to transfer to the appropriate shift for the long school holidays, and it granted unpaid leave in domestic crises. In the last resort, if the seriousness of the domestic situation required it, the Bermondsey mother put first things first and stayed at home till the emergency was past.

Though wives undoubtedly relied mainly on help from members of their family, on their own efforts, and on the flexibility of their conditions of work, mention was frequently made of the public

MARRIED WOMEN WORKING

services in the area. The four day nurseries were not much used by the typical mother who worked, partly because of the compulsory full day's attendance, the fees charged, and their association with the mother in severe financial need. At the same time Bermondsey's one nursery school had a long waiting list. The six L.C.C. play centres, numerous and efficient youth organizations, good public provision as regards playgrounds and parks, all eased the after-school and holiday problems.

If the public services provided in Bermondsey and the closely-knit, stable character of the area assisted the married woman to carry the dual role, she was also fortunate in the extent to which the small, part-time job at a wide choice of hours was available within easy reach. Half the Wives and Widows interviewed went out to work: of these workers, 56 per cent were employed under thirty hours a week, and 28 per cent under twenty hours. The Bermondsey woman was also able to select, from a varied timetable, those hours of work which fitted her domestic commitments; and she could adjust her hours as the structure of her family altered. Since it was easy to get a job fairly near her home, the journey to work was not a serious additional burden: in the Wives and Widows Sample a third of those in employment had a journey taking less than twenty minutes. This was an important consideration since the earnings from a part-time job were not high enough to justify a tiring and expensive journey. There can be no doubt that it was the wide choice of part-time work in the locality which made it possible for so many women to cope with both home and work without undue difficulty. Many wives, acutely aware of their duty to the family, would not have worked at all had only full-time jobs been available.

Finally, these wives carried on successfully by virtue of their own determination, efficiency, and sheer hard work. Among the Wives and Widows 30 per cent of those in employment reckoned to be up before 6 a.m., as were 45 per cent of the women in the Peek Frean Shifts Sample (on the day before they were interviewed). The wife who went out to work was compelled to plan her activities most carefully, and to stick to her plan whether she felt like it or not. In the last analysis, it was her own self-discipline and the sacrifice of her own leisure that enabled her to fulfil the dual role.

Did their families suffer?

Since the mother with a child under five worked in exceptional circumstances only, the problem of child care was chiefly connected with the children of school age. The mother showed her responsible attitude to the children's physical needs by working, whenever possible,

168

CONCLUSIONS

at times when the children were out of the house; by making sure that some minding agent was available in the after-school hours and in the long school holidays; and by the care with which she chose the minder. The crucial question, however, was not what arrangements were made, but what was the effect on the child of the mother going out to work? This vitally important issue is not one to which clear-cut and conclusive answers can be given. Facts, however, relating to 82 per cent of the dependent children of the Bermondsey households interviewed, enabled the team to compare the records of workers' and housewives' children with regard to health, school attendance, and educational progress; and to child neglect and behaviour problems as seen by the school and as leading to appearance in the Juvenile Court. On delinquency, information was obtained about the children of the whole of the Bermondsey sample households, i.e. whether they had accepted or refused the interview; and information on delinquency was also obtained for Bermondsey children as a whole. The factual material about the children was supplemented by the views of teachers and health visitors; of nursery-school, day-nursery, and play-centre staff; and of other people in close and continuous contact with the children of Bermondsey.

It can be said categorically that no evidence was found of physical neglect. The safeguards were many—the area's stability; the extent and warmth of family ties; the long tradition in these very poor homes of the conscientious mother who worked to augment the family income; the shortness and flexibility of working hours. On the other hand, the mother's rigid, loaded programme allowed her little time for playing with her children, listening to them, and enjoying their company. This may well have meant some deprivation for the child at a psychological level, but the team had neither the information nor the competence to assess such matters.

Detailed follow-up studies of the general health, from birth, of the children under five did not indicate that the worker's child had a worse history than the housewife's. The medical records of the children at school showed that cases of serious illness among the school children had been no more prevalent in homes where the mother worked than where she did not. Examination of school attendance records showed that the worker's child stayed away from school slightly less than the housewife's. This might have been due to a tendency for the mother who worked to send her child to school even if unwell; but there was no evidence that the health of the worker's child was affected adversely. Insofar as the educational progress of the eighty-one children at a secondary school could be measured by the type of school for which they had been selected at the 11 +

MARRIED WOMEN WORKING

stage, it was found that, of the eighteen at a grammar or technical school, as many as sixteen had a mother who worked. Though many factors need to be taken into account on this last point, the evidence in general did not support the claim that the worker's child was at any disadvantage educationally.

Since the alleged connection between juvenile delinquency and the employment of mothers is a matter of very great public interest, it is unfortunate that it was not possible to collect reliable figures on this vital point. Such facts as could be obtained throw a flickering light on this problem but provide no conclusive answers. It is certainly of interest that, in this area with a long tradition of mothers working, of the sixty-three Bermondsey children to appear in the South-East London Juvenile Court in the year ended April 1, 1958, twenty-eight were given an absolute or conditional discharge; and none was sent to an Approved School. For eighteen of these sixty-three children no information was available on the mother's work situation at the date of the offence, but among those for whom this point was recorded, more workers' than housewives' children appeared in court. An attempt to get detailed information on delinquency for the children of the total sample of households at 770 addresses produced the names of only fourteen children as having been on the Probation Office's card index of cases appearing at the court in the last ten years. As in the case of the Bermondsey children in general, the numbers in trouble appeared low, but again the mothers' work situation at the time of the offence was not known in a good many cases. In those where the particulars could be established, again the worker's child fared less well than the housewife's. The summing-up would seem to be that there was certainly no evidence of any acute delinquency problem connected with married women's employment.

In a matter so difficult to measure as the general well-being of children, considerable weight must be attached to the opinion of trained and experienced people in close contact with them. Teachers, health visitors, and social workers all agreed that the worker's child displayed no sign whatever of physical neglect, and practically no one could identify characteristics distinguishing the two sets of children. A rough synthesis of the views of the heads of forty-two of the fifty-three schools attended by the children of the Bermondsey sample showed seven of these head teachers strongly opposed to mothers working, fifteen seeing no harm 'provided that . . .'; and twenty approving in general, the headmistresses being rather more guarded than the men. All agreed that part-time work involved less

CONCLUSIONS

risk for the child than full-time, but they held no common view on the age at which the mother could safely start work. These relatively favourable opinions on married women's employment were surprising, especially since most of the heads pointed out that it puts additional responsibility on the school, quite apart from the extra work entailed. The schools' views were paralleled by public opinion in Bermondsey which favoured mothers working provided they had no children under school age, and provided that very careful provision was made for minding.

Freed from the criticisms of their neighbours and inheriting family traditions about mothers who had worked under far more rigorous conditions than obtain today, the wives were probably speaking the truth when they said they did not feel guilty about working. Indeed, many argued that the neglectful mother was the one too indifferent and too indolent to seize today's golden, and perhaps fleeting, opportunity to benefit the children by raising the physical standards of the home.

If there was no evidence that the children were harmed, neither could it be shown that the relationship between husband and wife was affected adversely. Few wives said that their husbands had expressly forbidden them to work, but many that the husband had disliked the idea when it was first mooted. He became reconciled as the advantages of the second pay packet grew evident, but always provided that the children were not neglected. Indeed the husband's practical collaboration in the work of the home testified to his approval. Partnership between husband and wife was thought to be growing closer and some people believed that married women's employment, far from threatening good relations, helped to improve them. They pointed out that sharing the domestic jobs and the day-to-day care of the children, jointly building up an attractive, well-equipped home, and enjoying together the new pleasures of the Sunday car ride and the family holiday, all strengthened the common bond. Joint income necessitated mutual consultation, and when a wife had money to spend which was indubitably her own, one potential source of friction was removed. The younger couples expressed such views more often than the older people, but all ages agreed that women today are not expected to accommodate their lives to men to the extent common in Bermondsey only a generation ago.

What enabled them to find work?

Though Bermondsey wives have always worked, their choice of employment used to be far more restricted than it is today. Demo-

MARRIED WOMEN WORKING

graphic changes, combined with the nationwide demand for labour and the expansion of local industry, have created new employment opportunities for the Bermondsey married woman who wishes to work. Employers have been forced to adopt more flexible attitudes, as in the case of Peek Frean's, where it was realized that a considerable proportion of married women would have to be employed and at hours adapted to suit their needs. This firm was exceptional in its high percentage of married women and part-timers and in the number of shifts offered, but other local employers too were driven to provide opportunities for part-time work, if on a smaller scale.

How did Peek Frean's adapt itself to the new type of labour?

Part-time work will clearly be available only if the employer is convinced that it is an economic proposition. Peek Frean's accepted part-time women workers because it was compelled to do so by force of circumstances. Conventional attitudes had to be abandoned: management realized that it would be impossible to recruit and retain large numbers of married women unless hours of work were adapted to fit domestic needs, and leave granted freely to meet domestic crises. Hence the development of an exceptionally elaborate and varied system of shifts, a re-interpretation of factory rules and regulations, and an acceptance of the added costs and problems created by large numbers of women working short and varied hours.

Management also realized that a careful policy of recruitment and allocation was necessary. Only a woman whose home circumstances seemed likely to enable her to hold down the dual job was engaged; while the probable absentee was not placed in a key position. Equally important was the necessity to pay as much attention to the initial introduction and training of the part-time worker as to the full-timer: this was essential if she was to become an effective part of the labour force despite her many commitments outside the factory.

How satisfactory was the married woman as an employee?

Some of the commonly held beliefs regarding part-time women workers were found to be justified. A very high absentee rate appeared to be inevitable among mothers with children of school age; this led to disorganization in departments, to increased difficulties for supervisors, and to dissatisfaction among the regular attenders who had to cope while their fellows were away. Labour turnover, though not exceptionally bad, was certainly high, especially in the early months of employment; this led to increased costs and administrative work,

CONCLUSIONS

and to inefficiency. On the other hand the stability rate was good on all except the 9.30 a.m.—4.00 p.m. shift, destroying the myth that part-timers are only birds of passage. Once she was trained for the job there was no sign that the part-time worker was either more or less efficient than her full-time colleague, while there was evidence that certain of the part-timers were highly-productive workers. There was no support for the general statement that the married woman takes things easily because she is not dependent on her pay packet for her livelihood.

In comparing the various shifts, the morning one appeared to be the most satisfactory from management's point of view, while the 9.30 a.m.—4.00 p.m. shift was of marginal value only, particularly as it involved idle plant and empty factory space for considerable periods of the working day.

The existence of so many shifts and so high a proportion of part-time workers undoubtedly complicated the organization of work, increased costs, and laid a heavy burden on the supervisors. The difficulties of the woman supervisor's job made it increasingly hard to recruit to their ranks women of the necessary calibre, especially as many of the married women were unwilling to tackle the job, fearing that the demands of work might conflict with the claims of home.

If the Bermondsey study showed that there was a real demand by married women for part-time work, Peek Frean's experience proved that it could be economically advantageous to employ women on this basis, provided certain limitations were accepted. A factory can be run satisfactorily with a wide variety in the hours of employment, and with generous arrangements for leave to meet domestic needs. Certain jobs cannot be economically staffed on this basis, but it is probable that there is very considerable scope for an extension of flexible working conditions over a wide range of occupations. Though labour turnover is potentially high among married women, much can be done to reduce it by careful selection and training and by studying the women's attitudes to employment. In particular, it is important to recognize that many married women undoubtedly want more social contacts and consequently dislike frequent changes in their work groups. Above all, the key to the effective use of this type of labour lies in supervision of a high calibre. To achieve this it may be necessary to abandon conventional ideas of the supervisor's roles and responsibilities, and to reassess the vital part she plays. This may well call for radical changes in the recruitment, status, and pay of the woman supervisor.

MARRIED WOMEN WORKING

Some implications of the employment of working-class wives

The desire of many wives to find paid employment is not a passing phase, but a permanent feature of modern society. The percentage of married women in work has increased steadily over the last decade, and shows no sign of dropping. As the surplus of women over men in the population continues to fall, the marriage rate is expected to increase; with the consequence that a still higher proportion of the potential female labour force will be married. In these circumstances married women's employment has to be accepted as an accomplished fact; the task now is to ensure that the dangers inherent in this new pattern of life are reduced to a minimum, and the advantages intensified.

The study at Peek Frean's and in Bermondsey confirmed the belief that many married women welcomed the opportunity to work part-time. It is interesting that this demand for part-time employment from the working-class wives of an inner London borough was also apparent in the national figures of Dr Klein's study,[1] in Mrs Hubback's[2] enquiry into graduate wives, and in an American study by the National Manpower Council.[3] Despite the strength of the demand, the most recent (1960) figures show that only 13·2 per cent of women in manufacturing industry in Great Britain are employed on a part-time basis. There thus is a strong case for reviewing employment policies for both industry and other types of work so as to extend the opportunities for part-time jobs.

The need for re-thinking is not limited to employers. Housing policy is one of the issues involved. This study demonstrates that the wife who worked depended greatly for help on relatives who lived close at hand. Where housing policy has disturbed the old types of community and broken up family ties, as in many new towns and housing estates, the employment of wives may well present problems that were not evident in Bermondsey.

Taxation is another issue. In wartime the State puts pressure on the wife to take employment, legally requires it of certain categories of women, and makes some provision for the domestic needs of the mother who has children to look after. In peacetime little is done to help the mother who works with her domestic problems. Indeed, by its insurance policy, the State tips the scales against part-time work. The full insurance which the employer has to pay for each of his

---

[1] Klein, *op. cit.*
[2] Hubback, *op. cit.*
[3] National Manpower Council, *Work in the Lives of Married Women*, Columbia University Press, 1958.

CONCLUSIONS

part-time workers is probably not a serious deterrent, but there is evidence that it discourages many small employers, and a change in this policy might do something to increase the number of part-time jobs offered. Although among lower-paid workers the taxation of married women's earnings is not an issue of importance, it becomes so as this group of women employees takes on more responsible posts. The full social acceptance of the married woman as a worker will lead to reconsideration of her tax liabilities and of her claim to tax reliefs for certain expenses incurred in carrying the dual job.

As the number of households with two wage-earners increases, there are likely to be other important social consequences, for this undoubtedly contributes to a rising standard of living, and may be a decisive factor in the blurring of distinction between middle- and working-class habits of spending and living.

The entry of a high proportion of married women into paid employment is bound to affect the life of the community, apart altogether from the more obvious and immediate consequences for industry and home. The possible effects of this on local activities have not yet been investigated. There is little evidence of previous active participation by working-class wives in local affairs, and their contribution may never have been very great. But if those who manage to run a home and go out to work tend to be women of capacity and determination, as this study suggests, some of them at least would seem to have potentialities for taking a responsible part in the local community. The combined demands of job and home, however, appear to have left these wives with little opportunity, or perhaps need, for any such interests. If this is so, local life cannot but be the poorer; and in the long run the family itself may suffer, becoming wholly engrossed in its new pleasures and new economic security.

In Bermondsey living standards are rising; but for the wife part of the price is the sacrifice of the possibility of increased leisure. To ignore the implications of married women's employment in relation to leisure is to ignore a most vital issue. The Bermondsey wives assume that going out to work is the sole way of profiting from their newly-acquired freedoms. More money means new possessions, and the excitement of seeing new faces and places. Set against the dirt, disease, and want of their own childhood, the vigorous response to the wider opportunities of today is natural and inevitable. They have not yet arrived at the stage when they question whether, for themselves and for their families, more leisure rather than more money, may not be the wiser choice.

This study has examined the advantages and disadvantages of

MARRIED WOMEN WORKING

married women's employment both for family life and for employers. There would be no jobs for married women were they not able to prove themselves effective workers. They would not be willing to continue in employment were they not convinced that they and their families were the better for it. The domestic and industrial issues are two aspects of a whole, and it is as a whole that this study has tried to understand the problems raised by the new trend. It has attempted to disentangle the various considerations involved in a locality where, for many years, thousands of women, their families, and their employers have faced, and have largely overcome, the difficulties that new ways of working and living must inevitably create.

APPENDIX I. *METHOD*

THE SETTING

At Peek Frean's

IN the last thirty years the firm has been increasingly mechanized, and though baking is automatic and wrapping semi-automatic, at the time of the survey the firm's chief labour user was packing, still largely a hand process. Until the early 1940's the firm had engaged married women for seasonal work only. Acute labour shortage forced it to lift this ban, and part-time work was found to be necessary if the housewife was to be attracted in any numbers. Post-war labour difficulties led to a continuation of this policy. At the date the team's interviewing began, part-timers comprised 66 per cent of all the women operatives, and 82 per cent of the women operatives were married. The total labour force was as follows:

Total Labour Force—Peek Frean's—March 1955

Operatives			*Total*
Men			1,280
Women	Full-time	1,020	
	Part-time	1,950	2,970
Clerical Staff			
Men			230
Women			430

Details of the average number of women operatives employed in 1955 and the size of the day-time shifts is given in Table 4 (p. 72).

In Bermondsey

Bermondsey, a dockside borough south of the River, with a population of 54,000, is an entirely working-class area with an unusually high proportion of social classes IV and V. It has long traditions of the poverty associated with casual labour, and of the wife working to help out family finances. Unskilled factory work locally, and domestic work in the City's cafés and offices, is normally available. Much of this is part-time work.

STAFF: OFFICES: TIMING

The study was undertaken by the London School of Economics and Political Science under the direction of Professor Richard Titmuss and with the co-operation of the directors of Peek Frean's (Chairman, Mr Philip Carr) and of its Works Committee (Chairman, Mr George Blackmore). The London County Council, Bermondsey Borough Council, and

MARRIED WOMEN WORKING

other public and private bodies gave invaluable assistance. The schools and health visitors were particularly helpful and so, of course, were the many individuals and families who provided the essential information on which the study was based. Three full-time staff, one of them clerical, were normally engaged during the period of the field work; together with a varying number of part-time and of short-term staff. In all about twenty people worked on the Peek Frean, and about thirty-five on the Bermondsey study.

Except for the writing up and the use of a Hollerith, all the work was done from offices in Bermondsey. A small house belonging to the firm and just outside the factory's main entrance was the first base; all the interviews with employees were held here. The team were given access to all departments of the factory and spent much of their time, at any hour between 7.30 a.m. and 10 p.m., among the women as they were working at their machines and benches. The team met the office and supervisory staff when consulting factory records, and in the various canteens which the firm kindly allowed them to use. The Bermondsey study was undertaken from three successive offices. The first was at a boys' club in an old congested area; the second in a terrace house on a main shopping street; and the last at a vicarage. This variety in surroundings provided a useful sidelight on local life: so did the senior worker's own house which was ten minutes' walk from the factory, in the dock area, and looked on to a day nursery and block of council flats. At the very beginning of the study, three of the team undertook a fortnights' paid work at Peek Frean's. Between them they worked on all five shifts, underwent the normal introductory process, and used the canteens and cloakrooms of their own departments. The senior worker also undertook three months' part-time paid domestic work in a Bermondsey hospital where nearly all her fellow workers were married women living locally.

The study's timing was as follows:

	Peek Frean Study		*Bermondsey Study*
Sept. 1954:	Planning.	Sept. 1956:	Planning
	Drafting schedules	Dec. 1956:	Consulting L.C.C.,
Jan. 1955:	Pilot		schools, health visitors.
Mar. 1955:	Main interviewing		Drafting schedule.
Feb. 1956:	Contacting key people		Pilots.
Mar.–Sept. 1956:	Analysis. Writing of interim report	Sept. 1957:	Main interviewing. Children's progress. Special studies
		July 1958– April 1959:	Analysis
April 1959– July 1961:	Preparation of full report for publication		
1960:	Interim report published on aspects of the Peek Frean study[1].		

[1] *Woman Wife and Worker*, Problems of Progress in Industry, No. 10. Department of Scientific and Industrial Research, 1960.

APPENDIX I

The timing misfired on two points. It took longer than was expected (March–July 1957) to make arrangements with the London County Council about enlisting the schools' help on progress studies of the children in the sample households; and the analysing of the Bermondsey figures proved more time-consuming than those for Peak Frean's.

THE PEEK FREAN STUDY

Data on domestic issues

The first stage of the study was devoted to an analysis of the factory's female population based on a 10 per cent sample of its employees as shown on the wages sheet at December 31, 1954. This gave an overall, if brief, account of the women employees as regards age, marital status, length of service, and shift. The material from this, together with information derived from the first three months' contact with management of different levels, suggested that shift was of key importance to both management and employees, and would probably provide the most useful tool to work with. It was therefore decided to base the study on comparisons between the five shifts, although this meant that the samples might contain spinsters as well as married women. Since the shifts were of unequal size, all figures had later to be weighted.

(a) *Shifts Sample.* A pilot set of interviews was asked of forty employees, their names drawn from the 10 per cent sample mentioned above. Since this pilot proved reasonably satisfactory it was decided to draw a stratified sample of 250 employees for the main interviews, fifty from each of the firm's five shifts. Six months later a second interview, on a different schedule, was requested from all who had taken part in the first one.

(b) *Newcomers Sample.* A one-in-three sample drawn from all women engaged as operatives for the factory between April 24, 1955, and June 6, 1955, provided 100 names. The team invited each woman for an interview within seven to twelve days of that on which she was due to start work. If she accepted this first interview, six months later they asked her for a second one. In both the above samples any employee who had left the firm between the first interview and the date due for the second was contacted for a second interview at her home address.

(c) *Visiting Families.* Certain women interviewed in the Shifts and Newcomers Sample had shown considerable interest, and had obviously enjoyed the novelty of taking part in a university research project. Thirty-six of them were asked if they would co-operate further by allowing a team member to visit their home on each of the days of one week to record a detailed diary of the women's day. Regular contact was maintained with about a dozen of these families during the whole of the factory study, and with about six local households (some of them members of the Visiting Families) throughout the enquiry. Most of these homes contained children. This helped to cement the relationship

MARRIED WOMEN WORKING

since the senior worker frequently ran across the children of these households in Bermondsey's shops, playgrounds, youth groups, etc.

(d) *Local people consulted.* About forty people holding responsible posts in Bermondsey, and selected on the ground that their work made them particularly conversant with local life, were consulted on certain of the local aspects of married women's employment. They were asked what major changes they had observed in the borough, how domestic life compared with that in other working-class areas where they had held an appointment, and any outstanding effects they had noted in the child of the mother who worked. Old Bermondsey residents, 'typical pensioners', were asked what changes in child-rearing practices they had seen, and how they felt about mothers going out to work.

(e) *Schedules.* The schedules were largely factual and were not intended to promote much general discussion. A normal interview, held at the team's office, lasted about three-quarters of an hour. That taking place at the woman's home might be no more than a door-step affair with the ex-employee, or it might last the whole evening and include other members of the family. The schedule for the Shifts Sample was based on pilot interviews with forty employees and related to about fifty points. It was found to need substantial modifications before it could be used for the interview proper: in particular all financial questions were dropped, and those on minding rephrased. The schedule finally adopted dealt with the structure of the woman's household, the hours at which each member was away from home, the family's daily routine, any minding provision made, and the main facts about the woman's life history and current job. It concluded with a few pointers to discussion on the pros and cons of married women working. At the re-interview six months later, the questions concentrated on the sources of domestic help that the woman relied on, the extra costs in which going out to work might entail her, and the changes that a paid job might have made in how she spent her leisure. The schedule used for the first interview with the Newcomers Sample enquired about the changes that working at Peek Frean's had made in the woman's routine, and what her expectations were about the new job. In view of the high proportion of newcomers who had left the firm before the second interview was due, the second schedule was chiefly devoted to the reasons that had led the employee to leave.

Data on managerial issues

(a) *N.B.1 (packing department): sample and departmental study.* After the research had been in progress for some months, it was thought desirable to make a special study of the employees of one packing department (known as N.B.1) which employed a high proportion of part-timers. Of the 241 women working there between 7.30 a.m. and 9.30 p.m., only twenty-six were full-timers. Interviews were held with

APPENDIX I

fifty-three women from the four main shifts (the evening shift, containing thirty-two women, was excluded as it had different supervisors). These fifty-three were from a sample of sixty drawn on a similar basis to that of the main Shifts Sample, i.e. equal numbers per shift. Matters investigated were the extent of the alleged transfer from job to job, and the minute-by-minute duties of the department's two women supervisors.

(b) *Leavers Group*. Since so many of the Newcomers Sample who had actually started work had left within six months, they were plainly an unsatisfactory set of informants from whom to deduce any general conclusions about leaving. Twenty-eight employees who had recently left after at least three years' continuous service were therefore selected for interview from forty of those leavers who fulfilled this condition. The women interviewed were the first twenty-eight of these former employees whom it proved possible to contact at their homes.

(c) *Management consulted*. Discussion with management, from the directors downwards, took place throughout the study. The production manager and staff of the Personnel Department were particularly helpful. Informal interviews were held with most of the managers above supervisory level, concentrating on the informant's views on married women's employment in general, and on the problems which it posed at Peak Frean's, especially in relation to turnover, absenteeism, output, and training. Management was most ready to provide factual information and to check impressions; the team received invaluable assistance from the women supervisors and relied on them extensively; while officers of the trade unions and members of the Works Committee also provided help. Indeed it was largely through the good offices of this committee in the early days of the study that the women in the various samples were prevailed on to take part in the interviews.

(d) *Schedules*. The schedule for the Leavers Group was primarily directed to the woman's reasons for leaving. That for the N.B.I. Sample, which took place towards the end of the Peek Frean study, aimed particularly at factual information on the point referred to earlier, job transfers. This cropped up in all the samples interviewed, and was a common grievance on the factory floor. It concerned the frequency with which women were said to be moved from one job to another. A second main topic explored in open-ended questions was what the woman herself considered to be a satisfactory job.

Approach to the factory: request for interview: refusals and no contact

The methods used to get the women to co-operate in the study are given in some detail, as a good many unforeseen difficulties were encountered. These affected the refusals which, in the Shifts Sample, were regrettably high.

The team made their first approach (for a pilot set of interviews) to

MARRIED WOMEN WORKING

the women through the following letter which they posted to her private address.

A STUDY OF WOMEN WORKERS WITH HOME RESPONSIBILITIES

Director: Richard Titmuss   Skepper House,
Professor of Social Administration   13, Endsleigh Street,
University of London.   London, W.C.1.
                                  Date—1955.

Dear ——

You may have heard about the above Study as a result of our meeting with the Works Committee last September. Your Firm is a large employer of women, full- and part-time, and has kindly allowed us to make our study here. Our office is at 155 Keetons Road, just outside the factory gate. Most women who go out to work nowadays have home responsibilities and we hope to talk over with people how they manage. They will be able to see us during working hours and with no loss of piecework earnings.

You will have heard a lot of talk in the papers and wireless on what running a home and a job really means to a woman. We want to try to get at the facts, which we cannot do without your help. Some of those who have already volunteered to come and see us have helped us a lot; and we look forward to meeting you too.

You will see that the study is being made by the University of London, and is independent of Peek Frean's. Everything told us will be kept confidential. Perhaps we should say, too, that we are not interested in P.A.Y.E. or income tax, and shall not ask questions about them.

You may wonder why we have written to you, and this is how we have come to do so. We have drawn the names of a number of people *at random* from each shift and yours happens to be one of them. Will you be willing to come to our office for a talk one day next week? Your Supervisor knows of our work and will let you know the exact time that will be convenient.

If you would like to know more about the study your Works Committee representative (Mrs/Miss ....) will explain it. Your Supervisor will also arrange, if you wish, for her to show you the way to our office.

                 Signed .... (Research team)

The letter was timed to arrive on a Saturday morning when the woman in question would probably not be going out to work. On the Monday following, the woman supervisor took a member of the team up to the recipient at her work bench, and introduced her as the writer of Saturday's letter. The team member then talked about the research, and asked if the woman would give an interview in connection with it. If she said 'yes', an appointment was fixed for a day or two ahead.

The scheme was not well received: by the end of four weeks all but twenty-seven of the forty women who had been approached had said

APPENDIX I

'no' politely but firmly. Interviewing was therefore abandoned for the time being while the reasons for its failure were investigated. One obvious difficulty in selling the idea of the interview, a delicate job at the best of times, was the setting in which the request had to be broached. The sheer din of the work rooms was a formidable handicap; so was the fact that the woman was acutely aware that to be seen talking with a supervisor and a stranger made her an object of curiosity and suspicion to everyone in eyeshot—was there anything wrong at home? had she won the pools? was something fishy going on? Another difficulty was that the majority of women were on piecework and impatient of even the briefest interruption. A more serious trouble arose from an unexpected source. It came to light that, in the previous year, another research body, studying incentives at Peek Frean's, had included in their interviews an enquiry into P.A.Y.E. This had been much resented. The team had themselves included in their very first interviews certain questions on finance and though they quickly dropped them the idea got round that this new study, too, was going to probe into financial questions. In view of all this the team came to the conclusion that their approach in the pilot had been too rapid. In the next few weeks, therefore, they did little beyond trying to get themselves known by sight in the various departments, at the same time renewing acquaintance with the twenty-seven volunteers who had risked the initial interview. They concentrated effort on some forty extremely busy people whom they judged to be key persons in the various departments —supervisors, checkers, trainers, Works Committee members, and trade union representatives. As the pilot had shown, it was impossible without the help of these key people to locate, let alone get, the goodwill of the 250 women of the Shifts Sample. A little experiment, a personal invitation to the forty people in question to come to a meeting and tea at the senior research worker's home in Bermondsey, met with unexpected success. About half of those invited spent a thoroughly informative and friendly evening with the team. Two such parties eased matters socially, while the talk there, forthright and shrewd, was a testimony to the speakers' own abilities and their grasp of the complex jobs they were doing. Their help with the study was plainly worth enlisting.

A more general difficulty was that deriving from the scale of the factory. Its physical size, the five different shifts, the frequent changes in production set-up, and the daily movement of certain workers, meant that people and situations were less static than the team had allowed for. The timetable relating to the interviewing was liable to unforeseen and unpreventable upsets. Despite the slowing-down process adopted as regards interviewing (which meant that three months elapsed before the interviews proper began) this introductory period was probably still over-short for a community of 5,000 people working on 800,000 square feet of ground, in thirty departments, and on six floors. This belief is supported by the fact that the samples and groups contacted at much later stages in the study proved easier to deal with. The N.B.1 sample,

183

MARRIED WOMEN WORKING

not undertaken until months after the study had been under way, had few refusals.

Brief comment on the early stages of the interviewing may be of interest. Forty-eight employees of the 250 in the Shifts Sample either refused the first interview, or could not take part in it for some good reason like illness. These refusals, though considerable, were an improvement on the thirteen in forty who had refused the pilot interview. Since no marked improvement took place as the Shifts Sample was worked through, it suggests that the women's reasons for refusing were firm ones, though whether this was primarily due to the team's fumbled initial approach, or to other unknown reasons, was never established. At the attempted re-interview of 202 employees, six months after the first, though various reasons (illness, etc.) made it impossible to get an interview from fifty-one, the actual refusals numbered only twenty-one. The refusals for the Newcomers Sample proved surprisingly different, as a first interview was obtained with ninety-six of the 100 employees in the sample. By the time this sample was contacted relationships between team and factory had had time to mellow: but it also transpired that this particular sample had, unknown to the team, taken the request for an interview as just one more of the many odd things required of the new girl. Six months later, as many as thirty-nine of the ninety-six newcomers refused a re-interview, but these refusals came largely from women who had not stayed at Peek Frean's for any length of time. In the N.B.1 study the response was:

	Full-time	Part-time a.m.	Part-time p.m.	9.30 a.m.–4.00 p.m.	Total
Interviewed	13	11	14	15	53
Refused	1	3	1	0	5
Absent	1	1	0	0	2
Total sample	15	15	15	15	60

All five refusals came from women working on individual jobs: of the group, none refused an interview.

No enquiries were made about the refusers since the team had guaranteed that the interview should be voluntary. Departmental grape vines indicated that they included those who were held to keep themselves to themselves; single women (who were often sore at the many privileges given to the wife who worked but denied to them whatever their domestic commitments); and teenage girls who could not see the point of taking part in a study on married women's employment.

THE BERMONDSEY STUDY

Data on households and the woman responsible for housekeeping

When the study came to be extended from Peek Frean's to the borough of Bermondsey, the team consulted some fifty people, both sociologists and those very familiar with the area, as to effective ways of obtaining

184

APPENDIX I

from Bermondsey's 54,000 population the factual material most likely to provide the data needed. On their advice, and since the interviewing technique used at Peek Frean's had proved satisfactory on the type of information produced, this method was continued. The sociologists advised using a sample of the borough's total addresses as given in the Electoral Register. Although this, of course, would include in the households interviewed ones which contained no married woman, the Peek Frean material had laid so much emphasis on the complex sources of help given and received by the wife who works, that it was thought desirable to interview all types of household. No particular attention was paid as to which adult member of the household was interviewed; if any one person could be classed as having provided the bulk of the material, it was the woman who was responsible for running the home. The interview was so often conducted in a room where others were present besides the initial person contacted, that these others inevitably joined in. This did not, however, apply to the factual questions on finance, nor to the opinion questions at the end of the schedule. The questions on both matters were directed at, and the answers given by, the head or heads of the household.

The team was advised that a general random sample would be suitable, its size to be determined by the degree of accuracy required and the interviewing resources available. Bermondsey has approximately 20,000 households, and a sample of 500 was deemed to be the minimum number needed to keep the sampling error within reasonable limits. A one in twenty-five sample of *addresses* (any one of which might of course contain more than one household), drawn from the 1957 Electoral Register, provided well above this minimum, viz. 770 addresses. Every household living at the sample address was asked for an interview, subsequent addresses being discarded on the procedure advised by Gray and Corlett in accordance with the sample design.[2] The technique used is explained in an extract from the instructions given to the interviewers.[3]

In those households which contained two or more women the detailed information on job history, etc., was as far as possible recorded for whichever woman appeared to be responsible for the main house-

[2] *Sampling for the Social Survey*, 1950. Gray and Corlett, 1955.

[3] 'Multi-household dwellings. The number of households at a given address should be determined. If there are n households they should all be interviewed, but the next (n – 1) addresses should be *omitted*. The interviewer must start with the first address on his first ward and must determine the number of households at this address. If there is no reply the interviewer must not go to the second address without finding out the number of households at his first address. For subsequent wards the address to be called at first is determined by the number of households at the last address interviewed in the previous ward, merely by using the (n – 1) technique. Any address which is definitely unoccupied or has been demolished should be noted as such but counted as one household only from the point of view of rejected addresses so that in each case the next address can be interviewed.'

185

MARRIED WOMEN WORKING

keeping. This total Bermondsey Households Sample from the 770 addresses of course contained some households with no woman. From this sample were derived two other sets of households, Wives and Widows, and Husbands and Wives. Their titles are self-explanatory.

Since the Bermondsey Sample related to the whole borough, the pilot studies, in order not to prejudice the sample, were undertaken in the neighbouring borough of Southwark. The interviews proper began in September 1957 and ended in June 1958.

(a) *Bermondsey Households Sample.* The 517 accepters of the full interview formed the Bermondsey Households Sample from which all other of the Bermondsey Samples were derived. Nine schedules were discarded when drawing up the tables because the woman's work situation was not recorded.

(b) *Wives and Widows Sample.* A subsidiary sample, numbering 465 households, and used chiefly to provide information about the employment pattern of any woman who was or had been married, was known as the Wives and Widows Sample. It included seventy-two widows' households and thirteen where the woman was a divorcee or living apart from her husband.

(c) *Husbands and Wives Sample.* A second subsidiary sample numbered 380 households. This was the sample from which the bulk of the data on the life of the 'typical' Bermondsey household was obtained, and that from which comparisons were drawn between the home where the wife did or did not go out to work. Known as the Husbands and Wives Sample, it included only those households which contained a wife living with her husband.

Two other small studies based on this sample were attempted; one, an experiment to see if the housewife would keep a brief record of her daily timetable, met with such a poor response that it was dropped. A second study consisted of an attempt to get twenty of the households already interviewed to keep a detailed record of one week's finances. The request proved successful in nineteen cases. A simplified version of the form used by the Cost of Living Survey was given to each family and, for the payment of £1, the housewife kept a detailed record for one week of the income and expenditure of each member of the household, and details of all food eaten at home and elsewhere. The filling in of these forms was checked throughout the week by a member of the team.

Schedule. A schedule of about seventy factual points was drawn up. It repeated some of the questions used in the Peek Frean schedules, and aimed at supplementing Census material as regards current and past employment. Fuller questions than those used at the factory were asked about the husband's job and the family income. Those on child minding, which had been found to put the factory employees on the defensive, were framed differently. One entirely new topic was introduced, the progress of the children in the sample households. At the end of any interview with a household found to contain a child under eighteen, the parent(s) was asked if the team might consult the child's health visitor,

186

APPENDIX I

school, and similar people about his progress. The parent(s) reply was recorded on the schedule. When all the interviewing was completed the relevant agencies were then consulted in the case of those children where the schedule indicated that parental permission had been obtained.

Request for interview. Bermondsey has forty-eight miles of streets situated in thirteen polling wards, and the latter were used as a rough division for the allocation and time-tabling of the main interviewing, which was undertaken by eight people. About half the initial contacts with the households, and two-thirds of the accepted full interviews, were undertaken by the senior (woman) worker and the two senior (men) assistants. The interviews were held on any week day, and at any hour from 8.30 a.m. to 10.30 p.m., reflecting the variety of the times at which the adults of these working-class households could make some time to spare. The initial approach was always a knock on the door: thereafter the interviewer used his own discretion as to whether he gave an immediate interview or fixed an appointment for later on. Some of the interviewers liked to leave the following letter on their first visit, but this, too, was left to the interviewer's discretion.

HOME AND WORK
A STUDY OF HOMES WHERE THE HOUSEWIFE DOES OR DOES NOT GO OUT TO WORK

Director: Richard Titmuss	107, Grange Road,
Professor of Social Administration,	London, S.E.1.
University of London.	Tel. BER. 1628.

This research is studying one of today's big changes, the increase in the number of married women who go out to work. We know, for example, that two million more married women are at work in Great Britain now than at the end of the war. We also know that research on this subject is going on in places as far apart as Canada, Holland, and India. It is a matter of world-wide importance.

This part of London has been chosen as a good place in which to make a fairly long study of how going out to work affects local life. We have already spent two years at Messrs Peek Frean's factory. We asked from the University if we might undertake research there since the firm employs a large number of married women. The directors kindly agreed. We are now going on to co-operate with a number of local families in order to get information from the home angle. We need the views and experience of families where the housewife does not go out to work to compare with the one where she does. We also want to know what the experience of the older generation has been; what are the views of the single woman worker; and how husbands and fathers feel about it.

We have chosen 700 addresses 'out-of-a-hat' for interview and yours is one of these. If you or any society you belong to would like to know more about the study, please get in touch with us at the above address.

187

MARRIED WOMEN WORKING

We should also be glad of offers of help in keeping short-term records for us.

What good is the research?

It will help to answer such questions as these:

1. What kind of work (hours, etc.) best suits the working mother?

2. What new arrangements could be made to help (during school holidays)?

3. How do a wife's earnings contribute to a higher standard of living for a family?

THANK YOU FOR YOUR HELP.

. . . .
Research Officer

If an interview could not be obtained at the first attempt or attempts, no more was done about it at the time and the case was classed as an interview lost (see p. 192).

Progress reports on the children of the sample households

The Bermondsey study tried to determine the progress of the worker's as compared with the housewife's child. Though originally it had been hoped to include the mother's past history of work since the child was born, this material proved too imprecise to be of much value; the mother's work situation at the date of the interview was therefore the criterion used for most of the comparisons. Details of this current work situation included the number of hours she worked, the time of day, and the length of her journey. Provided the parent was willing for the team to consult the relevant agencies, her work or non-work situation was later set against the assessment of the child's progress. Consultation with senior officials of the agencies concerned with Bermondsey children agreed that health visitors and teachers were the most likely source of relevant information for the children in general; heads of day nurseries and nursery schools for those children whose mothers had used official agencies to help with minding; the Children's Department, Probation Service, Care Committee, for any who had been in official difficulty; and the Youth Employment Service for those under eighteen at work. After lengthy consultations with the London County Council the Council gave permission for the team to approach those agencies with which they were concerned for confidential reports on the child, provided parental permission was obtained. In the case of the schools the Council left it to the head of the school to give the team what information he thought fit.

The Divisional Superintendent of day nurseries and other officials of the Public Health Department provided information on Bermondsey's four day nurseries and on any minders registered with the London County Council. In the case of those children who had been in trouble, and who might well come from the homes which had refused the interview, it was decided to match the list of households at the 770 sample addresses against the names of children on the current case loads of the

APPENDIX I

Probation Office and of the Children's Department. When all the relevant information was assembled for each of the children who were found to be matched, this was placed against what the records of the team and of the agencies could show of the mother's work situation at the date of the child's offence. Another set of children who were selected for more intensive study were those aged under eleven whose mother worked full-time. The point which the team held in mind throughout the whole of this part of the study was a negative one; had the worker's child fared worse—made poorer progress—than the housewife's?

(a) *Children under 5.* There were 127 children under 5 in those sample households which accepted the interview. Parental permission was given for a progress report on 100, and a report was obtained for ninety-two. Bermondsey's ten health visitors were found to be closely in touch with most of the homes concerned and with the minders, whether London County Council registered or privately arranged. The health visitors, therefore, had little difficulty in filling in the team's form from their personal knowledge as well as their records. Each health visitor later discussed the child's progress with a member of the team.

(b) *Children at school.* There were 297 children aged 5–17 inclusive in the sample households who accepted the interview. The team obtained progress reports for 224, parental permission having been obtained. They were found to be attending fifty-three schools, thirty-six in Bermondsey and none more than a few miles away. They were Primary Schools (27), Secondary Modern (16), Grammar (6), Comprehensive (1), All-Age (3) and Special (1).[4] By arrangement with the London County Council, the head of each school was asked, and practically all agreed, to co-operate with the study. The team sought the advice of the Divisional Education Officer and certain heads of local schools of different type as to what material was likely to be available from the existing records. The schools proved most co-operative, but it had not been envisaged that so many would be involved, nor that they would have so many different methods of recording pupils' progress. In the event it proved impossible to draw many of the comparisons hoped for.

(c) *Children at work.* There were known to be not less than twenty-eight, or more than thirty-three children in this position, the inexact figure being due to the difficulty of establishing the leaving dates of the 15-year-olds. The interviewers saw less of these adolescents than of the younger ones; the parents tended to exclude them when referring to 'the children', and Youth Employment Service records are not designed to show the youngsters' progress over a period. In view of all this, no comparison was drawn for these working children between worker's and housewife's child.

(d) *Children of the sample involved with the Probation Service and the Children's Department.* Fourteen children from the households at the 770 addresses of the total sample were found to be on the card index

[4] The Secondary schools, though not classified under different types by the L.C.C., were described as in the text by the team for the purpose of this study.

189

MARRIED WOMEN WORKING

of the Probation Office attached to the South-East London Juvenile Court. This index covered cases appearing in the last ten years. No child from a household at the 770 addresses was found on the Children's Department live records at July 1958, the date decided on for consulting these records.

(e) *Children under 11 whose mother worked full-time.* There were 280 children under 11, and twenty-five had a mother working full-time. All the material relating to these twenty-five was re-examined, particular attention being paid to the adequacy of their minding, the mother's reasons for working, and her past history of employment.

(f) *Request for progress reports.* The Bermondsey study provided the opportunity to get more detailed information than had been forthcoming in the factory enquiry into the effects on the children when the mother worked: it also enabled the team to explore what people other than the mother herself had to say. Though the matter was hedged with difficulties and the findings far from adequate, the attempt was held to be justified. Two issues involved were, first, the parental permission for the child's records to be studied by the team; second, in view of the confidential nature of the material, the agency's willingness to disclose information. The London County Council insisted on the family's permission being obtained. The relevant question, as written on the schedule, was 'We want to ask the headmasters, health visitors and similar people about the progress of all children in the families we interview. May we include your children?' The team guaranteed to make the point explicit to the parent, whether using this precise form of words or not. The question of confidence was also strictly observed. The schedules were kept under lock and key and no one but the team saw them or any of the reports from the agencies.

The team obtained follow-up studies for ninety-two of the children under 5; and for 224 of the children aged 5–17. Among this older age group were the thirty-odd boys and girls previously mentioned who had left school and were, therefore, excluded from the progress reports. Thus satisfactory information was obtained on 316 of the 394 relevant (dependent) children, i.e. on 80 per cent. The number of children from the total sample of 770 addresses (i.e. including households which refused the interview) involved with the Probation Office was fourteen; with the Children's Department, nil.

Bermondsey children in general involved with the Probation Service and Children's Department.

The case load of the Probation Office relating to the year April 1957–58 was examined, and the name of every child with a Bermondsey address extracted. The result of the court case in which the child had been involved was recorded, together with all the relevant information on the mother's work situation at the date of the offence, and her past history of employment. Sixty-three children were found to be involved, and the mother's work situation was known for forty-five of them. The

190

APPENDIX I

mother's past history of work was often not recorded fully enough to classify more finely than 'regularly', 'mostly', or 'not at all'. The live records of the Children's Department at July 1958, when examined, contained no child with a Bermondsey address.

General validity of Bermondsey data

The highly personal and controversial issues involved in married women's employment made it a somewhat uneasy subject on which to interview. It was noted how often tension mounted when questions on minding were introduced, and how they relaxed again when the talk turned to such things as the distant past. Bermondsey's entirely working-class character also added to the difficulties. In this particular study the interviewer was probably more likely than usual to be equated with the world of officials, with 'the man with the peaked cap' or 'the committee lady'. Also there were practically no interviews with middle-class homes which might have helped to interpret local patterns.

The sampling method was held to be sound, and the sample adequate in size. Here Bermondsey's homogeneity was probably an asset. The attempt to frame certain of the questions (e.g. those on minding) more precisely than had been done in the Peek Frean study, made for an over long schedule and this tended to produce an uncompleted one. An anthropologist who was working in Rotherhithe kindly checked the veracity of the interviews at nineteen households which she happened to be visiting shortly afterwards. She could find few signs of deliberate misinformation. The schedule's financial section, though the refusal rate to certain points was high, had a better reception than the Peek Frean study had led the team to expect. Questions on spending and saving were less satisfactorily answered than those on last week's earnings and the wife's housekeeping money. In certain cases, and at the interviewer's discretion, husband and wife were asked to give their replies according to a code card; this prevented them hearing each other's replies. One very unsatisfactory set of data was the woman's past work history. The older woman in particular found it hard to say how long ago her various jobs had been held, especially since relatively few had had anything to correspond with the straightforward career of the professional woman. Nor could much weight be attached to the opinion questions; in both studies the replies tended to be stereotyped. The validity of the progress reports on the children varied. Those on the children under 5 were limited to health in the broadest sense. The assessors, Bermondsey's ten health visitors, proved to be unusually knowledgeable about the children since eight of them had worked in the borough for 10–20 years, the senior one since 1924. They pointed out, however, that their information was less full on the older children than on those under one and on first babies; and also that they knew less about the child whose mother worked than the housewife's child.

Certain weaknesses in the material on the school child and in relation to delinquency were felt to be so important that they have been dis-

191

MARRIED WOMEN WORKING

cussed in the text. These weaknesses, however, did not debar the team from pin-pointing with some confidence one point of value, those children who had made *markedly* poorer progress than their peers in the sample.

There were obvious hazards in placing too much weight on any of the subjective assessments of the child's progress, though it must be emphasized that these were the judgments of people professionally trained, and, in most cases, of people very familiar with the area. Much of the material was, however, drawn from actual records—the health visitor's 'Child' and 'Family' card; the school's register, 'School Record Book' and 'Main School Medical Record'; and the files of the Children's Department and Probation Office.

Non-response

Both the Peek Frean and the Bermondsey study had to face the problem of non-response. To a large extent, at least at first, this was due to faulty technique in approaching for interview. There may also have been hostile emotions aroused by the subject of married women's employment. The Bermondsey pre-pilot had eleven failures in thirty-six requests for interview; the pilot eighteen in 104. The sample proper obtained 517 full interviews from the 770 addresses or maximum number of interviews aimed at. The remaining 253 consisted of homes where the people refused verbally; people who made two successive appointments and broke both; addresses at which contact was still not made after six attempts (at least two each in the morning, afternoon, and evening); addresses vacant or demolished since the 1957 Electoral Register was made up: and a small number of 'gaps' or numbers in the range 1–770 which were not used up when the appropriate number of interviews was allocated to each ward in the borough. The totals were:

Interviews obtained		517[5]
Interviews lost		
Attempted but not obtained	231	
Gaps (no attempt made)	22	
	253	253
Total		770

[5] See p. 188.

Analysis of 222 of the 231 interviews attempted but not obtained, showed that these households had characteristics distributed in much the same way as the interviews obtained, i.e. as the Bermondsey Households Sample. What differences there were did not appear to be ones which meant that the 'accepters', especially the vital Husbands and Wives Sample, was a distorted group.

After the whole of the sample had been approached, a secondary approach was made in 114 cases by a different interviewer and with a very much briefer schedule. Most of these 114 cases were original interviews lost (e.g. by refusal or no contact); a few were households from

APPENDIX I

which only rather sketchy first interviews had been obtained. In ninety-three of the 114, some amplifying material was obtained by this means. This was used in the analysis, but the size of the samples was in no way altered.

It is impossible to say how much weight should be attached to material derived from the long contacts with the Visiting Families. Their homes, incomes, children's education, and housekeeping appeared much like those of their neighbours; but they were probably rather more socially inclined than normal in that they had welcomed the team in the study's initial stages, and had continued to build up their side of the relationship. Presumably they were all homes which had nothing in particular to hide.

The fact that the study doubled itself in length had certain practical disadvantages. Only one person, the senior field worker, was engaged on it full-time, from 1954 to mid-1959: and practically no one working on the Bermondsey field work had had the advantage of taking part in field work at Peek Frean's. The load of work was necessarily uneven, necessitating numbers of short-term staff. Both office accommodation and a general secretary for the team, a key job with so transient a staff, were difficult to find in this part of London.

APPENDIX II. *TABLES*

TABLE 26

Estimated numbers of employees in England and Wales, 1951–1959[1]   (000's)

	1951	1957	1958	1959
		End May		
(a) All employees. Male and female	18,680	19,685	19,676	19,725
(b) Female employees	6,359	6,894	6,857	6,888
(c) Married women employees included in (b)	2,840	3,474	3,535	3,683
(c) As a percentage of (a)	15·3%	17·6%	18·0%	18·7%
(c) As a percentage of (b)	44·7%	50·4%	51·6%	53·5%

TABLE 27

Heads of household—Bermondsey households

Wife living with husband	380	Husbands and Wives	380
Wife living with husband	380 ⎫		
Widow	72 ⎬	Wives and Widows	465
Woman separated from husband, or divorced	13 ⎭		
Spinster	18	Spinsters	18
Widower	13 ⎫		
Man separated from wife, or divorced	4 ⎬	Household with no woman head	25
Bachelor	8 ⎭		
Total	508		

TABLE 28   'Wives and Widows'

Work situation of women heads of household who are or have been married

	Worker							
Marital status	Less than 10 hours per week	10–19 hours per week	20–29 hours per week	30–39 hours per week	40 hours and over	Non-worker, i.e. House-wife	Home worker or self-employed[2]	Total
Living with husband	9	44	61	36	48	172	10	380
Widow	3	10	3	3	6	46	1	72
Separated	—	—	—	—	8	3	—	11
Divorced	—	—	—	1	1	—	—	2
Total	12	54	64	40	63	221	11	465

[1] Ministry of Labour.
[2] Included with Housewife in all other tables.

APPENDIX II

TABLE 29   *'Wives and Widows'*

Woman's type of work in relation to time of day she worked

Time of day worked	Housewife	Job unclassified	Industrial worker	Domestic worker	Clerical worker	Distributive trades, nursing, teaching, entertainment and other services	Total
8 a.m.–5 p.m.		2	35	7	15	18	77
8 a.m.–12 noon		1	14	4	4	4	27
1 p.m.–5 p.m.		1	12	1	1	—	15
9.30 a.m.–3.30 p.m.			9	4	—	1	14
11 a.m.–2 p.m.			—	1	1	2	4
6 a.m.–9 a.m.			1	27	—	—	28
5.30 p.m.–8.30 p.m.			2	8	—	—	10
5.30 p.m.–8.30 p.m. and 6 a.m.–9 a.m.			—	9	1	—	10
Other hours than above		1	6	22	3	22	54
Hours not known, including non-workers	221	1	3	2	—	1	228
Total	221	6	82	85	25	48	467[2]
Those working on Saturday, Sunday, or shift work		2	3	47	6	36	

[2] Due to an error in classification, two schedules were included in this table which should have been rejected as they were insufficiently detailed in other matters. In this table the self-employed and home-workers, though normally classified as Housewife, are included with Workers.

TABLE 30   *'Wives and Widows'*

Woman's length of two-way journey to work in relation to her work situation

Length of two-way journey	Worker F.T.	Worker P.T.	Total	Housewife[4]	Total
Less than 20 minutes	28	38	66	2	68
20–39 minutes	33	44	77	—	77
40–59 minutes	15	12	27	—	27
60–119 minutes	19	28	47	—	47
2 hours and over	—	1	1	—	1
Housewife				230	230
No information	8	7	15		15
Total	103	130	233	232	465

[4] In this table the self-employed are classified as Housewife.

TABLE 31   'Wives and Widows'

Woman's main pre-marriage job in relation to her present type of occupation

Main pre-marriage job	Doctor, Teacher, Nurse, etc.	Supervisory level: e.g. Manageress of Shop, Book-keeper	Secretary, Typist, Student-nurse, etc.	Skilled Trade: e.g. Sewing Machine Operator	Office Clerk, Shop Assistant, Medical Orderly, etc.	Semi-skilled manual: e.g. Factory Operative	Unskilled: e.g. Office Cleaner, Miscellaneous Domestic Worker	Not at Work[b]	Total
Metal box assembly			1	1		6	8	14	30
Metal work: drillers, pressers, etc.							1	1	2
Soldering							2	5	7
Metal work: polishing, painting							1		1
Textile weaving					1	1	1		3
Rope making								1	1
Fur plucking or preparing				1		2		4	7
Leather machinist		1			1	1		1	4
Leather hand stitching							1	2	3
Dressmaking: designing, cutting, sewing	2	1		4	3	3	4	13	30
Dressmaking: pressing								1	1
Dressmaking: machine work				3	1	2	3	15	24
Making mattresses or bedding								1	1
Making biscuits or chocolate		1	1	1	3	2	4	8	20
Making jam				1		4	5	4	14
Other food making		1			3	4	6	6	20
Alcohol or tobacco manufacturer						2	1	4	7
Making wooden boxes							1	1	2
Paper making			1			1	1		3
Making cardboard boxes, paper bags, envelopes, etc.					1		3	2	6
Printing: compositors							1	1	2
Bookbinding						2		2	4
Other products (brushes, etc.)						3	2		5

196

MARRIED WOMEN WORKING

Painting, decorating								1	1
Bus conductresses							1	1	2
Messengers							2	2	4
Own shop		3				1		1	5
Shop assistants, saleswomen		1			2	1		7	11
Nurses, midwives, social workers	2							1	3
School meals supervisors, home helps	1				1	1	1	3	7
Opticians, laboratory assistants								1	1
Armed Forces				1				1	2
Cinema usherettes						1		1	2
Entertainment or sport							1		1
Barmaids								2	2
Waitresses				2	1	2	1	4	10
Restaurant counter-hands; including manageresses						1		2	3
Office cleaning			1			2	2	1	6
Laundry, dry-cleaning						1		3	4
Laundry, dry-cleaning (shop)								1	1
Cooks, housekeepers				1	1	1	2	7	12
Kitchen hands							2	4	6
Maids: domestic service		2		1	1	2	5	13	24
Typists, comptometer operators, etc.			10		1			9	20
Office clerks		2	3		2	2	2	10	21
Book-keepers, accountancy clerks		1	1					2	4
Packers in store, warehouse		1					1	2	4
Packers, labellers, bottlers in factory		1			2	9	7	14	33
Checkers			1					3	4
Soap, perfume manufacture								1	1
No information, or did not work		2	1	2	6	14	14	37	76
Total	5	17	20	18	30	71	85	221	465[a]

[a] Due to an error in classification, two schedules were included in this table which should have been rejected as they were insufficiently detailed in other matters

[b] In this table the self-employed and home-workers, though normally classified as Housewife, are included with Workers.

MARRIED WOMEN WORKING

TABLE 32 *'Wives and Widows'*

Woman's type of occupation in relation to her age[7]

Age	Professional; supervisory; senior clerical level	Skilled; semi-skilled; junior clerical level	Unskilled
	%	%	%
Under 20 years	50	50	—
20–29 ,,	25·93	59·26	14·81
30–39 ,,	23·44	50·00	26·56
40–49 ,,	11·59	56·52	31·88
50–59 ,,	12·73	43·64	43·64
60 and over	11·11	22·22	66·66

[7] In this table the self-employed are included with Workers.

TABLE 33 *'Husbands and Wives'*

Wife's spendable income (as % of N.A.B. figure) in relation to her work situation

Spendable income as % of N.A.B. figure	Worker F.T.	Worker P.T.	Total	Housewife	Total
0–100	—	1	1	10	11
101–150	—	9	9	53	62
151–200	9	30	39	40	79
201–250	12	26	38	20	58
251–300	15	12	27	2	29
over 300	22	2	24	1	25
Not normal week	1	2	3	4	7
No information	25	32	57	52	109
Total	84	114	198	182	380

TABLE 34

Family holiday (1957) in relation to wife's earnings   '*Bermondsey: Husbands and Wives*'

Wife's weekly earnings	No holiday away	Holiday away	No information	Total	Locality							Length of Holiday			
					British countryside	Thames Estuary	Yarmouth to Bournemouth	Any other British seaside	Ireland	Abroad	Total[a]	One week	Two weeks	Three weeks and over	Total
Under £3	20	28	2	50	8	8	10	2	0	0	28	17	10	0	27
£3 and under £5	16	34	3	53	6	6	17	8	0	0	37	13	17	1	31
£5 and under £7	12	35	2	49	7	7	12	5	2	3	36	18	14	2	34
£7 and over	3	14	0	17	5	0	6	1	0	3	15	2	12	0	14
No information (or does not apply, i.e. housewife)	85	106	20	211	21	20	36	14	4	5	100	43	48	8	99
Total	136	217	27	380	47	41	81	30	6	11	216	93	101	11	205

[a] The totals of the 'locality' and 'length of holiday' columns do not tally with the number of families who had holidays away because (*a*) in some cases there was more than one holiday per family, (*b*) information was not always obtained as to locality and length of holiday.

Annual holiday (1954)—'Peek Frean Shifts Sample' and 'Newcomers'

	Percentages	
	Shifts sample	Newcomers
No holidays away	35·8	47·4
Staying with friends, relations	9·1	10·5
Boarding house	43·0	21·1
Caravan/Bungalow	4·5	11·8
Car/motor-cycle touring	2·4	3·9
Holiday camp	3·7	5·3
Abroad	1·5	—
	100·0	100·0

MARRIED WOMEN WORKING

TABLE 35   'Husbands and Wives'

Possession of car and washing machine in relation to wife's work situation

	Worker		
	F.T.	P.T.	Housewife
(a) Car ownership			
Husband's income up to 200% of N.A.B. figure	7%	10%	11%
Husband's income over 200% of N.A.B. figure	12%	21%	5%
(b) Washing machine ownership			
Husband's income up to 200% of N.A.B. figure	20%	5%	11%
Husband's income over 200% of N.A.B. figure	27%	39%	7%

TABLE 36   'Husbands and Wives'

Amenities in household in relation to wife's work situation

		Worker			House-	
		F.T.	P.T.	Total	wife	Total
No. of families which have bought	Car	17	21	38	15	53
	W/machine	8	15	23	16	39
	Refrigerator	5	10	15	17	32
	TV	42	71	113	86	199
No. of families with	one item	35	48	83	70	153
	two or more items	17	31	48	27	75
Totals of families with wife's work situation as described		84	114	198	182	380

TABLE 37   'Wives and Widows'

Frequency with which families were in contact with relatives[a]

	%
Family met relatives "very regularly"	51
,, ,, ,, "quite a lot"	22
,, ,, ,, "a little"	27
	100

[a] Figures relate to the 252 families of the 465 Wives and Widows households who said they were in contact with relatives.

TABLE 38   'Wives and Widows'

Child or no child in the home in relation to the woman's work situation

	Worker			House-	
	F.T.	P.T.	Total	wife	Total
Child(ren) in the home	51	93	144	157	301
No child(ren) in the home	52	37	89	75	164
Total	103	130	233	232	465

TABLE 39

Minding of worker's child (in week previous to interview) in relation to his mother's part- or full-time work situation

| Mother's work situation | Minder | | | Total of children minded | Total of children not minded | No information or did not apply | Total of children |
	Maternal grandmother	Other relative	Other method of minding				
Full-time worker	6	4	6	16	37	8	61
Part-time worker	7	10	3	20	85	33	138
Total	13	14	9	36	122	41	199[1]

[1] Total of 199, not 196 as in Table 40, due to three children being minded by more than one person.

TABLE 40

Minding of worker's child (in last long school holidays) in relation to his mother's part- or full-time work situation

| Mother's work situation | Minder | | | Total of children minded | Total of children not minded | No information or does not apply | Total of children |
	Maternal grandmother	Other relative	Other method of minding				
Full-time worker	6	4	5	15	23	21	59
Part-time worker	8	11	12	31	49	57	137
Total	14	15	17	46	72	78	196

MARRIED WOMEN WORKING

TABLE 41

Attendance at clinic of mothers of children aged under five during child's first year of life, in relation to the mother's work situation

Attendance at clinic	F.T.	Worker P.T.	Total	Housewife	Total
20 times or more	2	5	7	20	27
10–19 times	1	7	8	19	27
5–9 times	1	—	1	9	10
under 5 times	3	1	4	21	25
No health visitor's report or no information	1	4	5	33	38
Total	8	17	25	102	127

TABLE 42

Illness during schooldays o j school child in relation to the mother's work situation at date of interview

Illness	F.T.	Worker P.T.	Total	Housewife	Total of children
Very little or none	10	21	31	21	52
Normal school ailments	17	23	40	39	79
One serious illness or accident: period of bad health: received special treatment	8	18	26	20	46
Did not apply or no information	27	82	109	158	267
Total	62	144	206	238	444[2]

' Total 444 not 424 (as in Table 18), probably due to duplication in 'one serious illness' group.

202

APPENDIX II

TABLE 43

Analysis of 222 of the 231 refusals to interview in Bermondsey Households Sample[3]

A. *Heads of household* (cf. Table 27)

Wives and Widows	172
Woman separated from husband, divorced, or spinster	14
Household with no woman head	25
No information on nature of household	11
Total	**222**

B. *Woman's age in relation to her work situation* (cf. Table 9)

Age of woman head of household	Worker F.T.	Worker P.T.	Total	Housewife	No information	Total
Under 20 years	—	—	—	1	1	2
20–29 years	1	1	2	9	2	13
30–39 ,,	10	8	18	8	1	27
40–49 ,,	2	9	11	10	1	22
50–59 ,,	8	11	19	10	2	31
60 and over	1	8	9	37	—	46
No information on age	5	4	9	15	7	31
Total	**27**	**41**	**68**	**90**	**14**	**172**

C. *Age of youngest child at home in relation to his mother's work situation* (cf. Table 12)

Age of child	Worker F.T.	Worker P.T.	Total	Housewife	No information	Total
Under 1 year	—	2	2	7	—	9
1–4 years	—	—	—	12	—	12
5–14 ,,	3	5	8	11	3	22
15–20 ,,	2	1	3	2	1	6
21 and over	4	4	8	12	—	20
No information on child's age	—	4	4	—	1	5
Total	9	16	25	44	5	74
Households without children	17	25	42	43	2	87
No information as to whether children in household	1	—	1	3	7	11

[3] In comparing Table 43 with other tables, note that it does not include in 'Wives and Widows' woman separated from husband, or divorced.

Index

Absenteeism, 74–5, 89; leave without pay, 75; increases job transfers, 76

Age and work situation: mothers, (tables) 95, 96, 198, 203; children, (tables) 138–9, 203

Amenities, household: and wife's work situation, (table) 118, 119, (table) 200

Armstrong-Jones, Antony (Lord Snowdon), 62

Baby-sitting, 144; and see *Minding*

Bermondsey, reasons for choice, 26–8, 35–7; homogeneous population, 38, 59; local loyalty, 39; location, 39–40; isolation, 40; growth, 40; respectability, 59–60; small-town atmosphere, 61; summary, 177

Bermondsey study (1956–9), 33–6; method, 178; chronology, 178–9; data and their validity, 184–6, 191–2; schedule of points investigated, 186–7; and see *Households sample*

Birth-rate, 21

Bomb damage, 52

Booth, Charles, 44, 59

Boredom, 108, 109

Borrowing, 102

Cadbury, Edward, 23

Catholic element, 60

Children, pre-1914 employment, 43–4; services and amenities for, 58–9; and mother's work situation, (tables) 97–8, 137, (tables) 138–9, (tables) 200, 203; smaller families, 106–8; share of housework, 126; method of survey of, 136–7, 145, 188–91; progress of under-fives, 145, (tables) 146–7, 189; progress of children of school age, 147–9, 189; leisure of, 152–6. care of, 156–63, 167–71; attitude to mother's employment, 159; expenditure on, 159–61; disciplining of, 160–1;

ambitions for, 161; children in employment, 189; and see *Delinquency*; *Minding*; *Mothers with young children*

Children's Department, as source of information, 35; children involved with, 149–50, 190–1

Class, see *Social structure*

Clinic attendance of babies, (table) 202

Cooking, see *Meals*

Cultural life, 60, 109–10

Day nurseries, 58, 143–4

Delinquency, 59, 149–52, 189–91

Demographic changes, 20–5

Diaries: mothers', 130–1; children's, 152–4

Disabled Persons (Employment) Act, 83–4

Divorce rate, 59

Dock labour, pre-1914, 43; Dock Labour Board, 52–3; present-day conditions, 56–7, 101

Do-it-yourself, 123

Drink, pre-1914, 47

Earnings, sharing of, 121–2

Employers, attitude of, 23–5; and see *Managerial problems*

Employment, general: in Bermondsey, (table) 55, 56–7; in England and Wales, (table), 194

Employment, women's: types of (England and Wales), 20; opportunities for, 21; pre-1914, 43–4; 1939–45, 53; today, 57–8; types of (Bermondsey), (table) 94, 95, (table) 195; pre-marriage jobs, (table) 196–7; and see *Wife's earnings*; *Wives and Widows sample*

Expectation of life, 21

Factory study, see *Peek Frean study*

Family life, 60–1, 106–8, 133; effect of wife's employment on, 168–71;

INDEX

Family Life—*cont.*
 frequency of contact with relatives, (table) 200
Flat life, 110–11
Full-time workers, output, 77; attitude, 86–90; and see *Part-time workers*
Furniture and furnishings, 117–25, 127

Games, provision for, 154–5
Group and individual work, 88

Health, pre-1914, 42–3; inter-war improvement, 48, 51; housekeeping strains, 128–9; industrial strains, 129–30; of children under five, 145, (table) 146, 147; of school-age children, (table) 202
Health Service, as source of information, 35
Hire purchase, 102
Holidays, 105–6, 131; importance to children, 156; wife's earnings and, (table) 199; type of, (table) 199
Hours of work, 138–40; and see *Shifts*
Households sample, 33–6, 92; method, 186–8; heads of households, (table) 194; and see *Wives and Widows sample*
Housekeeping, 125–32; adjustment to dual role, 166–8
Housewives, non-working, 112–14
Housing, pre-1914, 41–2; inter-war improvement, 48, 51–2; today, 54–5, 127, 174; and see *Furniture and furnishings*
Hubback, Mrs J., 23
Husbands, working hours of, 87; occupation, 98–9, (table) 99; earnings, (table) 103–4, 116–17, 121–2; share of housework, 126; attitude to wife's employment, 171
Husbands and Wives sample, 92, 186; and see *Wives and Widows sample*

Illegitimacy rate, 59
Immunization, (table) 146
Improvidence, see *Saving*
Insecurity, 38–9, 43, 101

Interviewing, difficulties, 181–4, 187, 192–3; analysis of refusals, (table) 203
Irish element, 41, 60

Journey to work, 93–4, (table) 195
Juvenile Court cases, 59, 151–2

Klein, Viola, 19, 25

Labour stability, defined, 72n; rate by shifts, 74; of part-time workers, 87
Labour turnover, defined, 72n; rate by shift, (table) 72; reasons for leaving work, (table) 73–4
Leavers sample, 33, 73–4, 181
Leave without pay, 75
Leisure, employment of, 109–10; lack of, 130–5; children's, 152–6 .
Lewin, Kurt, 78
London County Council, as source of information, 35; and see *Nursery school*; *Play centres*; *School meals service*
London School of Economics, study of kinship, 26–7
Loneliness, 110; and see *Sociability*

Management, attitude towards, 86
Managerial problems, 67–70, 172–3; shifts, 67, 69; part-time work, 68; and see *Absenteeism*; *Training*; *Transfers of job*
Marriage, early, 21
Married women in employment, see *Working wives*
Meals and mealtimes, 127–8
Mellish, R. J., M.P., 60, 61
Method of survey, 30–5; basic questions, 28–9; and see *Bermondsey study*; *Peek Frean study*
Minding, 141–5; types of, (table) 201
Missions, 49
Motherhood, changing attitude to, 106–8
Mothers' Meetings, 110
Mothers with young children : prefer evening shifts, 71; high turnover rate, 73; proportion at work, 95, (table) 96, 137–9; no evidence of neglect, 97–8

INDEX

Motives for taking work, 21, 87–8, 99–111; financial, 101–4; holiday money, 104–6; status, 106–9; 'makes a change', 109–12; furnishing home, 117–19; pin money, 120; expenditure on food, 120–1; expenditure on children, 121; summary of, 165–6

National Assistance Board, scale, 104n
National Insurance, extra cost of part-time workers, 83, 174–5
National Savings Committee, growth of savings, 120
N.B.I. sample, 32–3, 86, 180–1; absenteeism, 74–5; job transfer, 76–7; supervision, 78–83; disposition between shifts, 85; plan of room, 85–6
Neighbours, 110–11; assistance from, 126–7
Newcomers sample, 32; high turnover rate, 72–3; method, 179
Non-working women, 112–14
Nursery school, 58, 143–4

Output, part- and full-time workers, 77

Part-time workers: managerial attitude to, 68–70; output, 77; friction with full-time workers, 69, 88; attitude to management of, 86–7; stability, 87; percentage, 93; definition of, 93
Peek Frean & Co. Ltd., 26; reasons for choice of, 26, 27; early history, 63; personnel policy, 63–5; Works Committee, 64; labour shortage, 65–7; policy re married women, 66–7; shifts, (table) 67, 71; labour force, 177
Peek Frean study, 31–3; chronology and method, 178, 181–3; data, 179, and managerial data, 180–1; local people consulted, 180; schedule of points investigated, 180–1; management consulted, 181; and see *Leavers sample*; *N.B.I. sample*; *Newcomers sample*; *Shifts sample*; *Visiting Families*

Pieceworkers, unattracted by promotion, 68; piecework preferred, 88; over-work, 129–30
Play centres, 58, 154
Pocket money, 159
Population, decline in, 48
Poverty, pre-1914, 46–7; persistence of, 50–1
Pregnancy, frequency of, 21
Probation Service, as source of information, 35; children involved with, 149, (tables) 150–1, 152, 189–91
Promotion, married women refuse, 68

Refusals of interview, see *Interviewing difficulties*
Relatives, see *Family life*

Saving, 101–2, 119–20
School meals service, 58, 127, 143
Schools, in inter-war years, 52; types attended, (table) 147, 148; attendance, (table) 148
Shifts, at Peek Freans, (table) 67, 69, 71, 173; labour stability by shift, 74; relative efficiency of, 84; preferences, 88
Shifts sample, 31–3, 179
Sociability, as a motive, 87–8, 108, 111–12
Social activities, 132–3
Social structure, 35–6, (table) 54
Spinsters, diminishing number, 20–1
Status, as a motive, 106–9
Steele, Tommy, 62
Suicide rate, 59
Supervisors, married women as, 68–9; duties and efficiency of, 78–81; attitude towards, 81, (table) 82, 83, 88–9

Tallymen, 102
Taxation, 174–5
Television, children and, 155–6
Training, factory, 75–7; attitude to trainers, 89
Transfers of job, cause friction, 69, 87–9; high rate of, 76–7

Unemployment, (1932) 51

207

INDEX

Vaccination, (table) 146

Visiting Families Group, 33; method, 179–80

Vital statistics, 54

Voluntary services, 48–50

Wartime conditions, 23–4

Wife's earnings, how spent, 115–22; earnings and work situation, (tables) 116, 198; examples, 117

Wives and Widows sample, 92, 186; work situation, (tables) 93, 194; type of occupation, (table) 94; age and work situation, (table) 95; age of children, (tables) 96, 98; hours and type of work, (table) 195; and see *Husbands and Wives sample*

Working conditions, criticism of, 88, 89

Working wives, statistics (England and Wales), 20; criticism of, 22–5; Bermondsey pre-1914 figures, 44–5; summary of types of, 164–5; implications of increase in, 174–6; and see *Mothers with young children*; *Wife's earnings*; *Wives and Widows sample*

Youth Employment Bureau, as source of information, 35; statistics of placings, 96

Youth organizations, 58–9, 155